Beyond the
inner city

DAVID BYRNE

Beyond the inner city

Open University Press
MILTON KEYNES · PHILADELPHIA

Open University Press
12 Cofferidge Close
Stony Stratford
Milton Keynes MK11 1BY

and
242 Cherry Street
Philadelphia, PA 19106, USA

First published 1989

Copyright © David Byrne 1989

All rights reserved. No part of this publication may be
reproduced, stored in a retrieval system or transmitted in
any form or by any means, without written permission from the
publisher.

British Library Cataloguing in Publication Data

Byrne, David *1947–*
  Beyond the inner city
  1. Great Britain. Urban regions. Inner areas.
  Social planning – Case studies
  I. Title
  307'.14'0941

  ISBN 0-335-15872-2
  ISBN 0-335-15871-4 (pbk)

Library of Congress Cataloging-in-Publication Data

Byrne, D. S. (David S.), 1947–
  Beyond the inner city/David Byrne.
      p.   cm.
  Bibliography: p.
  Includes index.
  ISBN 0–335–15872–2   ISBN 0–335–15871–4 (pbk.)
    1. Urban policy—Great Britain—Case studies.   2. North Tyneside
(England)—Social conditions.   3. North Tyneside (England)—Economic
conditions.   I. Title
HT133.397   '989
307.76'09428'79—dc20   89–3302 CIP

Typeset by Scarborough Typesetting Services
Printed in Great Britain by
Biddles Ltd, Guildford and Kings Lynn

Contents

List of tables		vii
List of abbreviations		ix
Acknowledgements		xi

Part I The changing city and how to understand it
1	Introduction	3
2	Locality, social process and explanation	16

Part II The inner and outer city
3	North Shields and Cramlington: two localities and their city and region	39
4	Production and base in two localities	60
5	The question of land	82
6	Socio-spatial segregation in Northern Tyneside	99
7	The state and civil society in Northern Tyneside	121
8	The inner city and beyond in 1988	137

Part III Towards 2000 – strategies and tactics for change
9	Beyond the inner city: planning for a future	149
10	The sources of collective action for change	159

Bibliography	170
Index	177

List of tables

3.1	Industrial structure, Northern Region 1966–84	44
3.2	Population shifts on Northern Tyneside	45
3.3	Location of dwellings on Northern Tyneside 1921–81	46
3.4	Tenure and amenities on Northern Tyneside for 1971 and 1981	47
4.1	All employment in Northern Tyneside	63
4.2	Male employment in Northern Tyneside	63
4.3	Female employment in Northern Tyneside	64
4.4	Northern Tyneside industry–gender–time composition	65
4.5	Employment in North Shields and Cramlington	66
4.6	Tynemouth CB area economically active residents	67
6.1	Social deprivation in North Tyneside in 1971	101
6.2	Social deprivation in North Tyneside in 1981	103
6.3	Social deprivation in North Tyneside in 1981	105
6.4	Social deprivation in Cramlington in 1981	107
6.5	Census tract clusters, 1971	109
6.6	Census tract clusters, 1981	109
6.7	South Meadowell and Parkside	113
6.8	Cluster – vote correlations	119

List of abbreviations

BVDC	Blyth Valley District Council
CB	County Borough
CBC	County Borough Council
CDP	Community Development Project
CES	Centre for Environmental Studies
CSEU	Confederation of Engineering and Shipbuilding Trade Unions
DHSS	Department of Health and Social Services
DoE	Department of the Environment
DTI	Department of Trade and Industry
EDs	Enumeration Districts
GLC	Greater London Council
GMWU	General and Municipal Workers Union (later GMBTU)
HELP	Housing in Exchange for Land
ILP	Independent Labour Party
IMF	International Monetary Fund
LDDC	London Docklands Development Corporation
MSF	Manufacturing, Science and Finance Union
MDC	Metropolitan District Council
NALGO	National and Local Government Officers Union
NCC	Northumberland County Council
NRST	Northern Regional Strategy Team
NUT	National Union of Teachers

NUWM	National Unemployed Workers Movement
OPCS	Office of Population Censuses and Surveys
RAWP	Resource Allocations Working Party
SLD	Social and Liberal Democrats
UDC	Urban Development Corporation
TGWU	Transport and General Workers' Union
TWDC	Tyne Wear Development Corporation

Acknowledgements

A lot of people have helped me in the production of this book. These include the staff of North Tyneside Housing, Chief Executive's and Planning Departments, the staffs of the Blyth Valley Housing Department and Northumberland Planning Department, and the staffs of the Local Studies Libraries in North Shields, Newcastle and Gateshead and of the Northumberland County Records Office. Members of Blyth Valley and North Tyneside District Councils and Northumberland County Council made time to talk to me as did workers from the North Shields People's Centre and residents of North Shields and Cramlington and especially Steve Wyres and Peter Burnett. The Department of Employment gave me permission to use material from the Censuses of Employment in Chapters 3 and 4 and I am grateful to them for this. I would also like to thank my fellow workers from the North Tyneside Community Development Project, particularly David Corkey and John Foster, for their assistance and advice. Thanks also to Margaret Bell who helped in the typing of tables. Jane Byrne helped prepare the bibliography, and Christine Byrne helped in the production of the typescript. Both had to put up with me – which was not easy. The responsibility for what follows is, however, mine alone.

PART I

The changing city and how to understand it

1

Introduction

This book is about social change and its impact on a place. It is about deindustrialization, the restructuring of both capital and the working class, the emergence of 'disorganized' capitalism and the development of a post-urban society. It tackles this small set of problems and issues by addressing them in two localities – the old port of North Shields and the new town of Cramlington. There are many important questions which emerge in relation to comparative study which employs place or locality as the frame of reference and explanation. The debate which deals with these matters will be referred to and the conceptual apparatus which has been developed in that debate will be used where appropriate. However, this study is not primarily an exercise in the refinement of science. It was not undertaken to support, refute or criticize contemporary urban and regional theory. Rather, it is a project which comes from the author's biography and represents a return to an action-research exercise of the mid-1970s.

I hope that I might have undertaken work of this kind without the experience of working for North Tyneside Community Development Project (CDP) from 1974 to 1977, but I did and that experience shaped both the conceptualizing and the carrying out of this project. It has helped particularly in defining its nature. Action-research is a form of social scientific practice in which investigation is carried out in order to inform and facilitate a programme of social change as part of that self-same programme of social change. I was paid good money for 3½ years to do something about the problems of North Shields and a particular component of doing something was describing what things were like, giving an account of how they had come to be like this, and attempting to understand why the process had happened as it had. The singular virtue of action-research is that things could not be left at that – it was necessary to go on and do something about it all. The history of North Tyneside CDP and what it did can be found in the final reports of the project itself (North Tyneside CDP, 1977, 1978 a, b and c) and an account of CDP as a national exercise is given in Loney (1983). This book is not a recapitulation of events before 1977, although it will use the findings and experiences of the CDP as a baseline. It is about what has happened since, and why and what might be done about it.

However, my concerns did not begin with coming to North Shields in 1977. I am a native of South Shields and grew up in a locality which has much in common with its other half. What has happened to North Shields has happened to my world, my culture and my people. It has happened to the North East. I don't like it; I don't want it; I am against it; I need to understand it – and to understand it I have to describe it.

Since I find novelists tend to say it better than sociologists, let me quote from one who seems to have anticipated a good deal of what was to come after the period when we had never had it so good:

> All of this. . . . These streets an' these bloody awful shops, an' the muck an' filth an' everythin' second best because folk know nothin' better. An' the entire derelict bloody city an' all.
> Ah know we're buildin' multi-bloody-storey flats an' whatnot an' there's all sorts of clever bloody plans for the clever bloody future. . . . But its all surface show. All of it. We're livin' in the past, livin' of the fat of Stephenson, Armstrong, Swan an' all that lot. We're out of it now. We're just a branch bloody factory.
> (Chaplin, 1962: 105)

These comments date from the period of modernization associated with Hailsham's (1963) *The North East: A Programme for Regional Development and Growth* and the regional planning policies which stemmed from it. One product of this period was Cramlington. In the late 1980s we can review the situation in my two localities in terms of being 'after the planners', because the Hailsham programme consisted of planned accommodation with social change in the name of modernization and social progress. To use Jessop's (1982) terminology, it was a 'one nation' programme involving corporatist social strategies in the resolution of a crisis; at that time, the crisis engendered for the North East's social and industrial base by the pit closures under Robens in consequence of a shift in UK energy policy towards the utilization of (then) relatively cheap imported oil.

National policies for dealing with our contemporary crisis engendered by much more general deindustrialization involve the continued incorporation of the élite of the regional labour movement, but they are no longer 'one nation' in objective and orientation. I recently contributed to a book which was misnamed by its editors *Redundant Spaces* (Anderson *et al.*, 1983). It is not the space that is redundant but rather much of the population which occupied that space and worked in industries now regarded by UK policy makers and commentators as obsolescent and non-revivable. New uses are emerging for that space and new governmental and administrative forms and processes are being created which facilitate its reordering in a way which is analogous to the use of enclosure to expel a surplus peasantry, of the New Poor Law in England to dispose of a surplus of rural proletarians, of clearance to reorder the Highlands of Scotland for capitalist sheep farming, and of the Poor Law, eviction and the failure to relieve famine which was intended to transform the congested districts of Ireland from peasant to large-scale landlord-led capitalist farming. I have listed these processes because it was through their operation that Tyneside's industrial proletariat was created. Of course, high industrial wages were a pull factor, but our ancestors were pushed from their homes and their ways of life. It is my contention that a similar process is occurring for at least a significant part of the people of Tyneside today, although it is not affecting everyone in the same way and involves a complex process of what may be more apparent than real social differentiation.

This book is in three parts. The first part includes this introduction and Chapter 2, which deals with 'locality' as an issue in the understanding of social processes. This is now a fashionable field commanding the attention of very prominent social theorists. Despite my disagreement with the generally Weberian direction of much of this work, I think that it usually has virtues of clarity and relevance, and addresses a range of themes which are important in understanding developments in the places investigated in this book. In particular, it is necessary to pay close attention to the relationship of civil society (within which I will include much of what I mean by a specific urban culture) and state forms and processes, in a context of 'disorganized capitalism'. Despite its usefulness, I do see most of this sort of work as fundamentally flawed. This is illustrated by the enthusiastic endorsement of the range of writers working in this area of the content of Gorz's (1982) *Farewell to the Working Class*. This book will be highly instrumental in its treatment of contemporary issues of 'urban and regional and spatial' theory. It is not intended as an effort at resolving these debates: my objectives are specific and political – they are to do with action.

My attitude to another body of reference which will be addressed in Chapter 2 is different. The discussion of culture in Raymond Williams' (1983) *Towards 2000* has been very important in my consideration of where Tyneside is going and where it may be made to go. Williams always wrote in a way which deserves the label of 'political' in the sense in which that term is used by Cleaver (1979). There is much to be gained from integrating the considerations of culture and civil society in his work with the autonomist understanding of production and reproduction at the basal level which, at least for me, provides such a clear and coherent account of the capitalist relations of production and of the implications of those relations for class action. This is the only way in which a strategy for the political sphere can be developed. Thus part of the purpose of Chapter 2 is the getting together of a kind of conceptual tool-bag in advance of the specific case studies which are the content of the second part of this book.

The last part of this 'theoretical grounding' in Chapter 2 will be concerned with issues of understanding and in particular with the uses and potential abuses of realist epistemology (Sayer, 1984). A summary case will be argued for 'historical materialism'. This book is not a text in method and neither will its empirical core be used as a peg for methodological debates.

Chapter 3, which consists of profiles of North Shields and Cramlington in their regional and urban context, commences the second part of the book. An account is given of their development up to 1988. Present-day economic, social and political conditions are identified and an outline description of their origins is attempted. I place some emphasis on the 'urban' component of this location. North Shields and Cramlington are both parts of the Tyneside conurbation. North Shields has always been an integral part of Tyneside but the Cramlington area had a separate identity as part of the South Northumberland coalfield. Despite its physical separation from the continuously built up conurbation, Cramlington is now socially a part of Tyneside. This is of significance in itself, but it means that it is possible to advance a claim of some originality for this study. Most locality studies have been of relatively compact free-standing towns or of discrete neighbourhoods in great cities. There have been important studies of aspects of modern cities, but in my view there has been no recent study of a significant part of a great industrial city considered as a whole. Valuable as town or coalfield studies are, such as Urry and Murgatroyd's (1985) investigations in Lancaster or the work of Beynon (1982), Hudson (1986) and Cooke (1985) on coalfield regions, the great city is something different and needs special attention.

I am not claiming to have considered the whole of the metropolitan county of Tyne and Wear and its satellites. I have deliberately confined most of the detailed consideration in this study to the north bank of the Tyne. However, I do see the dynamics of the city as different and have tried to take some account of them in this study. This is not a matter of a reversion to the consideration of the city as a distinctive cultural form, an idea which is most generally associated with the work of Simmel but which was also essential to classic Chicago school urban ecology. None the less, there is a real sense in which the notion of urban culture in a particular locale is important. I have always been struck by the role of particular cities in certain works which have conveyed a very exact sense of historical location, e.g. Manchester appears in this way in accounts as diverse as those of De Toqueville and Engels, and Spring's enormously popular novels of the 1930s. The translator described 'the party' as the collective hero of Serge's (1978) *Conquered City*, but it has always seemed to me that in both that work and in *Birth of Our Power* (1977) the great proletarian cities of Petrograd and Barcelona are actors in their own right.

Tyneside has this character in the work of Jack Common and Sid Chaplin. The study of both Cramlington and North Shields is therefore not just a matter of the comparative examination of interestingly contrasted localities, but involves consideration of the way in which the real relationships between these localities constitutes the Tyneside of today. The work which best conveys this among recent studies is Ardagh's (1979) discussion of five European provincial cities including Tyneside.

The two localities which are the subject of this book are 'inner-city' and 'non-city' areas. The inner-city status of North Shields is apparent. It was the locale of a Community Development Project, part of the first major initiative by the central British State directed at inner urban problems. North Tyneside is a 'programme authority' for the purposes of urban programming, which puts it in the second highest division of local authorities for central assistance, which is inner-city related.

In contrast, Cramlington is 'non-urban' and was intended to be a more or less (there was always some equivocation about this and it grew over time) free-standing new town, located on a 'green field' site quite separate from the Tyneside conurbation. There are problems with 'inner–outer' or 'urban–non urban' dichotomies. *Faith in the City* (Commission on Urban Priority Areas, 1984) is the most recent study to remind us that for the non-London conurbations, the grimmest social conditions may be found on overspill local authority 'outer estates' (Centre for Environmental Studies, 1983). The 'social housing' (this term is used for all public and quasi-public rented housing, including the stock of local authorities, housing associations and development corporations) areas of Cramlington display clear signs of 'outer-estate' status. However, we cannot fall back on an 'outer estate'–'inner-city' dichotomy here. A large part of North Shields, the Meadowell Estate, is a 1930s 'outer-estate' which is now located in inner North Tyneside as a function of local government boundary changes.

The rest of the second part of this book comprises four comparative case studies of aspects of the two localities. These deal respectively with production and base, socio-spatial segregation, the question of land and state and civil society. I have been influenced in thinking about the comparative element in these chapters by Dickens *et al.* (1985: 23–31).

More will be said about this in Chapter 2, but it is necessary here to make a distinction between my comparisons and those which are associated with traditional case studies, including the case study material presented by Dickens *et al*. My case studies are comparative but they are also relational. This is a development of my earlier comments about the distinctiveness of this study in trying to get to grips with a great city. North Shields and Cramlington are different, and those differences are important and they help us to understand what is going on. But, and much more importantly, North Shields and Cramlington are related. The relations between them are what matter. I employ comparison in order to get to grips with relations rather than as a realist method of generating '. . . conceptually informed causal analysis' (Dickens *et al.*, 1985: 31). Here I will just assert that I think my comparisons are part of a 'historical materialist method'. This theme is developed in the last part of Chapter 2.

The case study themes have been expressed in this way because I am anxious that the political implications, the implications for collective social action, are to the forefront. Therefore, I do not have a chapter on 'industry' but rather have attempted a review of base. Base is here defined following Williams (1983), so that it includes not only production in terms of industrial structure and experience of it but also aspects of social reproduction, including elements of the domestic and of the welfare system.

None the less, part of Chapter 4 will be concerned with something which looks rather like the 'geography of production', although that term is inadequate in defining the nature of my concern. It will be necessary to look at the changing spatial organization of production in Cramlington and North Shields, and in the city region of which they are related parts. Useful as the ideas and examples assembled in Massey's (1984) work on this topic are, her approach pays too little attention to culture. Distinctive industrial/spatial cultures have very great importance as the bridge between base and civil society and particular attention will be devoted to the cultural derivatives of production in Chapter 4.

I can illustrate this best by example. A major concern will be a cultural set attached to what seems to be a disappearing base, at least if the logic of capital is allowed to determine the course of events. There has been a good deal written about coalfield culture but coalfield culture is not now (although it was very recently) central to either of my locales. What is still crucial on Tyneside is the maritime base and maritime cultures. It seems to me that Tyneside is a maritime locality or it is, literally, nothing. It is not just a great city; it is, or rather was, a great port and shipbuilding city, and that matters in understanding it and the places which are like it. There is an interesting comparison here with Liverpool and its 'class culture', but there is a difference precisely because of the much greater importance of 'marine manufacturing' on Tyneside compared with Merseyside. In addition, North Shields is a fishing port. All these things make their own contribution and add up in a complex way.

These theme categories are not mutually exclusive. They have the status of fuzzy sets. Thus housing is discussed in all the chapters in this part of the book (Chapters 3–8). There are aspects of the production of housing which are crucial to understanding basal relations, and the relationship between housing and land is obvious and will form a central part of Chapter 4. However, land will be considered in a more general sense following on from Ambrose and Colenutt's (1975) employment of Lefbvre's (1976) notions of a secondary circuit of capital.

I do not wish to nail my colours to this mast, but one of the characteristics of the last decade has been the shift of interest of innovative aspects of capital as displayed in my locales, from a concern with the restructuring of production (although of course this is still going on) to a concern with land and its potential. Not least important here is 'maritime land' and the operation of that new state form, an Urban Development Corporation. Obviously, questions of land are absolutely essential to an understanding of Cramlington which can be described in a brutally summary but not inaccurate fashion as the product of two private developers using the local state. What has surprised me, and is different from my understanding of processes as they were in the middle 1970s when I last worked in and on North Shields, is the centrality of land and development to an understanding of that place. I am not convinced that what is going on is a 'compensatory' secondary circuit of capital parallel to industrial production, but something is happening with residential and retail land development which appears to be separate from industrial production.

The work of the CDP suggests that there is a cyclical character to this importance of land. During North Shields' development in the second half of the nineteenth century, issues of urban land development were crucial, not least in relation to the politics of the local state. It seems that land has this centrality at times of change, either growth or decline. In this respect, the impact of the depression of the 1930s was somewhat different. Even then, there were land development issues associated with local state support for the new system of owner-occupation but, in comparison with developments after 1975, the 1930s seem to have been a period during which previous social forms were suspended rather than transformed. Actually, it is in relation to land and suburbanization that this statement is least true, even in the depressed North East. What is certain is that land and property development are where the action is today and that merits careful attention.

An important theme of empirical and theoretical work on contemporary social structure is that of social differentiation, and its spatial aspects. Forrest and Murie have written on the 'residualization' of council housing as a tenure in consequence of policies and basal developments. They have been careful to note that 'the analytical starting point must be labour market and economic restructuring' (Forrest and Murie, 1986: 49), a position which is not shared by neo-Weberian theorists of consumption cleavages such as Saunders (1982, 1986). Spatial and tenurial differentiation is a reality in my locales, although there are very great cleavages within tenures as well as between them. The two localities include sub-localities which are differentiated in relation to a typology of 'urban social areas' generated from social indicator data. Typological analyses based on clustering procedures are a means of *exploring* social reality (see Openshaw, 1983).

Such typologies are useful if, and only if, they bear some correspondence to social structure and social processes as perceived by social actors. Do people 'differentiate' in an active sense, in terms of attaching significant social meanings, among localities? It seems clear that they do and that a comprehension of such differentiation and its basis is part of the apparatus of significant agents, and in particular of speculative builders, in their own active differentiation of locales. However, there is an even more active sense of the notion of differentiation than that referring to marketing and planning strategies, although these are derivatives of this final process. I mean here the notion of differentiation as a crucial component of the *restructuring* of the working class as part of the restructuring of the capitalist system of production in these last decades of the twentieth century (see Byrne and Parson, 1983). Here I intend to extend and develop the analysis by looking at differentiation as the product of a process of underdevelopment in the sense in which that word is used by Cleaver (1977).

I want to emphasize that in my discussion of social differentiation I am not dealing with an 'underclass' in the sense in which that term has recently been employed by, among others, Dahrendorf (1987). Miller (1981) has pointed out the dangers of sloppy terminology here. It is appropriate to talk of 'marginalization' and 'peripheralization' because these terms are descriptive of social process, but the underclass model reduces capitalism to a description and confines action to moral outrage and good will. This is not to say it rules out action, but it fails to grasp the relation of action to capitalism. A central theme of this book will be a concern with the sources of action against peripheralization, and the role of the so-called 'underclass' as a classic reserve army of labour will be illustrated by examples of labour discipline and 'specially exploitative branches of accumulation'.

The actual empirical content of Chapter 5 includes a set of cluster analyses, a review of the implications of household surveys carried out recently in the two localities and the reporting of interviews with significant informants. North Shields and Cramlington contain an interesting set of sub-localities in which almost all the issues relating to residence in relation to base as an aspect of social differentiation can be investigated. There are residualized inner and outer public-sector estates, areas of marginal owner occupation in both pre-1914 and 'starter-home' stock, locales of gentrification, and clear instances of the importance of age cohorting in residence, which is itself an expression of different labour market, and hence production, conditions at the time of entry of different cohorts into work.

One absence on Tyneside, or at least in North Shields and Cramlington, is any real impact of race in relation to issues of differentiation. This is not least interesting, because before the mass New Commonwealth immigration after 1950, North Shields was one of the major locations of non-European settlement in the UK (Little, 1947). There is no way in which I would wish to minimize the significance of ethnicity in relation to differentiation and the action consequences of that differentiation. If race is not much of an issue in my locales it is in other areas, including West Newcastle where there is a significant Asian population and a history of very nasty episodes of racial attack. Perhaps even more interesting than the status of race as a demarcator of differentiation, is the absence of division around religion, and in particular around the ethnic–religious combination of Irish Catholicism. This is not true of places in Britain which otherwise much resemble Tyneside, namely Glasgow and Liverpool. I will pay attention to these things, but one aspect of the specificity of the locales I am dealing with is their relative unimportance.

Chapter 7 deals with the topics of the state and civil society. It is easier to define the first of these terms and lay out the implications of its consideration, than it is to deal with civil society *per se* or its relation to the state. What is characteristic of both locales is the de-democratization of policy formation and implementation. Cramlington, although a New Town, was not developed by a corporatist and appointed development corporation but by a partnership of two elected authorities (county and district) and two developers. In principle, there should have been a considerable democratic element. In practice, democracy was restricted and seems to be on the decline. North Shields has a long history of democratic local government and is currently under the political control of the most left-wing Labour authority in the North East. Here the significance of *authoritarian corporatism*, in the form of the new Urban Development Corporation (UDC), is enormous. Contemporary corporatist forms in the UK need to be distinguished from classical conceptions of this concept in some way because, while they incorporate working-class organization through the recruitment on a personal and unrepresentative basis of leadership figures, they are not responsive to any significant degree of pressure for working-class interests: hence, authoritarian corporatism. However, the UDC is not a bolt from the blue, rather, it is the logical next step in a process which began in the 1970s with the concept of urban aid and of central intervention in local affairs. The CDP itself was intended to be part of that process.

In North Tyneside, local politics there has been a transition of control involving a change in the dominant faction within the Labour group. An older faction, not so much of industrial workers as of municipal veterans with a 'collaborationist' attitude towards central government, has been displaced by a younger group including public-sector professionals and industrial workers with a recent and continuing history of trade union activism. It would be wrong to see this development as involving the replacement of the working class by the new urban left. Indeed, the new dominant group has many more real industrial links, and the extent to which industrial issues, and in particular job losses consequent on industrial restructuring, have been interpreted as local issues, is crucial to this aspect of politics in North Shields.

Cramlington's local politics are different. Within the coterminous Borough and Parliamentary Constituency of Blyth Valley, the old Labour hegemony based on the coalfield has been seriously threatened by the emergence of an Alliance challenge. The Alliance were briefly the controlling party in local government and just missed taking the Parliamentary seat at the 1987 election. There is an interesting history associated with the split in the Blyth Labour Party following Eddie Milne's deselection as parliamentary candidate and subsequent expulsion in the early 1970s. Milne's crime was to denounce systematic corruption in North Eastern Labour and Trade Union politics. However, reaction against Milne's treatment, although very important, is not the whole story. Cramlington, as a new social space, has had an impact. An understanding of the nature of the Alliance and Labour in both North Shields and Cramlington is crucial to any effort at grasping the form and content of the relationship between civil society and the state in these localities today.

I regard the form of political action as the most important connection between the state and civil society, and locate political engagement and organization as a component of civil society rather than the state. However, politics is not the sum of civil society. Aspects of the maritime culture described above belong to civil society and serve as a connection between it and the system of production. Likewise, many aspects of leisure and voluntary associations associated with residential location belong in the sphere of civil society. Although the central focus of Chapter 7 is on the connections between the state and civil society through political action, it will be necessary to consider these other aspects and their significance for politics. This *does not* involve a commitment to a notion of a politics of consumption à la Gorz or Saunders.

If this book was simply an academic text it would conclude with Chapter 8, which is a summarizing review thus far. However, I have made claims for the relation of this text to action and it is the final part of this book which bears the burden of substantiating that claim. Chapter 9 consists of the working out in a Tyneside context of an idea which derives from the work of Zusa Ferge (1979) and Alan Walker (1984). It can best be expressed by reference to Walker's (1984: 6) definition of 'structural incrementalism' which:

> is concerned with planning the transformation of existing institutions and with radical change in the distribution of resources, status and power between different groups. It sets out to question existing policies and services, not as an end in itself, but in terms of their adequacy as means of distributing resources.

Walker goes on to talk of 'structural incrementalism' as 'the basis of planning for need'. The idea is reminiscent of the transformational reformist principle of the best elements of the second international. This has to be distinguished very carefully from that kind of reformism which is simply concerned with the amelioration of an existing capitalist social order. Transformational reformism is about changing what is into something very different. Williams (1983: 272) identifies this process as:

> a socialist cultural revolution (which) has still to be rooted in potential majorities which can, by their own organization and activity, become effective majorities. The principle of cultural revolution offers an outline of ways in which there can be both effective association and new forms of negotiation beyond specific associations. In this assertion of possibility, against all the learned habits of resignation and scepticism, it is already a definition of practical hope. Beyond that, it seems now the only way forward in a situation of very general and dangerous unsettlement, where the taking of direct responsibility is not just an attractive idea but probably the only means of survival.

He also reminds us that what is to be attempted is a 'cultural *revolution* and not some unimpeded process of social growth' (Williams, 1983: 273). This is what 'democratic socialism' ought to mean, however remote it may be from the present practices of the Labour Party in or out of office.

Thus Chapter 9 is about what policies, both local and national, will be necessary as components of a structural programme concerned with the effective redistribution of resources and power and with the transformation of the existing social order through a process of cultural revolution. This is not just a matter of what is traditionally thought of as 'social policy'. While I take Walker's point about the trap involved in always predicating social policies on economic policies and their success, it is clear that any transformation must involve basal change. What may be unusual is my conviction that constitutional change, a reordering of the formal arrangements of political power and the nature of the British State, is a precondition for the achievement of the other changes, and that demands for this change may well be the vehicle through which other aspects of the strategy are developed and used as a stimulus to political action. I refer here to the urgent need for an effective devolution of central powers in the British State to elected regional governments. However, changes going the right way at any level are to be encouraged and demanded. Thus, there are policies which may lie within the present powers of an existing local authority, although these form part of the proper subject of Chapter 10 rather than a discussion of strategy.

It is conventional for such discussions to make reference to 'consultation' and 'popular planning'. I am all for planning from the bottom up but I am also convinced of the virtues of the presentation of draft proposals as a means for making discussion possible. In Chapter 9 I attempt an outline of the framework of a regional plan for economic regeneration which is a 'democratic alternative' to the corporatist proposals of the Northern Regional Strategy Team, (1979).

This sort of thing has been tried before and failed. Witness the experiences of the Greater London Council (GLC). This is where Chapter 10 comes in. If Chapter 9 is about medium-term strategies of social transformation, Chapter 10 is about short-term tactics of mobilization, and in particular about being 'in and against the state'. This is not a new idea, but what will be said here differs from the version of radical deviance theory which informed, for example, attempts by radical social workers to mobilize their clients as a self-sustaining force for social change. The rhetoric was always more extreme than the practice but it is the rhetoric which has persisted. I am not about to dismiss the poor as part of a force for change, but there is a great deal more to it than organizing the poor to help themselves. What is required now is a strategy for the socialist use of democratic control over the local state which, while never neglecting what efforts are possible at providing services in a socialist (i.e. humane and effective) fashion in the foreseeable future, pays a great deal of attention to the use of resources for the mobilization of forces. This is where community work becomes crucial. After all, one way of looking at it is that the job of the community worker is no different in kind from that of a revolutionary cadre. It is just that community workers get paid and do not have to go to gaol (Alex Robson of the 1930s NUWM in North Shields commenting on the work of CDP in the mid-1970s). The question is how do 'cultural revolutionary' cadres work within a framework of *democracy*, a word which is not emphasized for the purposes of irony but to indicate what still remains the central principle on which cultural revolution must be conducted.

Things are not made any easier by the removal for many people of 'organized' production as a central constitutive experience of their social being. In Chapter 10 I try to make some suggestions about the form and content of a practical politics of reproduction which could help in the mobilization of the social forces necessary for the implementation of a programme of structural social change. We need organization, and the central purpose of this book is to lay out an account of the nature of the social systems and processes so that we can get on with the job. The first two parts of this book are about understanding where things have to be done. Chapter 9 is about what things are to be done. Chapter 10 comes back from Utopia – and I am all for Utopia – to the question of 'How is it to be done?' That will be my conclusion.

2

Locality, social process and explanation

Introduction

This chapter will review recent debates so as to get to grips with some issues and ideas which are helpful in understanding the situation in North Shields and Cramlington. The point is to facilitate discussion of how to change things – how in terms of the title of this book to get *Beyond the Inner City*, both for Tyneside and for other places like it. The terms of the review are best illustrated by reference to the contrast between the *field* of social policy and the *discipline* of sociology. A discipline is a science. It is concerned with understanding the world and has a set of distinctive methodological devices for engaging in that process. In this sense, *sociology* is a discipline. A field is not a discipline. It is constituted by a set of problems which are approached using concepts and theories generated by disciplinary work. In this sense, *social policy* is a field in which disciplines are there to be used in order to enhance the development of policies, and policies are about changing the way things are now. The approach here is firmly in this tradition of emphasis on use for change.

One of the problems with the dominant Fabianism of UK social policy is its failure to take up the epistemological implications of this commitment to change. Instead, it has proceeded with a kind of respectful subservience to traditional science, which in the past extended to uncritical acceptance of positivist traditions and a self-identification as a sort of social engineering. More recently, social policy in this country has been informed by political economy – that tradition, primarily but not exclusively derived from Marxism, which identifies the ideological character of disciplinary boundaries and looks for explanations of the nature of social structure and social process in terms of the character of the dominant mode of production (see Gough, 1979). This is fine so far as it goes, but even Marxist approaches have not always taken things as far as they should go. In Cleaver's terms (1979), they have remained at the level of mere political economy by seeking to explain without making change central to their project.

This is even more the case with students of 'the urban', where there is *de facto* endorsement of political economy through the breakdown of disciplinary boundaries. However, in 'urban' and 'regional' studies, the issue of explanation for what has been prominent by its absence. The engagement with Marxism has been largely through contact with structuralist traditions and in particular with the work of Althusser as mediated through Castells (1977). This is best dealt with quickly and crudely in a book concerned with change. Structuralist variants of the Marxist tradition are characteristically informed by 'dialectical materialism', however sophisticated they may have become in their onward development. In other words, they assign a special status to 'scientific understanding' and allow for political engagement in the form of 'theoretical practice'. The debate about this in Marxism is old and important (see Avineri, 1965; Cleaver, 1979). The point is that structuralism is compatible with passive science.

Sociologists have a problem here. Although there is a strong structuralist tradition in sociology itself, there has always been a competing emphasis on action and on the voluntary will of human beings. (see Dawes, 1970). The cause of action has been upheld in 'urban' and 'regional' studies by those adhering to a broadly Weberian approach. Writers like Saunders (1984, 1986) have pointed out the problems of structuralism, but in their own work have often been guilty of endorsing profoundly capital logic accounts of social process. Despite a formal assertion of understanding the actions of human beings in the terms of those human beings themselves and, either explicitly or implicitly, an associated recognition of the capacity of collective social actors for changing the world, these authors have often seen the imperatives of the production process and capital's organization of it as absolutely overweening.

I have a soft spot for writers in the Weberian tradition or at the intersection of that tradition with Marxism and have learned a lot from them. However, I do think that the purpose of explanation in social science has been elided in work in this field. Geographers in particular (see Gregory and Urry, 1985) fall back on materialist accounts as merely superior explanations. If the issue of the relationship between action and explanation is addressed at all it is through an endorsement of 'realist' approaches to social scientific activity in general. Sayer (1984) identifies the problem and proposes an alternative objective:

> Academics generally occupy a place in the social division of labour in which the development of knowledge in propositional forms, in a contemplative relationship to the world, has unusual primacy.
>
> [The alternative] means more than merely a different way of 'doing social science'. It implies a different view of the social role of this type of knowledge and for 'intellectuals'. It means that social science should not be seen as developing a stock of knowledge about an object which is external to us, but should develop a critical self-awareness in people as subjects and indeed assist in their emancipation.
>
> (Sayer, 1984: 18 and 43)

The rest of this chapter deals with material organized around themes. The first will be that of the contemporary nature of capitalism as a system of production and reproduction which will be addressed by reference to the idea of 'disorganized capitalism'. The second will develop consideration of reproduction and go into the distinction between this concept and that of collective consumption with special consideration of the notion of consumption cleavages. This leads naturally to a review of the nature and potential of collective actors and the field of action in which they might be engaged. Next, the relevance of space will be discussed in relation to the concepts of locality and region and attention will be paid to the role of 'class practices' in constituting both of these domains. Consideration will also be given to the nature of culture and of civil society, of the domains of everyday life which are to be distinguished from 'economic' and 'state' spheres, but are crucial to the constituting of state and economy. An organizing term can be introduced here – post-modernism – to describe a new set of relations among economy, state and civil society *in crisis*. The discussion of the role of the state will focus on linkages between the state and civil society through political engagement and on developments in 'administration' considered in relation to crisis management. 'Post-modernism' will be extended to 'post-modernization' as a way of describing the development beyond 'modernization', the characteristic objective of state intervention in the localities and region with which this book is concerned from the 1930s to the mid-1970s. The chapter concludes with a review of modes of explanation in terms of a debate between 'realism' and 'historical materialism'.

The current condition of capitalism

This book is informed by a materialist understanding based on the premise that the organization of the productive system, and of associated reproduction, is the most important thing in a society. Other aspects of a society have to be understood in relation to that organization. With Williams' (1980) caveat that we must qualify the meaning of every term in the expression accepted, we can still best proceed if we understand that 'base determines superstructure'. The concept which has proved most fruitful in considering the nature and origins of contemporary capitalism in relation to the two Tyneside locales, is that provided by the contrast between organized and disorganized capitalism as discussed by Lash and Urry (1987), who distinguish between them in terms of a 14-point schemata. A brutal summary and paraphrase of this follows.

Organized capitalism is distinguished by centralization of capital and the increased interconnection between finance and industrial capital. It involves the separation of ownership from control and the growth of 'management' with an associated technical intelligentsia on the one hand, together with the increased organization of industrial workers on the other. Likewise, this pattern of organization extends into associations of employers, professioinals, etc. The phase is characterized by interarticulation between the state and productive capital and by the participation of collective organizations in the state which is increasingly a welfare state.

The world economy is dominated by manufacturing, which itself employs very large numbers of workers located in a key set of metropolitan capitalist countries. There is a considerable degree of regional specialization coupled with the growth of big plants and big cities. The dominant cultural motif is 'modernism', which emphasizes technical and scientific rationalism and its aesthetic realization.

Disorganized capitalism is characterized by the internationalization of capital in terms of production, marketing and control. Lash and Urry (1987) speak of a 'nearly universal decline of cartels'. This seems accurate enough, although one wonders if with trans-national companies in oligopolistic control of major industrial and energy sectors, cartels are in any way necessary. The class composition of formerly core industrial societies changes with a massive decline in the industrial working class and growth in white-collar service employment. Industrial relations become decentralized and local. At the same time, corporatist arrangements break down as does the class character of political parties. There is an erosion of the specialized character of regional economies and redundancy of big plants and associated big industrial cities. The dominant cultural motif is post-modernist.

Lash and Urry (1987) do not ignore the mass extension of industrial capitalism on a world scale. Indeed, this is one of their demarcators of disorganized as opposed to organized capitalism. However, it could be argued that they ignore the nature of industrial capitalism in its new locales and concentrate instead in descriptive terms on the impact on social relations in former metropolitan, specialized industrial city regions.

Given the topic of this book this does not lessen the usefulness of their formulation for our purposes but there remains a whiff of 'western-centricness' about any account which suggests that fewer people are experiencing that 'social being' which 'determines consciousness' through organized industrial labour. Lash and Urry are much less guilty of this offence than a group from whom they very specifically dissociate themselves – the proponents of 'post-industrialism'. Disorganized capitalism remains capitalism, and they make it clear that they are not bidding farewell to the working class. Indeed, 'disorganized capitalism' seems an unhappy term for conveying what they are dealing with. The idea of disorganization in social relations is important and accurate. What is manifestly not disorganized in disorganized capitalism as a set of social relations is capital, either in abstraction or as a 'system force' in crucial locations, but especially at the point of production. The concept of 'disorganized' capitalism is essentially sociological and political rather than economic and may require qualification at the political level. The form of relations among the state, capital and the organized working class is clearly changing, but the destruction of tripartite corporatism does not mean that instrumental connections between capital and the state do not persist. They may even be being strengthened.

The immediate utility of the notion of disorganized capitalism is descriptive in relation to the process of deindustrialization in the UK in general and on Tyneside in particular. The greatest force of the idea is in relation to culture as a component of civil society and hence to the sources of collective social action. It is worth pausing to consider 'deindustrialization', the destruction of what Rowthorn (1986) calls a 'workshop economy', and of the role of space in this as identified by Massey (1984). These themes are only noted here, because it makes more sense to develop them in Chapter 4 around relevant empirical information. However, they are the background to what follows – if 'social being determines social consciousness', then the changes in experience which derive from the reordering of production on Tyneside have profound significance.

The question of what is base and what is superstructure becomes relevant. There is no need for a detailed classificatory system. What is at issue is the location of reproduction. Capitalism is a system for the production of commodities, and to produce these commodities the things used to produce them must be reproduced, i.e. in its simplest sense, reproduction means the reproduction of labour power. However, the term is commonly extended beyond this simple meaning to include the reproduction of the willingness of the possessors of that labour power to work on capital's terms in a capitalist system, i.e. the reproduction of capitalist social relations (see Cockburn, 1976). It is important to note that reproduction is a source of dynamism, of change. As Lefbvre (1976) has put it, there is not reproduction of social relations without a production of social relations. If the term disorganized capitalism is useful in describing a new set of relations, then some of these relations have changed at a level which might traditionally have been assigned to superstructure – at the levels of ideology or civil society, although these terms will require subsequent careful discussion. Some things have, however, changed at a simpler and much more direct level. Offe (1984: 283) contends that:

> under modern capitalist conditions there is no one central condition that causally determines all other conditions on a base–superstructure or primary–secondary manner. The work role is only partly determinative of social existence.

Under capitalism, workers are paid wages for the use of their labour power and the simplest form of reproduction is to use those wages to reproduce their own labour power, i.e. those who do this for them (women), and that of future generations of labour power (children). One of the most fruitful recent contributions to Marxist theory has been that of autonomist writers who have identified the centrality of reproduction to capitalism and extended the concept of the proletariat beyond the directly employed worker to include the social proletariat (see Negri, 1979) engaged in the reproduction of labour power. This still keeps the wage–labour relationship and the work-role as determinative of social existence, even if this is at second hand (and its being at second hand is very important in relation to issues of patriarchy). What about the situation in which, on the one hand, many households have *no* contact with wage labour and are wholly dependent for reproduction on state benefits and, on the other, wage labour has penetrated far further into other households because of the importance of female employment?

Theorists of the social proletariat extend the term to include reproduction of capitalism's industrial reserve armies of benefit dependents (see Byrne and Parson, 1983), which provides a much more satisfactory account than notions of a residuum or underclass (this issue will be developed in Chapter 6). Here it is worth noting that one of the characteristics of disorganized capitalism as a social system is polarization and that this polarization is particularly apparent in relation to reproduction, with one set of households being dependent on state benefits and bureaucratic allocative systems and another being integrated into markets through the spending of wages.

An account of polarization in reproduction does not complete a consideration of production and reproduction under disorganized capitalism. Discussion about the nature of the state will follow below but there is a body of literature about the nature and form of the pressures on the state from the base in contemporary capitalism which is worth noting here. O'Connor (1984) proposed a capital derivative version of the state coupled with a 'consequences of action' modification. That sentence is a simplification of O'Connor's account and a gross simplification of a complex debate about the nature of the state in capitalism (see Jessop, 1982). However, there is a very considerable congruence between Marxist accounts and those of the new right who both identify much of expenditure on the welfare state as dysfunctional for capital accumulation (see Mishra, 1984). Under O'Connor's best known schemata expenditure, which either reduces the cost of labour power to capital or increases the productivity of labour for capital, is compatible with continued capital accumulation. What is dysfunctional is expenditure in the form of social expenses on system maintenance, either through legitimation or coercion, although discussion has emphasized the former.

Thus the demands of order (achieved through some combination of legitimation and coercion) are contradictory for capitalism. Without order, the system does not continue to exist, but spend too much and accumulation breaks down. Neo-liberal critiques have emphasized the dysfunctionality of legitimation expenditures in terms of 'crowding out'. One aspect of disorganized capitalism is pressure against general welfare expenditures for those not directly engaged in productive work. In this respect, the contemporary UK seems rather different from one aspect of Lash and Urry's description of disorganized capitalism. They refer to the development of class-specific welfare legislation as an aspect of organized capitalism and to the development of universalistic welfare legislation and subsequent challenges from both left and right to the centralized welfare state (Lash and Urry, 1987: 6) as characteristic of disorganized capitalism. In fact, universalistic welfare legislation coupled with the prioritizing of the retention of full employment as the key objective of publicly expressed economic policy seems absolutely characteristic of the organized capitalism of workshop Britain in the 1950s and 1960s. It is precisely the subsequent attack on this and the development of an exclusionary and residual welfare state for the poor, coupled with generous fiscal welfare for the non-poor, which seems characteristic of disorganized capitalism.

In disorganized capitalism, aspects of production's organization and of the organization of reproduction through welfare congrue in relation to segregation and social differentiation. This is not an original point. The conceptualization of system disintegration in ever more interrelated politico-administrative, economic and civil systems is central to the approach of the Frankfurt school and a number of commentators have noted the massive contemporary significance of social differentiation and segregation. All these things have to be brought together in relation to an account of crisis. For now we can proceed in terms of dealing with a fundamental social order which can be usefully described as disorganized capitalism.

Reproduction versus consumption: stratification and the origins of social action

Castells (1977) identifies urban problems as aspects of collective consumption in contrast to problems which derive from production. Urban issues are to be understood in terms of class conflicts over the character and extent of reproduction through collective consumption in the form of the provision of urban services and facilities, particularly housing. As Foster (1979) points out, Castells was concerned with mapping out the form of specifically urban contradictions, the contradictions which are created between privately owned means of production and collective aspects of reproduction. Castells was particularly weak on the question of how such contradictions were translated into social action. Foster indicates how commitment to relative autonomy of the political, ideological and economic generates accounts which look very like traditional functionalism. In a revealing passage, Castells (1977) dismisses any role for historical actors in favour of 'support agents expressing particular combinations of the social structure through their practice'. Foster's review is particularly good on the deficiencies of theorizations which fail to provide us with:

> some way of understanding what makes a contradiction 'deep' for one population and not another, of what *determines* (to use an unfashionable word) the material content of sectional consciousness and subjective perception.
>
> (Foster, 1979: 104)

Similar criticisms are made by Duncan (1982) and Mingione (1981) who points out the 'autonomy' component of Althusserian structuralism. While Castells' early work has usually been criticized for the absence of agency and consequent essentially functionalist explanation, this absence of connection between base and consciousness – an implicit dismissal of the notion that social being determines consciousness – is also a licence for action explanations in a Weberian tradition which completely sever the connection between the production system and social action around reproduction. Such accounts dismiss any notion of reproduction and treat consumption as wholly, as opposed to relatively, autonomous.

This approach is best known in terms of the concept of consumption cleavages as proposed by Saunders (1984, 1986). Saunders (1986: 156) distinguishes his account from traditional Weberian approaches to stratification and contends that he is dealing with:

> phenomena which have only arisen in the period of advanced capitalism in which the state has intervened directly both in the organization of production and in consumption. They are products, that is, of the use of state power in civil society and as such they have only appeared in the period since Marx and Weber were writing.

This matters because recent discussion shows Weber's conception of class (Wright, 1985) to be determined by production just as much as it is by Marx, but that Weber is concerned with consequences in terms of market exchanges, whereas Marx focuses on exploitation. Saunders begins by equating reproduction with consumption and by arguing that production-derived class is not determinant of consumption position. In large part, Saunders justifies his approach in terms of a questionable conception of what is meant by the term 'determine'. His retention of this argument is somewhat surprising given that Harloe (1984) took him to task for it in very exact terms in a rejoinder to an article on housing tenure, in which many of its central propositions were advanced. Harloe's point is the simple but necessary one which has already been cited in relation to Williams's discussion of base and superstructure, that 'determine' has to be understood in terms of the setting of limits, a usage which Saunders (1984: 207) himself employs in contradistinction to the 'one to one ism' of French structuralism to describe the relationship between tenure and production-derived class. However, this is water under the bridge. What matters is the contemporary nature of Saunders' claims, not in abstraction but, because at a superficial level they, in common with similar work by Dahrendorf (1987), Bauman (1987), Pahl (1984, 1985) and particularly Gorz (1982), seem to make a lot of descriptive sense.

Saunders deals with divisions which originate in differential access to consumption. He identifies these as 'material divisions which are every bit as "real" and every bit as pertinent as those which arise out of the relations between classes' (Saunders, 1984: 207). By 'real' and 'pertinent' Saunders means that these divisions are just as likely as class to be the source of significant social action. For example, owner-occupiers are considered to derive real wealth from houses as assets. This wealth is independent of production relations and owes more to household structure and position in the life-cycle. It is a source of cleavages which are as important for social action in general and voting behaviour in particular as production-derived social class.

Much of this has to be regarded as heroic in its assumptions. Its empirical basis is in questionable psephology (see Ball, 1986) and in an enormous edifice of theory piled on an admittedly important locality study in a rather unusual place (Pahl's (1984) description of Sheppey). Simple points are ignored or elided. No serious Marxist discussion of class has failed to recognize the importance of *divisions* within the working class. It is quite possible to present an academic and deductive dismissal of consumption cleavages without any real need to turn to empirical 'testing'.

However, the account goes further and this is what matters in relation to the study being dealt with in this book. Saunders does not stop at a description of social division as a source of significant social action. He goes on to identify:

new sectoral relations of exploitation (in which a relatively large number of people exploit an increasingly marginalized minority for whom collective provision remains the only and strictly second best, option).

(Saunders, 1984: 225)

Of these identifications of a new underclass as the victim of affluence in the two-thirds (affluent and Tory) versus one-third (not) society, Bauman's formulation is to be preferred to Saunder's because it sets up issues which are subject to empirical review and it continues to use a conception of reproduction:

the poor are less and less important to the reproduction of capital in their traditional role as the 'reserve army of labour'. They are no longer the object of concern for the twofold political task of recommodification of labour and limitation of working-class militancy. The previously taken-for-granted principle of social responsibility for the survival – and indeed well-being of that part of society not directly engaged by capital as producers has suddenly come under attack.

(Bauman, 1987: 21)

The traditional functions of the reserve army are alive and well in North Shields and Cramlington and the bidding of farewell to the working class is decidedly premature (see Byrne, 1984). However, the issue is a very real one. There are clear political and cultural cleavages in both the locales which could be identified in terms of consumption cleavages. Chapter 6 discusses these as revealed by patterns of social indicators, and action consequences are reviewed in relation to local politics and political culture. The question of 'reserve army or underclass' is crucial to any understanding of the potential for social action for change. It is addressed here in terms of historical evidence about the formation of the situation described, its present nature and its action consequences in terms of political behaviour.

Locality and region: the question of space

. . . it is a matter of distinguishing between those concepts which define the mode of production and which allow us to establish the nature of the classes and their relationships in the abstract from those concepts which allow a concrete analysis of these classes. The latter proceeds from an investigation of political history, forms of consciousness, and modes of organization of the classes. It is this dynamic which, by defining the forces in the field in concrete terms, allows the particular forms of the state to be determined.

(Gramsci, 1971)

In the introduction, emphasis was placed on the study of the city as a way of understanding social action for change. What was being dealt with was the significance of space in relation to social action. Space is now being employed in social science in relation to each half of the structure–action dichotomy *and* as a device for bridging the gap between them. The first aspect is represented on the one hand by the theme of 'uneven development' and on the other by the notion of 'local social system'. The connection is most often dealt with by some version of a realist explanation of their 'interaction'.

Uneven development is relatively easy to deal with. It is an example of a theme which will crop up throughout this book – that modes which originated as ways of describing and analysing international capitalism, and relations of domination within it, are being brought back home to be used in the understanding of developments within the former metropolitan power. What is being taken up here is Marx's account of 'combined and uneven development' in a spatial form. Changes within capitalism generate new forms of spatial organization at the same time as they create new forms of social organization. This applies both to production and to labour, which is reorganized both socially (see Braverman, 1974) and spatially. The best account of all this is given by Massey (1984), and her general argument will be discussed in more detail in Chapter 4. What is important is the idea that 'spaces' at a sub-national level within former metropolitan capitalism can be 'underdeveloped' just as the Third World has been underdeveloped by capitalist colonialization.

The idea of 'local social system' in its most recent form is not constructed around that phrase, which is more characteristic of the usage of an earlier generation of community studies (see Stacey, 1971). However, it is useful as a preliminary term because the preferred recent usage of 'locality' carries with it an account of process and, at least implicitly, an effort to resolve action–structure divisions. Urry (1982: 39) asserts that 'Localities are . . . the prime site in which social practices are made and sustained, social practices which constitute social systems'. His description is more sophisticated than that of the social anthropologically derived traditional community study which was rightly criticized for ignoring basal factors at the structural level. Dickens *et al.* (1985: 21) summarize the account very well:

> Simply put, capitalism may be an international system and its chief economic institution – the firm – is increasingly multinational and increasingly freed from time/space constraints. Labour, however, is not, nor are people's daily individual and communal lives.

Urry (1985: 35) identifies cities as being:

> not so much an interlocking economy of producing and consuming enterprises but a *community of subjects* who produce and consume in order to produce. . . . There is thus a substantial shift in the

structuring of each urban locality. Previously such localities were integrated within the production and reproduction of capital. However as each urban locality has been reduced to the status of a labour pool so they are now integrated not within the production process of capital but of wage-labour, within the sphere of civil society rather than of capitalist production *per se*.

What this amounts to is the underdevelopment of cities through a liberation of capital from spatial boundaries through the use of communications to allow very great spatial separation between aspects of the organization of capitalist production and the stages of the execution of that production, and a simultaneous 'peripheralization' of urban populations. The account makes a good deal of sense at whatever spatial level it is employed, but it seems most applicable at a level considerably beyond any modern residentially based labour market. However, *historically*, labour markets were by no means so residentially tied. If we employ the old expression used by so many organizations of capitalism itself and talk in a directly relevant way about 'the North East Coast', it is easy to identify a distinctive organization of capital on a regional basis in the era of organized capitalism and recognize a *tendency* (but by no means complete process) of deregionalization in the era of disorganized capitalism.

The discussion of space thus far has been somewhat backside foremost. Themes very closely related to the idea of 'locality' have been employed to bring us up to an account of region. Cooke (1985: 213) has defined 'regional' as 'a socio-spatial scale at which it is possible to place in focus the specificity of particular class formations . . . regional boundaries are largely coterminous with class practices'. This action-centred approach is refreshing but it would be wrong to regard Cooke's contribution as merely voluntaristic. In a careful schemata he identifies five elements which have to be taken account of, namely, productive base, labour process, ownership of capital, specific social relations (in civil society, although Cooke does not employ that term as a compendium) and institutional specificities. He argues that pre-industrial class experiences and the cultural forces which originated in them – 'the rich interaction of economy, community, culture and history' (Cooke, 1985: 239) – determine regional identity. We need to recognize the action centredness of the idea of region with boundaries defined in terms of 'the spatial edges . . . of social practices' (Cooke, 1985: 221). Cooke is not explicitly trying to resolve structure–action tensions but the approach he adopts implies a resolution, albeit one which is essentially historicist. Asserters of locality have addressed this question explicitly.

Human geography is undergoing an epidemic of 'unpicking' terms. The idea of locality has recently been the subject of two detailed examinations by Duncan (1986) and Gregson (1987). Both are concerned to see if the term has any value in explanation. Gregson (1987: 5) identifies eight separate ways in which the term has been used but considers that these fall into three broad categories, the first concerned with 'the scale at which certain social and economic processes operate and the way in which the local, in the form of particular places, might relate to this'. This is illustrated by Goodwin's (1986: 2) identification of locality as being concerned with 'those processes that have led to the uneven development and local differentiation of social and economic change', suggesting causal force as the strongest use of locality in both Gregson and Duncan's terms.

Another set of usages are concerned with policies and politics and employ the explanations generated in the first set of usages in their development. Finally, there is a sense of locality as the basis of a method. Gregson (1987: 5) asks 'whether locality can be approached as an object of study in its own right or whether it is simply another term for the case study method?' She plumps for the latter. In Gregson's terms this present book is concerned with place-specific studies. North Shields and Cramlington could be described in terms of localities, not least because to some extent they are based on a discrete organization for the sustaining of labour (see the discussion of Urry's approach in Dickens et al., 1985: 21). However, this identification is only 'to some extent', and it is easier to think of locality as a useful term in this study if it is extended, as Dickens *et al.* extend it in a way reminiscent of Cooke's discussion of the notion of region, to cover political and cultural relations. In the examination of North Shields and Cramlington the *interaction* of base, civil society and state will be investigated in order to understand what is going on. The fact that these things happen over time in the same place matters, even if this study does not draw on Giddens' (1981) notion of structuration to address this sort of question. Dickens *et al.*'s approach to locality, taken together with Cooke's account of region, indicates the need to consider culture and civil society before proceeding further.

Culture and civil society

The problem with old-fashioned community studies was that they lacked any systematic procedure for linking ethnographic observation with accounts of society as a whole. The term 'culture' could be used in this way in less complex, smaller-scale social systems, but it has other meanings in industrial society and seems inadequate for the task of relating everyday life to historical development. Historians and political theorists have another approach. This involves distinguishing the respective spheres of the economy/production, the state and civil society. Urry (1982: 16–17) provides us with a definition of the latter:

LOCALITY, SOCIAL PROCESS AND EXPLANATION

Broadly speaking the struggles of social classes to reproduce the material conditions of their existence are part of, but not exhaustive of, civil society. Also present within civil society are various other social groupings, particularly those based on gender, race, generation and nation. These groupings are not to be reduced to those of class, although the dominant relations and forces of production fundamentally structure the form that their struggles will take. These groupings derive from how in civil society individual subjectivities are constituted, of gender, race, generation, locality and nationality. The discursive and non-discursive structures within which such constitution occurs, particularly within the family, are in turn, related to, but not to be reduced to, the dominant relations/forces of production. Civil Society is not then to be viewed merely as the world of individual needs, but rather . . . as sets of structured, institutionalized social practices.

It is somewhat of a simplification but this definition seems to describe 'what is left of society after we get rid of consideration of production and the state'. Frankel's (1987) pertinent criticism of the usefulness of the notion argues that there are no real boundaries between the economy, state and civil society. Many of the social practices which are constitutive of civil society occur in relation to aspects of state administration and service provision. Social relations other than those of exploitation are also in large part constituted through contacts with the world of work.

However, starting from civil society has the virtue of starting from how people do lead their lives and brings us up against questions about how social changes have transformed the range of possibilities available to them. We can introduce the idea of culture here in relation to a special use of the term which was fashionable in the early 1970s. Considerable emphasis was placed on the idea of separate 'cultures' (or more properly sub-cultures) of poverty as a way of explaining the persistence of deprivation in societies which in principle were egalitarian and which certainly had seen massive increases in total welfare. The concept is both described and trenchantly criticized in Valentine (1969). Indeed, an early CDP inter-project report was devoted to dismissing such cultural explanations of the situation of areas like North Shields in favour of structural accounts centring on industrial change and its consequences. Valentine's pertinent comments about the origins of different behaviour originating in structural constraints which excluded the poor from the life-styles of the more affluent have lost none of their force, but any consideration of everyday life in Cramlington and North Shields has to address the issue of different and distinctive life-styles which are none the less embedded in a common cultural matrix.

What follows is abstract and will be developed in subsequent chapters, but the points are so obvious that they can be stated now. The culture of the North East, identified by Ardagh as being dominated by working-class values, was formed in an era of highly paid male employment in mining, heavy engineering and marine transport. It was based on 'family wages' and female employment was uncommon, and it flourished in the years leading up to 1914. That written, qualifications immediately spring to mind. The social world of the 1950s was profoundly different. Highly paid male employment re-emerged during the war and remained in the post-war boom, but women never retreated to the domestic sphere after 1945. The expansion of employment into new branches of manufacturing like clothing in the North East was almost entirely fuelled by mobilizing the latent reserve army of housewives. The North East of the 1950s and early 1960s was not the North East of 1914, not least in terms of domestic arrangements, demography and completed family sizes.

The best way to put this is by reference to the area of the CDP team's operations in 1974. This was still an employment-centred locale. In 1971 the census-defined unemployment rate for the project area was high at 13%, but this is lower than the national average as defined much less inclusively in 1988. The majority of the people in this locale, identified on a set of social indicators as worthy of special anti-poverty intervention, lived in households maintained out of wages. Things are very different now. Pahl (1984: 314) has referred to a situation in which:

> A process of polarization is developing, with households busily engaged in all forms of work at one pole and households unable to do a wide range of work at the other. . . . The division between the more affluent home-owning households of ordinary working people and the less advantaged under-class households is coming to be more significant than conventional divisions based on the manual/non-manual distinction.

This statement does not have to be taken as gospel to be of use. The existence of a sharply bipolar division of affluent and under-classes is not demonstrated by evidence from our locales when anything other then consumption is taken into account. However, the civil society and cultural values of the former CDP project area are likely to be profoundly influenced by the fact that most of the households resident in large parts of it are now dependent on state benefits rather than on wages for their reproduction. This is not an assertion of 'culture of poverty' – it is an identification of difference.

What is perhaps most interesting is the reality of Frankel's (1987) point about boundary collapse. We can *almost* distinguish between a cultural set constructed around employment and wages *for all adult members of the household* (which raises questions about the general applicability of Offe's, 1984, earlier quoted remark about the *lessening* importance of wages in relation to the determination of existence) and another constructed around benefit dependency. The distinctions are consumptionist but the determination of the differences is absolutely basal. One group of people have connections with production through employment and live their lives through patterns of consumption in civil society. Other people's lives are separated from employment but profoundly influenced by the administrative practices of the state, both local and national. The state is connected to civil society through aspects other than its role in administration and as a major employer, important as these are.

Where do we locate political behaviour in what is at least for the moment a mass democracy? By political behaviour is meant something more than just voting behaviour, although that is important and will be addressed. It includes all aspects of political participation, including formal parties, but also local and national pressure groups. Most political behaviour is in fact located in civil society at party meetings, community groups, CND meetings, tenants' and residents' meetings, etc. A good deal of straightforward social activity is almost always associated with the actual political engagement. The neglect of this area in work about the state is really rather remarkable. We will not understand what is happening and what we can do if we do not attempt a sociology of politics by paying attention to these things. They are not passive little sidelines but are the actual location of class (and if anything else other than class does matter, then that also) action in relation to the state. There has been a lot of assertion about the potential of action of this kind in civil society by what Frankel calls *post-industrial utopians* but very little account. Again the question of just what is disorganized about disorganized capitalism surfaces for our consideration.

State, class and corporatism

Although the fashion seems to be passing, the question of the nature of the state and of its relationships with economy and civil society generated an enormous amount of 'Marxist academic' consideration in the late 1970s. This will not be reviewed here. Instead, three themes will be identified as useful in relation to this study: What are the relationships between the state and the capitalist social order? What is the relationship between the state and social action? What political form is involved in decision making over crucial local policy issues? Discussion will be comparatively abstract and detailed elaboration will be left to Chapter 7, but the themes will be taken a little further forward in relation to a discussion of the transition of state engagement with society from modernism/modernization to post-modernism/post-modernization.

Offe has written on these issues since the early 1970s (see Offe, 1984; Jessop, 1982; Held et al., 1983). Held and Krieger (1983: 487) comment that, for Offe 'the most significant feature of the state is the way it is enmeshed in the contradictions of capitalism'. On the one hand, the state has to ensure the continuation of the accumulation of capital; on the other, it has to appear as a neutral arbiter of interests, thereby preserving its own legitimacy. Indeed, the state has an important role in the task of representing the legitimacy of the system as a whole. This resembles the account by O'Connor (1984) of state expenditures, but Offe goes further by considering the role of the state in relation to crisis management. Here he draws on a set of propositions derived from Habermas's discussion of crisis tendencies in modern society (see Roderick, 1986: 103).

Offe stresses the role of the state as a crisis manager and asserts that there is today a 'crisis of crisis management' itself which derives from the contradictions inherent in the state's efforts to compensate for failures in market mechanisms without challenging the private ownership of the means of production and the primacy of market mechanisms. Jessop (1982: 109ff.) points out that typically this dilemma has been resolved by the extension of non-commodity forms of social relations and refers to Offe's account of a process of 'administrative recommodification'. Offe (1984: 142) describes this as follows:

> The powerful political thrust to get rid of this administrative mode of control over labour and material resources is often, but not exclusively, motivated by the need to relieve the economy of the burden of taxation, and to overcome the fiscal crisis of the state. A second argument is of similar importance. It is the fear that the administrative form of control over material resources could become politicized to such an extent that it would no longer be subservient to, but subversive of the commodity form.

This seems a useful way of understanding the impact of the Thatcherite revolution on the nature of state (both local and national) activity in the two locales under study.

Offe's account of the state has to be distinguished from 'capital derivative' versions and offers an account of why the state favours capital within capitalism by pointing out that as the state apparatus depends on revenues drawn from capitalist accumulation, it depends on stable accumulation for its own functioning. As Held and Krieger (1983: 489) put it (noting 'the interesting parallel to the corporatist view'):

> the state selectively favours those groups whose acquiescence and support are crucial to the untroubled continuity of the existing order: oligopoly capital and organized labour.

This inherent tendency towards corporatism seems less inevitable in the late 1980s but we will return to it below. What about the role of action in relation to state forms and developments?

In Offe's work (see Keane, 1984), the origins of the contradictions of the welfare state in late capitalism are not located in class struggle, but in conflicts among the subsystems of socialization, economy and the state in late capitalism. In this respect, Offe is a post-modernist writer, essentially agreeing with Habermas that:

> What today separates us from Marx are evident historical truths, for example, that in developed capitalist societies there is no identifiable class, no clearly circumscribed social group which could be singled out as the representative of a general interest that has been violated. . . . Both revolutionary self-confidence and theoretical self-certainty are gone.
>
> (quoted in Roderick, 1986: 22)

Offe himself refers to the exhaustion of the potential of the labour movement and explicitly endorses Gorz's (1982) *Farewell to the Working Class*. This will be confronted in the empirical chapters. Here we need to note that there are accounts of state forms and practices which do address issues of collective action.

Any sociology of the state in the sense of empirical study of actual administration and events is bound to be instrumentalist. There are just too many processes and actions which directly serve particular class interests. Certainly, it is impossible to understand the form of the relationship between land and state agencies without paying attention to issues of influence. Perhaps this is why US writers on the state have paid such attention to action. Anderson and Friedland (1975: 48) have argued that:

> a theory of the state must contain a theory of . . . political class struggle, a theory of the ways in which class struggle itself transforms the internal organization of the state. In such a theory the state is seen as not merely helping to reproduce the capitalist system in contradictory ways, but as being itself shaped by the class struggle which results from those contradictions.

Historical accounts are almost invariably accounts of action. For example, Addison's (1975) *The Road to 1945* is an account of how individual *and collective* actors operating within a specific set of circumstances produced profound changes. In practice this book will endorse action accounts. It is written in a spirit of agreement with Cleaver's criticism of Critical Theory and extends that criticism beyond the immediate conflict between labour and capital (which Cleaver himself does implicitly):

> Critical Theorists have remained blind to the ability of working class struggles to transform and threaten the very existence of capital. Their concept of domination is so complete that the 'dominated' virtually disappears as an active historical subject.
>
> (Cleaver, 1979: 42)

Most of the discussions about the relationships between class, state, economy and civil society proceed on the basis of a 'unitary conception' of the working class. The implications about the relationship between the state, economy and a differentiated working class have only really been taken up in a way which derives from radical labour market theory. Clearly, this is important and the relationship between the state, civil society and different sections of the working class is one to which we will need to return.

Before getting to grips with the corporatism as such, it is worth looking at the idea of the *local* state. Local government in the UK once regarded as irredeemably boring (as Cochrane has commented), has become a focus of both academic and political attention. Goodwin (1986: 3) takes up an idea which originated with Milliband: 'some local state institutions and in particular local government both represent local interests and, at the same time, represent the social interests dominant at the centre'.

This action centred-account can be extended to allow for conflict between local interests and system forces expressed through the state system and becomes analytically interesting when there is a radical working-class political domination of local government. UK local government as part of the political system of franchise democracy has been an important area for organized class politics. This politics matters and has been addressed by a series of locality studies, notably that of Dickens *et al.* (1985). At the same time, local government and even more directly administered or corporatist elements of state action at the local level (DHSS local offices, Manpower Services Commission, Health Authorities) are, as Goodwin (1986: 3) puts it, 'important in administering and implementing locally the decisions reached in central government, where weaker and subordinate groups are *not* dominant'. The nature of democratic politics at the local level is straightforward enough in principle, whatever the actual nature of administration through corporate management in local government (see Cockburn, 1976). However, one of the important themes in this book will be the developing *de-democratization* of local political decision making and consequent administration. This is most usually addressed through a discussion of corporatism (see Panitch, 1980: 173).

A discussion of regional policy in the North East since the 1930s could be conducted in terms of an almost classical illustration of corporatist political structures. They were exactly characteristic of the era of 'modernization' (I am grateful to Tim Blackman, 1987, for this usage) in which the leadership of the local Labour and Trade Union movement actively collaborated with regional capital, regional representatives of trans-national capital and the central state in promoting a series of strategies designed to facilitate the operations of trans-national capital, while simultaneously providing jobs and improving the environment. Cramlington is a product of this era.

However, non-democratic corporatist forms have a much greater role in administration. At the same time the representatives of the organized working class are either being excluded from such bodies or rendered impotent in influencing their operations. An example of the latter is provided by developments in training and of the former by the Urban Development Corporations. This 'authoritarian corporatism' is clearly much removed from Scandinavian corporatism proposed as part of reformist political objectives by Mishra (1984).

There are interesting contrasts here. In the Health Service, authoritarian corporatist administration is a way of responding to system pressures for restricted public expenditure. With the UDCs we find a very straightforward pork barrel subsidizing of particular development capital interests through the use of public resources. This is more than just instrumental self-aggrandizement, because this 'market forces' approach is an important ideological device in 'recommodification', but the form of involvement is highly instrumental for many participants. If post-modernism is a critical theory with the working class written off, then post-modernization is authoritarian corporatist administration of urban issues with the working class written out.

Realism versus historical materialism

Spatially orientated social science has been much engaged with epistemological questions which revolve around how what is, is to be explained. Realist approaches (see Sayer, 1984) have been used to provide an alternative to positivism on the one hand and historicism on the other. Dickens *et al.* (1985: 254) indicate why this approach has proved so popular:

> The tension between structure and agency, necessary and contingent recurs in political activity; any political outcome is far from being predetermined or even appropriate. Similarly, epistemologies also have their political implications. Empiricism reproduces the present world. . . . Structuralism ends up in passivity, although sometimes more the passivity of despair rather than acceptance. . . . This world view forgets that people must live now, and, even if capitalism is inevitably to break down, there will be considerable room for manoeuvre over how this happens and what will replace it. . . . The realist approach implies the possibilities for more meaningful action between these two extremes.

There is much to sympathize with here, but this study will not adopt a realist perspective. Sayer clearly wishes to move beyond explanation to transformation but the problems that realism poses for me derive from its confinement in practice to being simply a better system of explanation. This is illustrated by a claim by E. W. Soja (1985: 121–2) that:

The realist philosophy of social science seems almost ready-made to sustain and rationalize the theoretical directions taken by contemporary materialist interpretations of spatiality. For this emerging form of realism revolves around a particular interpretation of the relation between appearances and essences. . . . Realist science is a means of conceptual discovery based on the movement at any given level of analysis, from manifest phenomena to knowledge of the structures and mechanisms which generate them. . . . Empirical analysis is thus given an alternative explanatory methodology.

Outhwaite (1987) comes to a similar conclusion. Realism offers a way of explaining what is observed, which, for example, allows us to account for observed socio-spatial polarization in residence in terms of the generative mechanisms of the capitalist mode of production. I am not at all persuaded that if offers a way of coping with human agency.

This section is not so much demonstrative as assertive, but this present study is informed by a remark of Gramsci's (1971: 465):

It has been forgotten that in the case of a very common expression (historical materialism) one should put the accent on the first term – 'historical' – and not on the second, which is of metaphysical origin. The philosophy of praxis is absolute 'historicism', the absolute secularization and earthiness of thought, an absolute humanism of history. It is along this line that one must trace the thread of the new conception of the world.

This book is directed toward informing action. It may seem pretentious to say so but it is intended in Gramsci's terms as an *organic* intellectual work. It is not about explaining what is, but rather seeks to give an account of what is as the basis for developing a set of practices for getting us to what might be. Thus it is informed by a kind of pastiche of reading from 'unorthodox Marxism', from the black books of the 1920s, because all of these emphasized the importance of conscious collective actors in changing the world.

PART II

The inner and outer city

3

North Shields and Cramlington: two localities and their city and region

Introduction

North Shields and Cramlington are separate but related. The relationship derives from the way in which Cramlington is in part a product of planning policies directed towards the solution of problems of urban congestion on Tyneside. Hence the logic of discussing the two places as part of a 'city', even if the effect of planning policies and spatial reorganization in a more general sense has been to complicate the definition of just what constitutes the 'city' of Tyneside. Obviously, North Shields and Cramlington are part of the same region in that they both lie within a single UK standard planning region. However, emphasis has already been placed on the value of Cooke's conception of a region as defined by 'class cultural' practices in civil society. Here again Cramlington and North Shields belong within the same region, but region in this sense has different geographical boundaries from the standard planning region. Before proceeding to description, it is necessary to sort out some definitions.

The two localities both lie within the standard planning region of 'the North of England' which comprises the counties of Northumberland, Durham, Cleveland, Cumbria and Tyne and Wear. These exact boundaries date from local government reorganization in 1974 but something like the present administrative area has existed since the establishment of regional commissioners for the maintenance of supplies in the 1920s. This is the 'region' for which extensive social and economic trend information is available and it has a practical reality as the area of responsibility of the Northern Regional Health Authority and as the regional level of organization of central state departments. The North is the most clearly defined English administrative region in terms of congruence of administrative boundaries.

The modern notion of a distinctive regional identity dates from the 1930s and was reinforced by the involvement of significant local élites in regional planning, etc., after 1945 (see Chapman, 1985). Contemporary expressions of this sense of 'The North' include the northern group of Labour MPs, the Northern Association of Councils and the Northern Development Company. Typically, this level is corporatist in its political forms and practices. However, despite the construction of a *regionalist* culture at élite levels, this is not really a culturally distinctive region.

The entity which corresponds to 'South Wales' in Cooke's discussions is the 'North East Coast'. Geographically this runs from South Northumberland to Cleveland and extends inland to include all the coalfield and former coalfield areas. Its origin is in coal, the marine transport of that coal and the industrial structure of engineering and shipbuilding which developed from coal and its transport. Although there are significant differences within it (particularly between Teesside and Tyneside), it is marked culturally by what is, to outsiders at least, a distinctive single local accent which is used by natives of all classes except the land-owning upper class.

The North East is almost uniquely industrial. Its only rival for 'industrial determination' in Britain was West Central Scotland – both zones received massive immigration in the nineteenth century. This immigration was so great, that it is difficult to conceive of a 'Northumbrian' culture, other than as a middle-class construct. What is 'North Eastern' is the absolute dominance of industrial class relations. The mining and marine transport of coal created a distinctive capitalist class *and* one of the oldest and most organized working classes in the world. The immigrants arrived in a world organized socially around the conflict between labour and capital. It is often said that the North East was populated by successive generations of industrial scabs. This makes for a remarkable degree of working-class homogeneity, at least for the descendants of those who arrived before 1920 when what had been the world's wealthiest and most productive industrial region outside the USA went into a very rapid decline. In any event, the significant 'cultural' region is the north east coast, but this has no separate administrative existence except, interestingly enough, in some of the oldest organizations of labour and capital. What then of the City?

The idea of Tyneside is at least as old as the middle of the nineteenth century when modern industrial interests combined with local radical politicians to wrest control of the river from the city of Newcastle which until then had exercised a medieval monopoly. The first Tyneside agency was the Tyne Improvement Commission which transformed the river by deepening it, rechannelling it (to such an extent that a piece of Durham ended up North of the Tyne) and building the largest harbour on the east coast and the only harbour of refuge accessible in all weather and tide conditions. Certainly, the idea was in common use by the 1930s, (Mess, 1928). However, Tyneside has never had administrative unity. The term 'Tyneside Conurbation' has been employed in relation to census data since the inter-war years but this contained four county boroughs and significant parts of the counties of Durham and Northumberland. Even after 1974 with the establishment of the Metropolitan County of Tyne and Wear, not only was the separate Wearside area incorporated into the County, but significant overspill locales (notably Ponteland, which is a very affluent Newcastle suburb, and Cramlington) remained in Northumberland.

The area of the former Metro County is now only residually an administrative city (in the form of successor joint boards) and never really was a cultural city. Sunderland is distinctive. As with the Region data is available for the administrative county and not for Tyneside. Even here much of the relevant economic and employment data is by 'travel-to-work' area, and it is noteworthy that the Newcastle travel-to-work area, which includes both North Shields and Cramlington, extends up into Northumberland and down to include the Derwent Valley in County Durham, but does not include South Tyneside and Wearside. In this book the city is Tyneside and its environs by which is meant the areas of the four metropolitan districts of Newcastle, North Tyneside, Gateshead and South Tyneside, together with overspill suburbs in South Northumberland and North Durham.

The introduction of the idea of overspill raises issues of change. Cramlington is the exact location of a planned transformation of 'overspill'. Blyth was historically a separate place from Tyneside, although very much a part of the North East Coast. Now it is within the Tyneside ambit. In the detailed examination of the spatial organization of Tyneside, use will be made of the idea of 'Northern Tyneside', by which is meant the metropolitan districts of Newcastle and North Tyneside together with the adjacent county districts of Blyth Valley and Castle Morpeth. This area was the basis for coordinated planning by Northumberland County Council, Newcastle and Tynemouth in the 1950s and 1960s and includes all the types of residential districts found in the city and its overspill suburbs. It is this 'half' (actually in terms of population rather more than half) of Tyneside which will be used for trend analysis.

It would be a mistake to identify the metropolitan districts as urban-industrial and the periphery as rural. North Tyneside Metropolitan District Council (MDC) includes the seaside suburbs and resorts of Whitley Bay and Tynemouth. Newcastle City now includes the very wealthy suburb of Gosforth. Much of the peripheral area is former coalfield rather than rural. However, with all these reservations and qualifications noted there is a city called Tyneside and in 1989 North Shields is part of it as it always has been and Cramlington is as it has been since the early 1970s.

The easiest definitions to provide are those of North Shields and Cramlington. Both are identified in terms of particular sets of local government wards by the Office of Population Censuses and Surveys (OPCS) and are described as 'urban areas'. The use of the OPCS definition for Cramlington is no issue but OPCS distinguishes North Shields from Tynemouth. There is some justification for this in terms both of spatial layout of settlements and of cultural conceptions. However, for many years North Shields and Tynemouth were combined as the small County Borough of Tynemouth (70% of which was made up of North Shields). Much of the historical data relate to the County Borough area. In this study an effort will be made to focus on North Shields in terms of the OPCS-defined urban area, but where this is not possible it will be made clear just what space is being referred to.

A region in decline

> It is perhaps hard for us to realize after the years of the inter-war depression that for sixty years before 1914 the Durham pitmen and the shipyard workers of Tyne and Wear were among the most highly paid workers outside the USA. . . . The decline into the poverty of the inter-war years was from the heights into the depths.
>
> (Hughes, 1970)

Any understanding of the North East has to be grounded in terms of the nature of industrial development and of the class and other social relations which derived from a very particular industrial experience. The North East was by 1914 a locale of a particularly organized capitalism. This system no longer had quite such a regional character as it had had in the 1890s because local banks were already becoming part of the national system of clearing banks which was to take shape during the First World War. If any single factor can be identified as crucial in the destruction of a 'regional integration' in the economy, it might well be this delocalizing of finance capital. Be that as it may, the North East had organized capital, organized labour and until 1920 was growing apace. Its social problems in the pre-1914 years were problems of growth rather than decline. Thus in 1910 Gateshead was identified, along with Coventry and Clydebank, as an area of acute housing need because all three were boom towns and were drawing in massive amounts of labour, attracted by high wages. Tyneside in particular and the North East in general was a zone of great prosperity. This is not to deny the reality of urban poverty based on a significant differentiation within the working class (see North Tyneside CDP, 1977), but the theme was high wages and rough and ready urban conditions.

Accounts of the problems of this region usually begin by pointing out that after the 1914 War the overheated heavy industries of the North East were severely affected by a change in market demand away from their products, that these problems were exacerbated by central government's exchange policies, and that in consequence the integrated economic structure – the organized capitalism – of the pre-war and war years collapsed. Any consideration of the North East has to pay attention to the severe reverses of the depression and their consequences for industrial organization, particularly in terms of a continuing delocalization of industrial control through amalgamation in heavy engineering. However, it is important to remember that after 1935 the traditional industries recovered in the run up to a second war and continued to be prosperous until the early 1960s.

It is this second period of affluence which sets the level against which recent developments have to be set. As McCord (1979: 262) puts it:

> The most diligent student of the region's past will find it extremely difficult to fix upon any period in earlier times in which the condition of the people can be seen as more attractive than the point reached by the early 1960s.

The actual industrial structure of the mid-1960s, by which time the massive Robens-led reduction in mining employment was already underway, is given in Table 3.1 and compared with the situation in 1976 and 1986. The changes over the period 1966–76 are interesting.

The transition from the post-war boom in traditional industries to a modernized branch plant structure occurred after the Hailsham Plan of 1963 and changed the nature of the origins of the region's economic problems from overspecialization by industrial sector (i.e. over-reliance on old basic industries particularly affected by changing market demands and the new international division of labour) into overspecialization by corporate function (i.e. under-representation of control and research and development functions). From 1945 until 1963, national priorities actually operated against the modernization of the North's industrial structure. In particular, the emphasis on maximizing coal production meant that the National Coal Board systematically opposed the importation of industries employing male workers. Most new industrial development from 1950 to 1963 was based on mobilizing the reserve army of female labour both in manufacturing (particularly clothing) and in white collar services. With the beginning of the closure programme in the pits the situation changed dramatically.

Table 3.1 Industrial structure, Northern Region 1966–84 (in thousands, with percentages in parentheses)

	1966	1976	1981	1984
Agriculture, etc.	23	16 (1.3)	14 (1.3)	15 (1.4)
Mining	107	50 (4.0)	41 (3.6)	33 (3.1)
Total manufacturing	461	438 (34.9)	344 (30.5)	281 (26.5)
Chemicals, etc.	57	51 (4.1)	49 (4.4)	41 (3.9)
Metal manufacturing	62	47 (3.7)	30 (2.7)	17 (1.6)
Engineering	114	118 (9.4)	114 (10.2)	85 (8.0)
Shipbuilding, etc.	58	48 (3.8)	34 (3.0)	21 (2.0)
Other manufacturing	171	175 (13.9)	117 (10.2)	117 (11.0)
Services	687	751 (59.8)	714 (63.8)	735 (69.3)
Construction	105	96 (7.6)	72 (6.4)	61 (5.8)
Transport, etc.	237	210 (16.7)	197 (17.8)	180 (17.0)
Professional, etc.	130	180 (14.3)	174 (15.6)	179 (17.0)
Public admin., etc.	71	91 (7.3)	81 (7.3)	75 (7.1)
Other services	144	174 (13.9)	190 (16.7)	240 (22.6)
Total	1277	1255	1114	1064

The branch plant manufacturing industries which arrived after 1963 were attracted by generous regional subsidies (see Robinson *et al.*, 1987) and extensive infrastructural development. Table 3.1 illustrates the impact of this period. Mining employment in the region declined by more than 50% between 1966 and 1976 but manufacturing employment held up with an overall decline of just 5%, despite a significant decline in the major traditional sectors of shipbuilding, chemicals and metals manufacturing. After 1976 there was a massive decline in manufacturing as a whole with a fall of over a third in total manufacturing jobs in the region between 1976 and 1984. These falls have been due to a combination of production decline and productivity improvements, and this aspect will be explored in more detail in relation to the case studies in Chapter 4.

Associated with the decline in manufacturing employment has been a change in the gender–'time' composition of the workforce. It must be remembered that these changes have had a complex effect. The workforce has become increasingly female-dominated, but the numbers of full-time women workers has declined considerably because of job losses in manufacturing. Another point to note from Table 3.1 is the slow decline in public employment and welfare state employment in terms of absolute numbers since the mid-1970s. There was growth here between 1966 and 1976, but since 1976 there has been a decline of more than 10% in total employment in these sectors. Thus we can see the regional consequences of welfare state expansion and of post-1975 (and IMF intervention) cuts.

The contrast between the 1930s and the last 10 years cannot be

Table 3.2 Population shifts on Northern Tyneside (in thousands)

Date	Centre	Inner ring	Outer ring	Total
1901	330	48	72	450
1911	367	71	84	522
1921	382	72	89	543
1931	393	88	91	572
1951	407	107	97	611
1961	390	138	116	644
		158	*96*	
1971	337	153	134	624
		179	*108*	
1981	310	160	127	597

Note: North Tyneside comprises the areas of the 1971 Newcastle City, Tynemouth County Borough and Wallsend Borough (the centre), the remainder of the present authorities of Newcastle and North Tyneside (the inner ring), and the areas of Castle Morpeth and Blyth Valley Districts (the outer ring). Figures in *italics* indicate the implications of the transfer of part of the pre-1971 outer ring to the Metropolitan Districts of Newcastle and North Tyneside.

emphasized too strongly. The 1930s saw a mothballing of both human and physical capital, whereas the recent period has seen an actual destruction of physical plant, especially shipbuilding berths, and non-replacement of skills. Seen in these terms, the present peripheral status of the region is new and disturbing.

Population and housing change in 'Northern Tyneside'

Table 3.2 documents population changes in Northern Tyneside in terms of absolute size and location. It shows the post-1951 absolute loss of population from the riverside core areas to both the inner-ring suburbs within the metropolitan district areas and to former coalfield areas. In 1951 more than two-thirds of the population lived in the river corridor (this includes the middle-class Victorian and inter-war suburbs of Jesmond, Tynemouth and Cullercoats), whereas by 1981 this proportion had fallen to just over half of a smaller total. In contrast, the population of the inner ring is now nearly four times the size it was at the beginning of this century and the population of the outer ring is nearly twice the size. The outer-ring figures result from the complex interaction of loss of coalfield status (which implies population decline) with suburbanization and population growth.

Table 3.3 shows the enormous growth in the 'domestic'-built environment in the twentieth century. Even in the urban core where there has been massive population loss associated with slum clearance, there were

Table 3.3 Location of dwellings on Northern Tyneside 1921–81 (in thousands)

Date	Centre	Inner ring	Outer ring	Total
1921	77	14	20	111
1931	83	14	26	123
1951	114	31	29	174
1961	123	44	36	203
1971	119	53	45	216
		60	36	
1981	118	63	45	225

Note: see note for Table 3.2

almost as many dwellings in 1981 as there had been in 1961 and, as Table 3.4 shows, the area now has a far higher standard of amenity. The background to this has been the decline of private renting as a consequence of slum clearance and the transfer of dwellings to owner-occupation. Housing growth in the inner and outer rings has been dramatic, particularly in the inner ring with a doubling of the numbers of dwellings in the post-war years. The tenure data for the rings shows that here there has been an increase in owner-occupation at the expense of 'other tenures' which in these former coalfield areas included colliery housing. The inner core is now characterized by a preponderance of public tenants (nearly half of households), whereas the rings show a majority of owner-occupiers in line with national patterns. Too much should not be made of this polarization. It is overlain with a more detailed pattern reflecting the location of overspill estates, which will be described in Chapter 6. However, the inner–outer city distinction is a real one. In these terms North Shields is part of the inner city, whereas Cramlington is part of the outer city.

Cramlington and North Shields provide examples of a core and outer locale respectively, but they do not provide us with an account of 'inner-ring' developments. The essential character of the inner ring is that having ceased to be a coalfield it became a suburb without a specific local industrial base. This is as true of nineteenth-century Whitley Bay (which literally ceased to be farmland) as it is of almost all of Longbenton, developed as a Newcastle overspill after 1945. The inner ring is economically dependent on core Tyneside for the bulk of its employment opportunities. There are some interesting service exceptions regarding offices, e.g. the massive head office of the DHSS at Longbenton, the North's largest single employment establishment, and the Regent Centre out-of-town office development at Gosforth. However, there is no major industrial location in the inner-ring areas apart from a riverbank development at Newburn which is just a linear extension of West Newcastle.

Table 3.4 Tenure and amenities (percentages) on Northern Tyneside for 1971 and 1981

	1971	1981
Core		
Owner-occupied	30	36
Public tenant	39	47
Other tenures	31	17
All basic amenities	77	99
Inner ring		
Owner-occupied	45	52
Public tenant	38	38
Other tenures	17	10
All basic amenities	91	99
Outer ring		
Owner-occupied	40	51
Public tenant	38	35
Other tenures	22	14
All basic amenities	85	99

The point is that this suburbanization developed entirely in response to housing pressures. In the late 1940s and early 1950s these pressures derived from a concern to resolve the crisis of housing need and, simultaneously, to begin the process of reducing inner-conurbation population and housing density. Hence the provision made was in the form of public sector overspill, particularly at Longbenton, but also within Wallsend and Tynemouth County Borough. There was not a sharp transition to the next phase because public sector overspill of a 'simple housing kind' continued into the early 1960s. After 1955 an increasing amount of inner-ring suburbanization was produced by developer builders in response to market demand. This aspect became even more important after 1963 when public sector intervention took the form of the provision of mass housing ('large flatted estates of a form never built for the market'; Dunleavy, 1981: 1) on redeveloped inner sites and in inner-ring locales like Killingworth. At this time modernization as a planning theme emphasized job creation and industrial diversification, but only at Killingworth, which is right on the outer edge of the inner ring, was there any integrated public sector planning in which even in principle housing and industrial development were associated (see Byrne and Parson, 1983).

The massive amount of activity by developer builders after the mid-1960s, which continues to this day, cannot be described as unplanned, given that it was carried out in relation to land-use planning and the provision of infrastructure. However, invariably in practice, and with the single exception of Cramlington in principle, it was not part of strategic planning for modernization. Even in Cramlington, the activities of the developer builders were seen largely in terms of providing a population to serve as the basis of demand for services, rather than, as was clearly the case for the public sector, in terms of providing housing so as to assemble a labour force for new industries.

Hence, although Cramlington is in the outer ring and has a distinctive industrial zone of some importance, the actual development of its owner-occupied locations was close to that of inner-ring locations like Westerhope (see Banim, 1987). Thus an account of housing development in North Shields provides us with a background to inter-war and immediate post-war developments in both owner-occupied and council housing, whereas Cramlington's owner-occupied estates can be thought of as suburbanization produced by developer builders.

The recent administrative history of Northern Tyneside is that of the short-lived Tyne and Wear County which was created in 1974 and abolished in 1986. Even this did not include the whole of the area because the Tyneside suburban areas in Blyth Valley and Castle Morpeth, particularly Cramlington and the very wealthy suburb of Ponteland, were left under Northumberland County so as to maintain the viability of that Shire. Hence Structure Planning could not provide a unified scheme for the area. In any event Structure Planning is now dead and has been replaced, within the former Metropolitan County Area, by the Unitary Development Plan in which the strategic guidelines are imposed by the regional office of the Department of the Environment (DoE). This is really not much more than a local plan for land use over a larger area, so there is now no strategic mechanism for the City of Tyneside.

North Shields: an old port

An account of North Shields' industrial, urban and political history is given in the final reports of the North Tyneside CDP (1977, 1978 a, b and c), which form the baseline for this study. It is not proposed to repeat all this here, but a summary is appropriate, particularly since it provides an opportunity for the discussion of trends and developments of a general kind after 1974.

Although there has been a settlement of some sort at North Shields since the Middle Ages, the modern town is a product of the addition of industrial capitalism to mercantile capitalism. It was always concerned with coal shipment but in the nineteenth century the work of the Tyne Improvement Commission transformed the capacity of the port, and a modern transport infrastructure including a rail network was developed. North Shields became the export base for much of the South East

Northumberland coalfield. The last North Shields pit closed in 1929, although Backworth colliery which was just over the boundary of Tynemouth CB survived until 1979.

The development of the Port was associated with a range of new or transformed industries. The most important was ship-repair at Smith's Dock Yard, the town's largest employer from the 1890s to the 1960s. North Shields has always been a fishing centre but the construction of the new fish quay in 1886 and the invention of steam trawling by the tug-boat firm of Purdies led to a big growth in activity in the late nineteenth century and the development of a distant water fleet. In addition to these directly maritime activities which set the town's character as a port, the nineteenth century saw a considerable development in engineering. In contrast, the once important glass and ceramic and clothing and textile industries declined to the point where they almost disappeared.

The net effects are best demonstrated by looking at the population. Between 1801 and 1851 the area's population doubled and it doubled again from 1851 to 1921, the year that saw the culmination of the first phase of the town's development as a capitalist urban locality. Its distinctive status as a locality derives exactly from the nature of its development. It is easy to see this in the nineteenth century because the development of local government reflected economic organization and the political processes which derived from it. Tynemouth was a separate county borough from 1849 to 1974 and this reflected its distinctiveness as a port-town from the coalfield which surrounded it.

The scale of urban development in the nineteenth and early twentieth centuries was considerable. In 1801 North Shields consisted of the old 'low town' at the bottom of and extending up the very steep bluffs at the river mouth. This contained 55% of the area's population in 1801 but only 11% in 1901. However, not much in the way of working-class housing was constructed on the banktops until the 1850s, when housing development began in earnest and continued until the First World War with the construction of 'By-Law' housing by builders of a variety of scales but always using land 'developed' by large-scale investors. This period saw the building of areas like the Triangle, Ropery Banks, Gardiner Street and North Trinity, which were important for housing action by the CDP. Most of this housing took the form of Tyneside flats, an unusual type of construction in which what appears to be one reasonably large terrace house of a kind very commonly built in industrial cities in Northern England in the late nineteenth century, is in fact two flats. This reflected both the very high cost of land on Tyneside and the very high wages of the skilled workers for whose families they were built (see North Tyneside CDP, 1978a; Byrne, 1980).

The relationship between industrial and urban development in this period was more complex than simply being a matter of industrial development attracting workers who were housed in a uniform fashion.

Instead, there was a clear socio-spatial differentiation which reflected distinctions within the working class and took effect through differences in housing forms and standards and consequent rent levels. The banktops of Tyneside flats, to be described as 'decent means streets' by a 1930s Medical Officer of Health, were occupied by skilled workers and the highest paid seamen. Labourers and more poorly paid seamen lived on the banksides and in the 'low street' in single-room tenements in industrial and pre-industrial slums.

Interestingly, the first organized political movement of labour in North Shields originated because of agitation about housing conditions and the failure of the private system to provide an adequate number of dwellings (see North Tyneside CDP, 1977; Byrne, 1980). Local trade unionists and labour (ILP) activists organized themselves in an effort to force the local authority, which was dominated by 'urban capitalists' (housing landlords, builders, estate agents and others who derived their living from private rented housing), to implement its powers under the 1890 Housing of the Working Classes Act. Previously, lib-lab trade unionists had merely been a part of a bourgeois-led radical coalition directed mainly at contesting parliamentary elections. This significance of reproductive politics as a basis of working-class organization is typical of the period.

By 1918 North Shields was a clear locale of modern organized capitalism with very large industrial establishments in Smith's Dock and the docks of the Tyne Improvement Commission, with a highly organized capitalist class, particularly in shipping and in urban development, and with a working class organized around production in trade unions and reproduction through *ad hoc* organizations, especially around housing. The combination of port activities and maritime industries produced a rather different civil society from that found in a 'pure' port like Liverpool. North Shields had highly organized workers in the yards and on the railways. These two groups provided the 'steady' leadership of labour but were always complemented by the unskilled and the seamen and by socialist intellectuals (most of whom were manual workers in this period) working around reproductive issues.

Discussion of the inter-war years usually centres on industrial change, but North Shields resembles the rest of the North East here in that while it is true that the 1920s saw a good deal of structurally induced unemployment which reflected the position of traditional basic industries, and the 1930s saw the impact of work recession, these same basic industries began to recover in the run up to the Second World War in the mid-1930s and were to remain basic to the area until the early 1960s. This is not to deny the importance of inter-war industrial change – just to get it in perspective relative to the much more profound restructuring of the recent past. What were unequivocally dramatic were changes in demography and urban structure.

Until the end of the First World War the North East experienced massive population growth through immigration. After 1920 immigration to the region ceased. Such population growth as there has been since then comes from a natural internally generated increase and there has been significant out-migration. The population of North Shields shifted from a period of very rapid growth to one of slow growth. At the same time the quantity and quality of the urban infrastructure was transformed. In 1920, what is now North Shields, consisted of the banksides, the banktops, the industrial villages of Percy Main and East Howden, and the villages of Chirton and Preston. The villages were separated from the town by farmers' fields. By the outbreak of the Second World War this was a continuous built-up area.

There were two processes involved here. One was suburbanization by addition. This term is used to cover both private sector building for owner-occupation and (for a period in the late 1930s) for rent, and the non-slum clearance council house building of the 1920s, i.e. further stock was being added to that which already existed. Most of this stock in the 1920s was subsidized – given the existence of subsidies to builders under the 1919 Housing (Additional Powers) Act – and it went to the relatively well-paid skilled and white-collar working class. It was generally built on land assembled by the local authority. Nearly half of all private development in North Shields and Tynemouth took place on land originally owned by the council. Access, however, was market related. Council housing rents were subsidized, as were most house prices for owner-occupiers until 1931, but both were beyond the reach of the unskilled.

The effect on overall housing standards was by filtration. As households moved into the new stock, better pre-1914 dwellings became available for rent by poorer households. Thus, with only minimal slum clearance, housing overcrowding (percentage of persons living at more than two per room) declined by nearly a half in the 1920s from 35 to 24%. In the 1920s over 900 council dwellings, over 900 subsidized private dwellings and over 450 unsubsidized private dwellings were built. Almost all were semi-detached houses on pleasant 'garden'-style estates, exemplified by council and private housing on the local authority's Balkwell estate.

This process continued, without subsidy, in the private sector in the 1930s when builders took advantage of falling construction costs and cheaper land. Over 2800 private sector dwellings were built between 1931 and 1940. However, quite a different process occurred in the public sector. There had been a small number of 'slum clearance tenements' built in 1924, but there was major slum clearances in North Shields in the 1930s after the Greenwood Act, when the banksides were almost totally cleared and some 9000 people were moved out, the bulk of them to the Meadowell Estate where 1961 dwellings were built, of which 84% were flats. This process of redevelopment and movement was quite different from that of suburbanization by addition. As it happens in North Shields, it remained suburbanization. The Meadowell was build on a green field site and, as such, is an overspill estate, although it is quite close to North Shields centre. However, slum clearance and replacement was for the poor. While what was provided was massively superior to what it replaced, it was much inferior to the public and private sector dwellings produced by suburbanization by addition. There was very little if any social distinction between the subsidized private estates and the 1920s council housing. This was not the case with the relocated banksides on the Meadowell where the existing distinction was perpetuated.

The inter-war years saw a good deal of activity in North Shields by the local branch of the National Unemployed Workers Movement (NUWM; see CDP, 1978), whose main base of support was on the Meadowell. It would be a grave mistake to identify this estate in the 1930s, and indeed at any time before the 1980s, as a locale in space of the residuum. Its population was less likely to be comprised of skilled workers but many of the men were seafarers and traditions of innovative and flexible organization were strong. The leadership of the NUWM had acquired much of their experience in the Seaman's Minority Movement and the present left leadership of the NUS is in direct line of descent from them.

It is not an over-simplification to describe the industrial experience of the inter-war years in terms of mothballing until about 1936 and then as hell-for-leather toward war. There are, however, two necessary qualifications. British shipbuilding was never to recover the world pre-eminence it had during this period, although the yards were to do well until the late 1960s. The other qualification relates to initial efforts at industrial diversification. One of the first of what is now English Estates trading estates was built at Chirton in North Shields under the 1930s special areas legislation. There was an emphasis on the generation of female employment as well as on the general need for diversification but there had been little development by the outbreak of war.

It is almost conventional for discussions of localities to miss out experience of the Second World War, although First World War experiences are more commonly considered. This is probably because the focus of much of locality based history has been reproduction and the important political initiatives in relation to reproductive issues during the Second World War were national in origin and response. However there were very important productive developments. This was not just a matter of revival of basic industries in previously depressed areas. Despite its relative closeness to Germany, Tyneside was very defensible against air attack. Thus it was a good location for dispersal of engineering and sites were readily available on estates like Chirton. Much of this new employment was for women. Shortages of labour in the immediate post-war period meant that this pattern of female industrial employment was not reversed overall, although it was in traditional basic industries, and any discussion of production post-1945 has to take account of a far larger North Shields female employed proletariat than had existed pre-War.

The industrial history of North Shields in the 1950s and 1960s broadly resembles that of the Northern Region. There was decline in primary industries with a 70% fall in employment, but this was from a small initial base. Far more important was the growth in manufacturing employment which increased overall by 31% or more than 1700 jobs for men and by 1600 jobs or 54% for women between 1951 and 1966. In this period employment in shipbuilding and repair actually increased, so there was no crisis in basic manufacturing industry. Much of the employment for women was in a variety of food and clothing concerns located on Chirton industrial estate which had a predominantly female labour force. The 1950s and 1960s were prosperous years for manufacturing capital, with a successful experience of industrial diversification.

The most significant incoming employer was the De La Rue–Formica plant on the Coast Road which employed nearly 2000 workers at its peak. De La Rue have had a major commitment in the North East but the company is not in any traditional sense local and Formica was sold to American Cynamid in 1977. The new plants tended to be non-local in control. Thus, while the 1950s and 1960s saw a growth in employment, they were also a period of significant delocalization and the manufacturing sector was increasingly composed of 'branch plants'. This term is in fact misleading because it implies that there were central plants elsewhere. As capitalism had developed its disorganization, the tendency is for there to be no central manufacturing plants. Thus the diversified structure had its own in-built fragility.

Urban developments were more complex. The significant issue remained housing. Again the two models of suburbanization by addition and redevelopment are useful but the pattern of their application was rather different from the inter-war years. From 1946 to 1950 almost all suburbanization by addition (89% of the 2126 dwellings built) took place through the construction of very high-quality estates of semis by the local authority. The 1950s resembled the 1920s experience with a roughly equal balance of public and private construction, almost all of which was suburbanization by addition and which produced 3732 dwellings. The 1960s resembled the 1930s, with most public sector construction being associated with slum clearance while suburbanization by addition was a private sector phenomenon. During this period the local authority built 930 dwellings to the private sector's 1915.

While all the local authority construction of the 1940s was of very high quality for general needs, the late 1950s saw the first non-traditional units in the form of Wimpey's point blocks built at Hunters and Murrays Closes in Percy Main. This development, privatized using an Urban Development Grant in the early 1980s, was not originally associated with slum clearance and was actually more expensive per unit than the traditional housing being built at the same time. Tynemouth CBC was late in the game in getting into post-1957 slum clearance and particularly slow in addressing the issues posed by the condition of the oldest by-law housing. Its major slum clearance programme of the early 1960s was in the area of Dockwray Square where an early nineteenth-century development of very fine terraced houses had degenerated into tenemented slums. The history of continuing post-war pressure by officers for a flatted development in the East End of North Shields is a fascinating one but for our purposes here what matters is that nearly 1000 flats and maisonettes were built, again at a higher unit cost than that of the contemporary construction of traditional dwellings. These flats were demolished in the early 1980s and the history of the use of the site is an important part of this study's concern with land.

Housing issues in the 1970s were more concerned with existing stock than with new developments. The modernization of the Meadowell estate, which transformed it from flats to terraced houses and dramatically reduced the density of occupation, was a consequence of the availability of central government assistance intended to stimulate employment opportunities in the construction industry as a corrective to general problems of unemployment in the early 1970s. Likewise, the major part of improvement of pre-1914 stock was based on the availability of 75% grants which had an identical objective. It is important to note that this older housing was being improved rather than rebuilt. The bulk of the money went on the addition of amenities and not on structural repairs. However, housing conditions were much improved by this and by the clearance of some 700 slum dwellings. There has been some rebuilding on the site, but the effect has been a massive reduction in residential densities.

The politics of the 1950s and 1960s were not as dramatic as those of the 1930s. There was a spontaneous revolt against the local authority by Meadowell tenants over rents and repairs but, until 1974, Tynemouth was a small non-Labour controlled authority with a quiescent and right-wing Labour party.

Cramlington: a created community

At the beginning of the nineteenth century, Cramlington was a scattering of farms and a small village. During the course of that century and with the extension of the Great Northern Coalfield it became a mining area. Since the early 1960s it has undergone a transformation as great as that of the nineteenth century and has become a new settlement with virtually no connection with agriculture or coal. As a New Town, Cramlington has always had a dual function. It is related to the conurbation and to the inner city, but it is also post-coal. The two were combined at the planning stage, as illustrated by the written analysis to the County Development Plan of 1962. Here, the first planning objective was identified as controlling urban sprawl from the Tyneside conurbation:

> In its place the aim was to build up communities on the periphery equipped with all the necessary facilities, including local employment and to set a firm limit to the size of these communities. Further expansion would then have to take place away from the present urban area. . . . The second decision was to locate the major expansion in a North Eastern direction from Tyneside and to plan North Tyneside and the coalfield area as essentially one unit.
> (NCC, 1962: 1)

The necessity for this arose from the catastrophic collapse in mining employment. In 1951, 75% of all employment in Seaton Valley was in coal mining. Throughout the early and mid-1950s when national fuel policy emphasized volume of production this remained, but by the late 1950s with a national shift towards cheap oil the NCB had began a series of closures. In the early 1960s county planners were estimating that mining employment in the Cramlington area would fall to about 2500 jobs by 1971 compared with the 6000 jobs which had existed in 1955. This reflected the fall in the Northumberland coalfield as a whole. Between the mid-1950s and 1967, 17 000 mining jobs were lost from an original total of 42 000. In the early part of this period most job losses were managed by 'natural wastage', with 80% of miners from closed pits being transferred to those that remained open, but the overall loss of employment opportunities was dramatic.

The other factor was the need to cater for population moving out of the Tyneside conurbation. The desire to reduce densities in the conurbation had been part of the background to planning since the 1930s and was reemphasized in Northumberland's current development plans for the North Tyneside area (corresponding broadly with what is called Northern Tyneside in this book). Indeed, the overspill factor had a longer history than a concern with post-coal industrial restructuring, since the plans of the 1940s and early 1950s had assumed stable employment in coal. In 1958 the written analysis of the North Tyneside District Town Map identified a potential overspill from Newcastle and Wallsend of 40 000 people. At this time the population of the Cramlington area in the pit villages of Cramlington itself, Nelson Village and Klondyke was some 6000.

The immediate origin of the new development was in negotiations between Seaton Valley UDC and Northumberland County around the implications of the North Tyneside District Town Map. In 1958 the three actors in the process were all on the scene. The county and urban district were discussing settlement patterns and William Leech Ltd., a large Newcastle developer builder, was 'taking an interest' in housing land in the area. In October, Leech was refused planning permission for housing development to the south-west of Cramlington Village but did not appeal against this decision. The refusal was associated with another decision by Seaton Valley UDC to allow Leech to make representations at a suitable time in the future when overall development was being considered. By the early 1960s Leech was a major landowner in the area of what was to be the New Town.

After this things moved fast. By early 1959 the County Council was proposing to designate Cramlington as a Comprehensive Development Area and this was supported by representations from the UDC. The Seaton Valley District Town Map of 1959 contained proposals which closely resemble the New Town as it was to develop. The twin elements were the provision of industrial estates for new industries to replace lost mining jobs and ensure the diversification of the industrial base *and* large-scale housing development to cater for 40 000 people of whom 29 000 would come from Tyneside with the rest originating in Seaton Valley itself. The other crucial factor is represented in the written statement in support of the Town Map:

> a master plan for the new town is to be prepared by a consultant, working in close consultation with the local planning authority, since the bulk of the development will be carried out privately.
> (NCC, 1959: 3)

This is the essential point about Cramlington. It was not a New Town under the New Towns Act created through the agency of a Development Corporation, and it was never intended that it should be. It was instead the product of a partnership between a county council which provided industrial estates and infrastructure, a district council which provided public sector housing and infrastructure and two major developer builders working in tandem who provided a very large element of private housing. The actual legislative status was as a Comprehensive Development Area under Section 5(3) of the Town and Country Planning Act 1947. Resources were obtained from central government under the 1952 Town Development Act and the 1961 Housing Act which subsidized the importation of an overspill population, but these were far less than would have been provided to a designated New Town where all infrastructure costs would have been borne by central government.

The important consequence of this was for the operation of the developer builders. If Cramlington had been a designated New Town then all their housing would have been built on land which was designated as housing land before it was sold to them. They could not have made change of land use profits. In Cramlington they could and did, not only from housing land but also through their subsidiary which developed the town shopping centre, which again in a designated New

Town would have been a development corporation function. All this was above board and the developers reached an agreement to pay a per acre developed contribution to the district council towards development costs, as did the county council. They also sold infrastructure and public sector housing land to the councils at historic cost plus interest rather than developed land value. There is a good argument that the exclusion of a development corporation has in the long term been to Cramlington's advantage, but the opportunity for land development profits was very important. The authorities did seek reserve powers by making all land subject to compulsory purchase, although they intended to leave most of it in the developers' hands. In practice it seems that the land transactions were by agreement.

The scheme was approved by the Ministry of Housing and local government in March 1963 as Amendment 13 to the County Development Plan. The Comprehensive Development Area comprised a total of 5670 acres of which 424 were available for industrial development. The ultimate projected population total was 49 000. This target was revised to 60 500 (to be achieved by 1984) in 1966 and the area of the CDA was extended to 6010 acres, of which 2520 acres were subject to compulsory purchase, if necessary.

The development of the industrial estates by the County Council began in the mid-1960s with an advance factory for Wilkinson Sword. By 1968 four Board of Trade advance factories had been developed and allocated on the Bassington Estate. In 1966 the County Council extended its role from land development to include the provision of small nursery factories in partnership with English Industrial Estates (as it then was). The Nelson Estate was also being developed in the late 1960s. By 1974, when Seaton Valley was incorporated into the new Blyth Valley district, there were 8061 jobs on the industrial estates and 2033 elsewhere in the New Town area. The locational division corresponds pretty well with a manufacturing–service distinction.

The new District Council received a useful report on the status of the new town in 1973 when it was in 'shadow' existence (BVDC, 15/10/73). This repeated the sets of priorities established in the original plans, i.e. to secure a diversified industrial base in order to create employment, and to achieve related 'secondary objectives', namely,

> to provide (a) an attraction for new residents to the area to provide a basic pool of manpower for the new industries, (b) a new and attractive environment in which to work and play, (c) an alternative quality of life to that normally associated with Tyneside and the declining industrial areas in South East Northumberland, and (d) a strong reservoir to meet the recurring economic crises which have been suffered by the North East since the last war.
>
> (ibid.)

This report was distinctly optimistic about employment growth. The planners' survey of the 24 incoming firms established in the New Town by 1973 indicated that these had expansion plans which would lead to the creation of a further 7000 jobs by 1991 and it was anticipated that additional incomers would provide a further 3000 jobs. The central implication for Blyth Valley was with regard to housing provision because 'the local authority will need to secure the building of more rented housing to meet the needs of new industries' (ibid.). This is a clear indication of a central principle of planning for Cramlington. It was the public sector which was to provide housing for the locally employed workforce. This was represented in the very early stages by allocations of new council housing in Seaton Valley to workers of incoming firms on a much more generous basis than a simple 'key worker' system. In addition, Seaton Valley cleared most of the existing colliery housing in the existing pit villages and rehoused their residents in new developments in Cramlington. This involved at least 1000 colliery and 'temporary' dwellings and was achieved without any of the controversy associated with the Category D policy in County Durham (see Blackman, 1987), largely because residents got good modern dwellings close to their original homes. These relocated households were 'post-coal', and were a crucial part of the labour force for the new industries.

In contrast, private sector development was geared to overspill residents from Tyneside and the implicit assumption (and certainly reality) was that most of these would commute back to the conurbation for work. By 1976, Leech's and Bell's had built 4267 dwellings at Cramlington compared with 205 built by other private sector developers, 1103 built by Seaton Valley/Blyth Valley and 788 built by housing associations. Information was collected on the origins of households moving into the area in connection with the requirements of the legislation under which Cramlington was attracting central aid as a recipient of migrants. A total of 75% of the households moving into new owner-occupied dwellings were from the County of Tyne and Wear and the greater part of these were from the Newcastle and North Tyneside MDC areas.

Therefore, by the mid-1970s, Cramlington was proceeding much according to plan, with a number of firms being attracted to the area and the consequent job creation being associated with extensive housing developments by both the private and public sectors. All the housing development took the form of low-rise, garden city-style estates. In the mid-1970s Cramlington looked to be succeeding in its industrial and environmental modernization, which simultaneously resolved the 'post-coal' problems of South East Northumberland and provided a pleasant overspill mechanism for reducing residential densities in the Tyneside conurbation. However, a cautionary note had been sounded right at the beginning of the whole exercise:

In 1962 at the time the Master Plan was submitted the *Architect's Journal* reported briefly on the proposals and questioned whether Cramlington New Town would ever materialize in the form recommended by the planning consultants. Quite rightly the *Journal* emphasized the importance of attracting industry to the town, and warned that if unsuccessful in this respect Cramlington would be in danger of becoming a dormitory town, resulting in social imbalance.

(Elphick, 1965: 66)

In the mid-1970s things still seemed to be going well. We will deal with what has happened since then in subsequent chapters.

4

Production and base in two localities

Introduction

This chapter takes up the theme of industrial determination introduced in relation to the Northern Region in Chapter 3. The character of the Northern Region cannot be understood apart from its industrial history and the same holds for the Tyneside conurbation and the two locales which are the subject of this study. What reason is there for North Shields without an industrial base for employment? In 1988, that question is far from academic. North Shields could well have no industrial base of any kind by the end of this century. Similarly, we have already encountered the question posed by *The Architect's Journal* when Cramlington was first proposed in its modern form: will this place have any industrial, and hence employment, base which will make it more than merely a dormitory suburb? The chapter begins with 'trend' information drawn from the Censuses of Population and Employment to describe the changing employment structures of the two locales, and the 'Northern Tyneside' area of which they are a part.

There are two necessary qualifications here. First, employment data is a derivative of production, not a complete account of it. For example, employment in plants in a given industrial sector could halve while productivity tripled. From the point of view of capital the sector would have increased in importance by a half. This is the phenomenon of job loss growth as experienced by a good part of the 'modern' industrial base of Northern Tyneside. Census of Production figures are not disaggregatable to the spatial levels which are possible for those from the Censuses of Population and Employment. Attention will be paid to production in terms of outputs in this chapter, but locating this is not easy, particularly when dealing with branch plants for which no separate returns are made. Even if the plant is a free-standing subsidiary, within-group pricing policies make determination of real outputs difficult. Much of our evidence about outputs will be based on anecdote and hearsay. However, the structure of employment is crucial for class structure. Discussions of deindustrialization are as often discussions of the deindustrialization of the employment location of the working population as they are of the declining importance of industrial production as a part of total production.

The second qualification relates to the boundaries of the areas studied. Northern Tyneside was identified so as to incorporate all types of residential locale. It is, more or less, the northern half of the Newcastle Metropolitan Region, as identified by Robinson *et al.* (1987), but its only real existence was as the spatial basis for collaborative planning in the late 1950s and 1960s. That administrative reality is important, because it played a large part in determining what things are like now. However, the area is not a 'journey-to-work' area. It is part of the 1981 Newcastle journey-to-work area and there are considerable in- and out-flows from it. In 1981 these amounted to an inflow of 65 000 and an outflow of 34 000, compared with a resident and working-in-area total of 220 000. These figures are derived from Census of Population figures and produce a different total workforce from Census of Employment figures. However, it is patterns which matter: 87% of the residents of Northern Tyneside who work, work in the area; 77% of the area's workforce lives in the area. The four districts' boundaries do correspond roughly with an aggregation of employment exchange areas and this allows for the construction of employment time-series from Census of Employment data. The reality is that we are dealing with half of a metropolitan region because it is manageable on this scale for the study of residential patterns and it makes sense to review base at the same level. Thus the study of reproduction is determining the pattern of the study of production.

The intention is to present an empirical account of what things are like and how they got there before addressing bodies of theory which might help in understanding. This was the procedure the CDP adopted in the 1970s and it will be repeated here. Of course, even the most empirical study is informed by a problematic – if only at the level of choice of what is significant, and this study is a good deal less innocent than that, but the story will be told first.

Following the presentation of trends, a more detailed account will be given of developments in key areas, selected so as to cover the productive base of North Shields and Cramlington. Here, productive base includes some aspects of services, if they have traditionally been part of the reason for an area as opposed to a consequence of the accumulation of population in some area with a pre-existing rationale. Marine transport was crucial in the formation of North Shields and will be reviewed as an aspect of production. In contrast, the construction industry is centred locally and will be dealt with in relation to a discussion of land, as will retailing. Local authority and health services will be discussed in relation to the state. This is not to downgrade their importance in social relations but it does put basal production first.

The production sectors to be reviewed at North Shields will be divided into the traditional and the products of modernization and diversification. In Cramlington, only the latter sector exists, given the disappearance of coal so early in the life of the New Town. North Shields' traditional sectors are: marine transport; marine manufacture, including shipbuilding, ship-repair, 'offshore' work for oil and gas extraction, and related sub-contractors; and fishing with related food processing. The modernization/diversification sector is all other manufacturing which is almost invariably the product of regional policy, has no inherent geographical rationale for its location and is characteristically based on industrial estates. This is important in both localities.

Deindustrialization in an industrial city

Tables 4.1 to 4.6 present a range of trend information about the composition of the employment base of the population resident in Northern Tyneside, North Shields and Cramlington and the workforce of establishments in those areas. Let us deal first with the Census of Employment data regarding the large inclusive area of Northern Tyneside describing workforce by location of establishment, in other words the people who work within this area but who do not necessarily live within it. Here, this is defined by an amalgamation of those Employment Exchange Office areas which have at least part of their area within the districts of North Tyneside, Newcastle, Blyth Valley and Castle Morpeth. There is quite a good correspondence between Office area boundaries and district boundaries but it is not exact. In Table 4.1, a crude estimate of 'population available for work' has been constructed by adding the total workforce, as taken from Census of Employment figures, to the total number of unemployed. This both ignores major changes in the definition of unemployment over the period covered by Table 4.1 and compounds residential-based information (unemployment) with workplace-based information (employment). However, crude as the exercise is, some of its products are so gross that its crudity can be ignored. From Table 4.1 we can see that the 'total working and available for work' in Northern Tyneside was roughly the same in 1984 as it had been in 1972,

Table 4.1 All employment in Northern Tyneside (in thousands)

	1972	1976	1981	1984
Total of employed and unemployed	294	306	288	297
Total employed	279	286	250	253
Total mining	6	4	3	3
Total engineering and shipbuilding	39	36	29	23
Total clothing and textiles	6	7	6	5
Total transport and communications	27	20	17	14
Total welfare and state	70	78	68	74
Primary (%)	2.8	2.1	2.6	2.6
Manufacturing (%)	29.2	27.3	24.5	20.8
Construction (%)	7.5	7.3	6.7	5.7
Services (%)	60.5	63.3	67.0	72.0
Full-time (%)	85.0	81.9	81.0	77.7

Note: Percentages are of total employed as recorded by the Census of Employment.

Table 4.2 Male employment in Northern Tyneside (in thousands)

	1972	1976	1981	1984
Total of employed and unemployed	182	181	168	163
Total employed	169	165	146	135
Total mining	6	4	3	3
Total engineering and shipbuilding	34	31	25	20
Total transport and communications	18	16	13	12
Total welfare and state	30	30	27	29
Primary (%)	2.8	2.5	2.4	1.8
Manufacturing (%)	36.5	37.1	33.2	30.0
Construction (%)	12.1	12.2	11.1	10.2
Services (%)	44.3	47.3	52.7	58.0
Full-time (%)	96.5	95.6	95.0	94.1

Note: Percentages are of total employed as recorded by the Census of Employment.

i.e. under 300 000. However, in 1972 there were 279 000 jobs, whereas in 1984 this had fallen by nearly 10% to 253 000. Major job losses came in manufacturing where, in 1972, there were 81 000 jobs in Northern Tyneside; by 1984, this had fallen to 53 000, a loss of more than a third. This included the loss of 16 000 shipbuilding and engineering jobs and 1000 jobs in clothing and textiles. Table 4.2 shows that the decline in male

Table 4.3 Female employment in Northern Tyneside (in thousands)

	1972	1976	1981	1984
Total of employed and unemployed	112	125	120	129
Total employed	110	120	109	117
Total clothing and textiles	4	5	4	4
Total retail	23	23	21	31
Total welfare and state	40	47	41	45
Primary (%)	0.3	0.2	0.1	0.1
Manufacturing (%)	18.2	15.8	13.8	12.9
Construction (%)	0.9	0.9	1.1	1.1
Services (%)	80.9	82.5	84.4	85.9
Full-time (%)	68.1	62.5	60.5	58.9

Note: Percentages are of total employed as recorded by the Census of Employment.

employment in manufacturing involved the loss of 21 000 jobs and Table 4.3 shows that nearly 4000 female manufacturing jobs disappeared over the same period. Whereas 30% of all jobs were in manufacturing in 1972, by 1984 the proportion – of a smaller overall total – was 21%.

Not all 'industrial' jobs are in manufacturing. Conventionally, employment in mining, transport and construction is also included. Using this definition, in 1972 104 000 men and 22 000 women were employed in the industrial sphere in Northern Tyneside. Thus 62% of men, 20% of women and 45% of all workers were employed in 'industry'. However, by 1984, this number had fallen for both men (69 000) and women (18 000). Thus the proportion of industrial jobs fell between 1972 and 1984 to 52% for men, 14% for women and 34% overall.

Table 4.4 shows the changes in the proportional composition of the total workforce by sector, time (full or part) and gender. Definite tendencies can be identified including the decline in full-time male employment; the steady state of full-time female employment as a proportion of all employment, despite a substantial decline in the total of women employed full-time; the growth in part-time male employment in services; and the dramatic growth in part-time female employment in the service sector. This is not the disappearance of work emphasized by 'post-industrial' theorists. However, this does not mean that changes do not have class segmentation consequences, given the operation of UK benefit regulations in relation to households.

Growth in employment in the service industry has been concentrated in particular sector–gender–time locations. Employment in construction fell by 7000 over the period and employment in transport and communications fell by the same amount. The growth areas over the period 1971–84 were financial services, with an increase of 11 000 jobs (more than twice the 1971 figures), and distribution, etc., with an increase of 12 000

Table 4.4 Northern Tyneside industry–gender–time composition

	1971	1976	1981	1984
Totals (thousands)	277	286	250	252
Primary				
Male full-time	2.7	1.9	1.5	1.4
Male part-time	0.0	0	0.0	0.0
Female full-time	0.0	0	0.0	0.0
Female part-time	0.0	0	0.0	0.0
Total	2.9	2.1	1.6	1.5
Manufacturing				
Male full-time	22.6	20.5	18.5	15.4
Male part-time	0.0	0.0	0.0	0.0
Female full-time	6.1	5.5	4.8	4.3
Female part-time	1.1	1.3	1.1	1.2
Total	30.1	27.3	24.5	20.8
Services (including construction)				
Male full-time	33.8	32.8	33.8	33.1
Male part-time	1.8	2.6	2.4	3.5
Female full-time	20.1	20.9	21.4	22.6
Female part-time	11.2	14.3	16.1	17.8
Total	67.0	70.6	73.7	76.8
All				
Male full-time	59.2	55.2	53.9	51.5
Male part-time	2.1	2.7	2.6	3.5
Female full-time	26.3	26.4	26.3	27.6
Female part-time	12.3	15.7	17.3	19.0

jobs, or an increase of a third. In each of these sectors the largest relative growth was in part-time female employment. Overall part-time female employment in services increased from 31 000 to 45 000 between 1971 and 1984. Over the same period, full-time male employment in the service sector fell by 10 000, with little growth in other services to replace job losses in 'industrial services'. Full-time female employment in the service sector grew by just 2000 or 4% between these years. This was less than the absolute growth in part-time male employment in services which more than doubled from 4000 to nearly 9000. All these are rounded figures. The oscillating pattern of 'Welfare and State' employment (covering public administration and defence plus professional and scientific services) is worthy of note.

Developments in the two localities follow a very similar pattern. We have a longer run of data for North Shields thanks to the earlier studies of the CDP, although there are major difficulties in comparing data from

Table 4.5 Employment in North Shields and Cramlington (in hundreds)

	ER II			Census of Employment			
	1961	1966	1971	1971	1975	1981	1984
North Shields							
Primary	11	6	5	2	1	0	0
Manufacturing	108	114	108	100	95	72	56
Construction	14	20	15	11	15	9	11
Services	128	143	133	127	132	130	146
Cramlington							
Primary	n.a.[a]	n.a.	n.a.	0	0	0	0
Manufacturing	n.a.	n.a.	n.a.	43	80	51	57
Construction	n.a.	n.a.	n.a.	9	7	5	5
Services	n.a.	n.a.	n.a.	17	30	41	44

[a] n.a., not applicable.

earlier 'card counts' with that produced by the Census of Employment (Table 4.5). Figures for 1971 are available on both bases and are given to indicate the potential disparity. The main trend is represented by the overall loss of very nearly half of the total manufacturing jobs. Industrial employment in North Shields declined from its 1966 peak of 16 500 jobs to 7500 by 1984. Overall there were 5000 fewer jobs in 1984 than in 1966. The number of males employed had declined by over 6000, whereas female employment increased by 1000. However, full-time female jobs had declined by nearly 1400 since 1971. As with Northern Tyneside as a whole, the growth in employment had been in part-time employment for women with a significant growth in part-time employment for men. Care should be taken with these figures because of the different methods of collection already cited, and there are discontinuities which derive from the absence of non-responses in the job-centre area data for 1981. There were also changes in industrial classification. Again it is the gross pattern which matters.

Cramlington has a different pattern because of job creation on green-field sites in the 1970s. Employment here peaked in 1975 and had somewhat recovered from its lowest level of 1981 by 1984. However, the pattern of shift is as with Northern Tyneside as a whole. Cramlington lost over 2300 manufacturing jobs between 1975 and 1984, all from new industries, and gained over 1400 service jobs. This again followed the overall pattern, i.e. a decline in full-time male employment in industry and an increase in part-time female employment in the services. In Cramlington there were actual job losses for women in full-time employment.

Table 4.6 Tynemouth CB area economically active residents (in hundreds, with percentages in parentheses)

	1966	1971	1981
Employers and managers	31 (9.8)	27 (9.5)	28 (11.2)
Professionals	10 (3.1)	9 (3.0)	7 (2.8)
Intermediate non-manual	18 (5.6)	18 (6.3)	24 (9.3)
Junior non-manual	69 (21.8)	65 (21.8)	59 (23.4)
Supervisors and skilled	81 (25.7)	71 (24.8)	56 (22.3)
Personal service and semi-skilled	65 (20.6)	57 (19.9)	47 (18.8)
Unskilled	35 (11.6)	34 (12.0)	22 (8.8)
Own account	7 (2.1)	7 (2.3)	6 (2.5)
Other	1 (0.2)	1 (0.4)	3 (1.3)
Total	317	289	252

Table 4.6 provides information for residents of the area of the former Tynemouth County Borough derived from population censuses. It shows the decline in economic activity by men over school leaving age from 88% in 1951 to 77% in 1981. Over the same period the percentage of men working fell from 84 to 63%. In contrast, economic activity for adult women increased from 31 to 45% and the percentage actually working rose from 29 to 36%. Table 4.6 also shows the changes in the occupationally derived socioeconomic groups of the Tynemouth CB area workers. The most notable decline is that of the supervisory and skilled manual group, which comprised nearly 3000 fewer residents in 1981 than in 1951. The only absolute increase has been in intermediate non-manual workers. These residence-based figures confirm the general story of deindustrialization provided by the workplace-based information from Census of Employment figures. No equivalent figures are given for Cramlington because of the irrelevance of the information given for Cramlington before the late 1970s.

Maritime industries in North Shields

Marine manufacturing, the largest traditional employer in North Shields, comprises shipbuilding, ship-repair and 'offshore' fabrication for the oil and gas industries. All require similar labour and riverfront sites. In addition, there is significant employment in off-river subcontracting. The post-1977 history of marine manufacturing can be divided into two. First, there is the post-nationalization history of shipbuilding and repair; secondly, there is the history of the offshore, which was never nationalized. All the elements on Tyneside are now in private hands and have similar structural problems. Essentially they operate on a short-term basis in the context of intense international competition. The effects of this have been massive job losses, the casualization of the labour force, a profound erosion of trade union power, and the virtual cessation of training to replace human capital in the form of skilled labour.

The history up to 1977 is given in North Tyneside CDP (1978b). In 1977 the shipbuilding yards were nationalized. Ship-repair was excluded and Smiths Dock in North Shields remained a private company with 1300 employees. The Wallsend ship-repair yards were sold to British Shipbuilders by private treaty as they were embedded in the building yards. At nationalization British Shipbuilders employed some 12 000 workers on the Tyne in building and repair. All the Tyne elements have now been reprivatized by management buy-outs. In April 1988, Swan Hunters Ltd, which includes all that is left of Tyne shipbuilding, had some 3000 employees. Tyne Ship Repair, which includes all the nationalized repair yards, employed 850 in March 1988 compared with some 4000 a decade earlier. In December 1987, Smiths Ship Repair had a workforce of 700 compared with 1300 at nationalization. All the yards now employ from order to order with minimal 'retained' workforces. The *Journal* of 10 November 1987 described the situation in Smiths thus:

> The company has an agreement with its workforce that when work is short employees will be laid off for two weeks on full pay [and] after that they will have to apply for unemployment benefit. . . . That applies to the core workforce of 200. Temporary employees over and above the 200 are simply paid off when work is short.

In 1978 the core workforce exceeded 900. The situation in ship-repair is straightforward. The Tyne yards have lived from order to order with a steadily decreasing total workforce. In 1978 Tyne Ship Repair had 6 repair yards, 18 dry docks and employed 3500. It was down to one yard and 343 employees in August 1987, although with new orders the workforce increased to 850 at the beginning of 1988.

The shipbuilding story has been more complex. Swan Hunters was reprivatized in January 1986 and is now reduced to a workforce of some 3000 and one building berth at Wallsend, although other yards are being used for preliminary fabrication. The company is almost entirely dependent on Royal Navy orders, although it has built the odd merchant ship of a more complex kind. The *Journal* (8 January 1985) commented that:

> Short of building merchant ships for free, British Shipbuilders [this was before privatization] can never hope to compete with the merciless competition presented by the South Koreans and the Japanese.

In the year before reprivatization, over 2500 workers had volunteered for redundancy and the very large Hebburn Yard had been abandoned, despite an occupation by workers of all the Tyne yards. The immediate aftermath of privatization was a dispute over pay, with the workers claiming a basic wage of £195 in contrast with the then current level of £135. Paul Stockdale, the Secretary of the Confederation of Shipbuilding and Engineering Unions (CSEU) for the Tyne yards stated their position in the *Journal* of 24 March 1986:

> This action [strike] followed 8 weeks of negative negotiations with a company who it now appears are determined to impose Dickensian conditions in their shipyards. . . . The four entrepreneurs who have privatized the company appear to be underfinanced. They cannot however expect the Swan Hunter workforce to accept the imposition of such working conditions at any price.

Management won and this official himself took redundancy in November 1986.

Since then issues have revolved around the allocation of Royal Navy and Royal Fleet Auxiliary orders among the Tyne yards, Harland and Wolf in Belfast and other privatized warship yards. There have been two recent debates about the industry in the House of Commons (1 February 1984 and 19 May 1988). In both, the relatively unsubsidized position of British yards in comparison with competitors, including Korea, has been made clear. The chief opposition spokesman, Brian Gould, MP for Dagenham, pointed out that there were actually signs of an upturn in demand for shipbuilding. The amount of capacity laid up was falling and much of the world fleet would require replacing in the mid-1990s. However, Kenneth Clark, who replied for the government, was not encouraging and seemed to accept the pessimistic view of Neville Trotter, Conservative MP for Tynemouth, who blamed all the problems on Korean labour costs which were only 20% of those in the UK. We can describe Tyneside ship-building and -repair as reduced to almost a minimum with a cowed workforce accepting the logic of management's competitive position. This is illustrated by the response of the CSEU to the 1980 action of a GMWU official who blacked the *BIAKH* at the request of the International Transport Workers Federation when the ship came into Jarrow Mercantile Dock. The crew of this flag of convenience vessel were owed a substantial amount in wages, but the official was disowned because of the threat posed by this act of international solidarity to future orders.

Offshore is a post-shipbuilding and port activity. It requires riverside sites vacated by traditional shipbuilding and port functions and is absolutely dependent on a workforce which got its initial training in ship-building and -repair. The first offshore construction facility was developed by William Press at Howden in North Shields in 1972. This company has now expanded to three other yards including the former British Shipbuilders Hadrian Yard (Clellands) at Wallsend, and the Wallsend Slipway which had been operated by Howard Doris Ltd. for the offshore industry until the demise of that operation in 1986. Newspaper coverage in December 1987 identified a workforce of 1300 in Press's Tyne Yards but there has been considerable fluctuation in numbers depending on the state of contracts. Thus the management in August 1987 referred to having employed twice as many workers 2 years previously. The nature of operations is illustrated by the closure of Howard Doris with 650 job losses and by the experience of Charlton Leslie offshore which, in June 1987, had only 11 employees, down from a previous total of 700, but on receipt of a new order expanded to some 300 in partnership with McNulty Offshore. Press's have had only one 6-week period without an order (in 1984), but their workforce has fluctuated between 700 and 2500 employees. At the present time, Tyne offshore facilities include Press, Charlton Leslie, McNulty and Dunlop Armaline's pipe coating facility at the former Walker Navy Yard which employs some 160 workers. In December 1987 Peter Morrison, Minister of State for Energy, estimated that the North's (including Wear and Teesside) offshore industry was expected to exceed 4000 jobs in 1988–9. This seems reasonable and about 50% of these are situated on the Tyne.

Marine manufacturing is almost wholly dependent on skills acquired before 1980. In the early 1970s there were some 800 apprentices a year recruited into Tyneside ship-building and -repair with others acquiring relevant skills in engineering and plating factories. British Shipbuilders last seems to have recruited a significant number of apprentices in the late 1970s. Recently, there has been virtually no recruitment. The Careers Department in North Tyneside were last able to identify any recruitment in 1986, when Swan Hunters engaged 25 apprentices; however, they never started work. The offshore industry has trained a handful of apprentices, but these do not compare with its labour requirements. There is plenty of skilled labour available and given the short-term view nobody will train.

In the 1984 debate on the shipbuilding industry Peter Shore, the opposition spokesman on Trade and Industry, said: 'I can think of few industries where the medium to long-term view of demand is more necessary.' This seems to be precisely what is lacking on Tyneside with regard to all aspects of marine manufacturing. The Booz-Allan Report of 1972 identified the need for state intervention if the British industry was to survive world competition. The unions looked to nationalization to achieve a strong industry. Instead, the experience of nationalization under a government committed to free-marketism and opposed to subsidies, has been one of restructuring and run-down. The UK gives the least subsidies of any major marine manufacturing country and only warship yards are regarded as of strategic significance. Most of the shipbuilding companies are small. Nationalization's successors on the Tyne are made up of two management buy-outs and Smiths, which is the fag-end of the original Swan Hunter empire. These are not small yards, but they are small companies in the sense of not being part of large conglomerates with access to substantial investment. Only William Press, which merged with Fairclough to form AMEC in 1982, has large corporate resources. It seems fatuous to condemn companies like this for functioning as they must in the industrial and political context in which they find themselves. However, the actual and potential role of the state requires consideration in different terms.

The other marine aspects of North Shields, marine transport and fishing, are also in decline. In 1901 more than a quarter of all employed males in North Shields worked in and around the port and there were nearly 2000 seamen and 600 dockers and coalheavers resident in the town. The last census for which comparable figures are available for Tynemouth CB was 1971, when there were 330 resident seafarers and 160 dockers, etc. The basis of the Tyne as a port was the export of coal, much of it through the Northumberland Dock in North Shields which exported the coal from Cramlington and other South Northumberland collieries. However, the port also handled general cargoes including the import of wood and trade from Scandinavia (for developments until 1977, see North Tyneside CDP, 1978b). Today, no coal is exported from North Shields – the old Northumberland Dock has been filled in and is the site of a gas treatment station, an oil depot and Velva Liquids, which handles chemicals, etc. There is a significant passenger and cargo trade with Scandinavia through Albert Edward Dock. More recently, this dock has been used for the importation of Fiat cars (it used to be used for the export of British cars). All these trades are quite healthy but they employ very few people given the innovations in cargo handling and the dominance of Scandinavian companies in shipping.

Much of the cargo trade is now handled as roll on–roll off, as is all the passenger trade. The port's operations are subsidized to some extent by the local authorities but in the main the port is financed by port dues and this had led to a demand that any port land released for development should yield significant port use in order to generate revenue. We will return to this in Chapter 5. The main point here is the relatively minimal impact of employment in port-related activities. In 1987, a consultant's report estimated that some 250 jobs (including road haulage, etc.) were generated by Scandinavian trade. Other trade at North Shields can scarcely add another 100 to this total. There is a considerable contribution to retail employment in Tyne and Wear by the Scandinavian shoppers who use the ferries. However, the overall picture is of minimal port employment in a series of capital-intensive and land-requiring uses, several of which are, at least potentially, environmentally unpleasant.

The position with regard to merchant seamen on Tyneside is rather complex. Traditionally, the Tyne has been one of the bastions of British maritime power. Until the last war, Tyneside shipowners owned an important part of the British merchant marine. However, the last North

Shields firm, *Stag Line*, merged with *Hunting and Son* in 1981 and closed its North Shields office. After the closure of *Common Bros* of Newcastle, there is now no major Tyne-based shipping company.

This abandonment of a Tyneside base by shipowning interests would not necessarily reduce recruitment of merchant seamen from the Tyne. Men are now recruited into a national labour pool and their home base is largely irrelevant to where they take ships. North and South Shields remain the home base for many British merchant seamen and officers with important training facilities at South Tyneside College. A decline in employment has followed a decline in the overall level of employment in the British Merchant Navy deep-sea trades. This is in part a function of reduced manning levels on modern ships, particularly container vessels, but it also reflects the flagging out of much of the fleet to flags of convenience. The British Merchant Navy now consists of 545 vessels compared with 1682 vessels in 1975. The merchant marine now totals 14 000 ratings and 9800 officers, compared with 50 900 ratings and 34 800 officers in 1975.

The importance of the merchant navy in the formation of the maritime culture in North Shields was very great. There was a direct connection with the shipyards, not only in terms of orders by British owners (who now build abroad to a far greater extent than any other non-flag of convenience maritime nation), but through the training of engineering officers who traditionally served their time as fitters in the yards or engine works before going to sea. The Tyne seamen have had some sort of union organization since the seventeenth century. The present-day National Union of Seamen was founded on the north east coast, which was also a major centre for the Seamen's Reform Movement which recaptured the union for the rank-and-file in the mid-1960s. Tyneside maritime culture is rather different from that described for Liverpool by Lane (1988). It has never been docile – the press was resisted with great violence in both North and South Shields in the early nineteenth century – but it has always been ordered. In the late eighteenth and early nineteenth centuries, the Shields-based Loyal Standard Association operated as a Friendly Society for sick, injured and elderly seamen under the patronage of a senior Royal Navy Officer of flag rank. However, it also functioned as a trade union in defiance of the Combination Laws.

The Tyne atmosphere, in the formation of which merchant navy officers have played a major role (before the war transition from seamen to officer was not uncommon although it is very rare now), is well reproduced in a number of memoirs (see *Before the Box Boats* by Captain A. W. Kinghorn of Cullercoats, 1983). Tynesiders see themselves as a seafaring people with all that implies. Present trends indicate that by the end of this century, this will no longer be the case.

The fishing and fish-processing industry in North Shields is a comparative newcomer. It dates from the invention of steam trawling in the port in the late nineteenth century and had its heyday in the great steamdrifter herring fishery of the early twentieth century. In the 1930s fishing and fish-processing were second only to Smiths Dock as an employer and the total engaged rose to 3000 at one point. The focus has almost always been on the North Sea, although between 1965 and 1973 eight distant-water freezer trawlers belonging to Ranger Fisheries, a subsidiary of P and O, were based in the port. North Shields is very well placed in relation to the North Sea grounds. In the late 1970s there was considerable pressure on landing facilities at the fish quay and a serious proposal for a replacement on a much larger scale (see North Tyneside CDP, 1978a). However, since 1978, the pelagic fishery (fishing for open-water species, i.e. herring and sprats) has collapsed in the North Sea. Local fishermen blame the Danes for hoovering up young fish for fishmeal.

The industry's crisis led to a nationwide blockade of ports by UK fishermen in 1981 protesting at the importing of foreign fish. Irvin's, the port's largest fishing company, closed in 1980. This company had purchased two new middle-water vessels, the *Ben Loyal* and *Ben Roy* but had been unable to make them pay and was obliged to sell them in May 1980. In 1983 North Tyneside Council commissioned an examination of the industry in North Shields by the Sea Fish Industry Authority. This wrote off the need for any large new harbour construction. Despite the advantages of the Tyne, accessible in any weather and at any state of the tide, it had missed its chance to be a major North Sea fishing port. The North Shields fleet was dominated by day-trip vessels. Whereas in 1972 there had been 462 persons employed in the catching sector, this had declined to 217 by 1982. Deep-sea fishing had entirely disappeared, but there was some expansion in the inshore sector, much of it in fishing for prawns. In addition to the catchers, a further 286 were employed by fish merchants and 131 in ancillary services.

The report identified 67 vessels based in the port, although these were much smaller than the vessels of the early 1970s. By October 1986 the local press was describing the fleet as consisting of just 40 boats. The 1983 report had identified the crucial issue for North Shields as the need for the development of an adequate marketing facility in the port to attract larger visiting vessels which were responsible for 54% of landings in 1982. The consultants saw a steady state of landing for demersal (white) fish and nephrops (prawns), but commented on the poor state of premises around the fish quay. Subsequently, the MBC has made available a number of new premises for rent to processors and has generally tidied up and improved the area using Industrial Improvement Area procedures. The Port Authority has also invested £300 000 in major repairs. Local authority figures for 1986 showed that landings from British vessels at the port were valued at £5.6 million.

The North Shields fishing industry, life in which is interestingly and sympathetically described in Peter Mortimore's (1987) *The Last of the*

Hunters, is now pretty much what it was in the mid-nineteenth century. The boats are diesel-powered rather than sailing cobles, but the fleet is small and scarcely serves its local market, let alone an important part of what is in any event a diminishing national fleet. The largest fish-processing plant in the area, Findus at Longbenton, came from Hull and has no direct relationship with the North Shields fishing industry. It is part of the 'modernizing' sector rather than of traditional maritime activities. The rest of the industry, and particularly the catching sector, could be described as having been 'underdeveloped'. Fishing was always pretty rough and ready but for most of the post-war years the core was a modern sector with employed and unionized labour working for large capitalist enterprises. North Shields fishing could now be described as a peasant activity. This is almost a classic illustration of underdevelopment in the autonomist sense.

Indeed, the whole of the maritime industrial base of North Shields could be described as underdeveloped. In fishing this literally means that the catching sector has been forced back into a more primitive, earlier phase. In marine manufacturing one has the sense of a kind of using up of existing facilities and skills without much new investment, although the Tyne does have R and D capacity in this sector. The port is surviving at a limited kind of level. A full analysis of the situation will be postponed to the end of this chapter, but it seems worth noting that recently the Tyne shipped its largest ever cargo – an export load of scrap.

The 'modernized' industrial sector in North Shields and Cramlington

The problems which derive from the decline in the industrial structure which gave rise to the North East as an industrial region have been recognized since the 1930s, and until the coming to power of the present government the same core strategy informed attempts to resolve them. The problem was the narrow and old-fashioned character of the traditional industrial base and the states' solution was to modernize and diversify (see North Tyneside CDP, 1978b). Recent regional policies originating from central government are described in Robinson *et al.* (1987). The focus in this section will be on the present state of the modernized industrial structure as represented by developments on the Chirton and Tyne Tunnel industrial estates in North Shields and on the industrial estates in Cramlington. This concentration on industrial estates is not accidental. Most of the modernized sector is on industrial estates because industrial land development, particularly by what is now English Estates North, has been a central part of state efforts at modernization since the Special Areas measures of the 1930s. The use of 'industrial land' provides us with a bridge to the issues to be considered in Chapter 5.

Of these spatial concentrations of modernized industry, Chirton Industrial Estate is the oldest. There was some pre-war and wartime development but the real growth began in the 1940s. Part of this was the continuation of the mobilization of the very large reserves of female labour on industrial Tyneside, particularly in the clothing industry, but there was also the Formica plant which was opened in 1947. By 1961 total employment on the estate stood at 5000. Despite a turnover of plants in the 1960s and early 1970s, employment was maintained until the mid-1970s when a CDP study estimated it at about 4800 of whom 50% were women. A survey of industrial guides, directories, etc., enabled the present author to calculate some sort of employment statistics for the mid-1980s for some 80% of identifiable establishments on the Chirton Estate, including all of the larger plants. These statistics totalled some 2800. I believe that total employment in manufacturing on the Chirton Estate is unlikely to exceed 3000, although there are some jobs in retailing.

Part of the reason for this is closure without major replacement. Establishments which have closed include the Levis Jeans factory (July 1984 with the loss of 283 jobs) and General Foam Products (1981 with 300 job losses). Firms who have substantially reduced their workforce include Formica (with 550 employees in 1987, compared with more than 1200 in the early 1970s), Welch's (a locally owned sweet manufacturer with 130 employees, compared with 200 in the early 1970s), Universal Bedding (with 350 employees in 1982, compared with 500 in 1973), and Great Northern Knitwear (with 75 employees in 1987, compared with 115 in 1973). Obviously, these totals vary and indeed sometimes increase. For example, Great Northern Knitwear seems to have increased its total number of employees from 80 to 105 in September 1987 following £717 000 of new investment. However, the general trend is down. An interesting comment on the background to this is provided by a statement from the Managing Director of Norfran Aluminium which employs 60 people on the Chirton Estate. He is the former production manager of British Die Casting which in 1973 employed 143 at Chirton and was quoted in *The Shields News Guardian* on 26 May 1988 as saying: 'We are producing double the output of the old British Die Casting with half the workforce.'

The other major location for modernizing plants in North Shields is the privately owned Tyne Tunnel Trading Estate. In the mid-1970s the CDP estimated total employment here to be some 1600. Much of the activity on the Tyne Tunnel Estate has always been in small warehousing and distribution depots but the two large manufacturing employers are Cape Insulation and Twinings Teas (a subsidiary of Associated British Foods). In 1977 Twinings employed more than 330, compared with 165 in February 1987, when the creation of an extra 30 jobs was announced. Almost the only identifiable employer in North Shields with significant job gains is the electronics company Elmwood Sensors. Employment here increased from 200 in the mid-1970s when it was established, to some 380 in 1987. Most of these jobs are for women working part-time.

The general picture in North Shields is one of some closures with considerably reduced employment levels in most remaining plants caused by a combination of poor trading conditions and productivity gains. The situation in Cramlington is essentially similar. In 1974 there were 8061 employees on the town's industrial estates; by 1981 this had fallen to 5337. A 1987 document prepared by Cramlington Libraries Service identified 'almost 5,550 jobs'. The decline to 1981 had involved 1217 jobs lost as a result of closures and 2218 lost from establishments reducing their workforces, with 805 gains from new establishments and 234 from establishments increasing their workforces. The picture since 1982 has been one of net zero change although there has been at least one new arrival, Boots PLC.

This approximate total of 5500 jobs is to be compared with the 1974 estimates of 17 000 jobs by the early 1990s. A substantial part of the industrial land has been developed but the job yield has been far below initial expectations. This is very much a function of productivity gains in modern manufacturing. Cramlington's major employers include: Lonhro Textiles, who manufacture bed linen (1300 employees); American Air Filters, who manufacture exactly that; House of Mayfair/Commercial Plastics, who together employ some 950 in the manufacture of specialist plastics and decorative plastic wall-coverings; Bristol Myers, Merck, Sharp and Dohme Ltd. and Boots PLC, who are all manufacturers of pharmaceuticals; and a range of modern general engineering, computing and chemical companies. It is indeed a diversified system with only interrelated aspect represented by the pharmaceutical element, which is part of a substantial development in employment in this sector in South East Northumberland in the post-war years.

Industrial culture

The Tyneside industrial culture has emerged out of the long-term association and interaction of practices which derive from a range of industrial experiences *as these come together in civil society*. Tyneside has almost a unique congruence of a range of industrial traditions for men. Thus it was a great port with a very long-established seafaring tradition. Urban Tyneside still has mining employment and in the recent past this was of great significance. Finally, there is the 'engineering and ship-building' tradition of skilled worker syndicalism. People did move between these industries: engineering workers went to sea, as did in the course of a lifetime, some miners; seamen came ashore and worked as scaffolders and riggers in the yards. Individual cross-experience was much reinforced by family connections in which siblings and sons worked in a variety of industries. Such family connections were very different from those in one-industry occupational communities and are important precisely because they are the basis of interaction in civil society and relate to political action.

At the level of political action two components have to be carefully distinguished. One is the tradition of industrial politics at or immediately derived from the point of production; the other is formal state-related politics, which includes the activities of trade union officials in corporatist engagement with the national and local state. The first on Tyneside was syndicalist, organized around shop-stewards in engineering and the shipyards with lodge officials and the activists of the Seaman's Reform Movement playing a similar role in mining and shipping. This kind of organization was also important in the construction industry but never had the same force in 'process' plant production. It did exist in those parts of 'modernizing' industry which were part of the engineering industry and involved skilled labour in manufacture, as distinct from the Fordist production practices of process plants. Interestingly, female clothing workers were associated with the syndicalist tradition, although much of the leadership of industrial action in the early 1970s came from male cutters.

It was this tradition, frequently 'unofficial', which maintained Tyneside industrial militancy in a range of important disputes in the 1960s and 1970s, including the 1966 seamen's strike, and the 1972 and 1974 miners' strikes. Although the main basis of action was immediate issues, the leading militants were frequently part of the wider socialist movement in the area and many were associated, however loosely, with the ideas of the Institute for Workers Control. The Communist Party never had much influence on Tyneside other than among seamen. The leading 'rank-and-file' activists of the 1960s and 1970s generally regarded themselves as anti-Stalinist leftists. This was in no small part a remnant of ILP influence from the 1930s and 1940s. The last flowering of this tradition was in the Tyne Conference of Shop Stewards, established in 1975 in relation to the Labour Party's White Paper on Industrial Strategy and the consequent Industry Act (see North Tyneside CDP, 1978b).

This tradition has by no means wholly disappeared, although the power of the shop-stewards movement is now massively reduced by the changes in its traditional locations described above. It survives in some remaining large-scale engineering plants and in the pits and has also been taken up in public sector employment in the National Civil Service (particularly at the Longbenton Head Office of the DHSS), the Health Service and Local Authorities. This transition and survival resembles the developments described for South Wales by Cooke (1985) and is often mediated through family connections. It is commonly said in the North

East today that more miners' children are teachers than miners. It is certainly true that most north-eastern white-collar workers and para-professionals' family origins are in the skilled working class.

There has been little sociological work on this topic but there has been a good deal of interesting history, much of it carried out under the aegis of the North East Labour History Society. However, the North East has another related tradition of ultra-incorporated labourism in local government and involving trade union officials in corporatist regional boards, etc. This requires extended consideration as part of the subsequent discussion of the state, but it is not by any means dissociated from industrial culture, although it has frequently been in opposition to it.

In the 1960s and early 1970s, the left on Tyneside regarded trade union politics as massively more important than local government politics. The leading lights of the working class were plant convenors and lodge secretaries, not elected councillors, who were generally, and not wholly inaccurately, regarded as a collection of third-rate nuggets. In 1975 when North Tyneside and Benwell CDPs attempted to locate 'change agents' with sufficient force to have some impact on the structural origins of the situation in the two locales, the obvious target was the rank-and-file organizations of the traditional industrial working class. It would be very difficult to arrive at the same conclusion in 1988.

During this syndicalist period the 'official' movement was wholly committed to participation in the programme of modernization in which it participated with regional capital and the associated regional élite (see Benwell CDP, 1978). The net effects of all this are well described by the Northern Trade Union Labour Left (1984) culminating in efforts to establish a 'Regional Executive' on explicitly corporatist lines. What matters here is the effect of all this. What do the changes which can be summed up as 'modernization plus deindustrialization' amount to in terms of consequences for people?

Conclusion

The writer who has had most to say about this sort of issue is Massey, particularly in her *Spatial Divisions of Labour* (1984). Massey's work attempts to do two things at once: it is part of the revolution in human geography in which there has been a transformation of explanation in that discipline and at the same time, it is intended to inform the construction of political strategies. There are some problems here. Massey's realism is implicit rather than explicit but she remains committed to what looks like a traditional and reflective, rather than revolutionary and transformational, conception of explanation. This epistemological criticism is not directed at her political intervention but at her recourse to structuralist account and emphasis on the capacities of capital rather than of class. In common with much of the writing on which this present book draws for useful insights, Massey focuses on capital as the *active* agent in the processes with which she is concerned. There is really more to this than necessary pessimism of the intellect associated with optimism of the will. Her work lies within the tradition characterized by Cleaver (1979) as political economy, casting the working class as merely 'a spectator at the global waltz of capital' (p. 27).

Thus what we have is a first-rate account of the use made by capital of space in conflict with the working class which underplays the extent to which this use is a *response* to working-class organization.

This is an important point, even if it results in a somewhat excessive criticism of Massey. Massey's schematic description of the forms of organization of capital in space, or more particularly of productive capital in space, is exceptionally useful, but its very utility means that her general account has to be qualified before it is employed.

What we have in North Shields and Cramlington looks very like Lash and Urry's description of disorganized capitalism. We have, in particular, a modernized sector of production which is certainly not organized on the basis of locality. Massey's schemata is useful here, especially if we follow her instruction to be concerned with the real relationships among our objects of study rather than formal legal relations. In other words, we need to recognize that many apparently independent units of production are, without being legally owned subsidiaries, so dominated through subcontracting and purchasing arrangements, that they are effectively part of a single unit of capitalist production. A good example is provided by the relationship between Marks and Spencers and its suppliers, which is relevant to the clothing industry on Northern Tyneside, but many engineering plants which operate as subcontractors are in the same position.

Massey (1984: 77) identifies three types of spatial structure in production. There is the locationally concentrated structure in which all administration and control are located coterminously with the total process of production. Examples in Northern Tyneside include ship-building and -repair as part of the maritime industrial structure, and those local plants which are independent and not tied to a particular customer. These categories are not in practice sharply edged and enterprises can shift their location in both directions. Thus the shipyards were not 'locationally concentrated' when they were part of a nationalized structure, but rather represented an example of the 'cloning branch plant spatial structure' in which there is a separation between head office administration and control and branch administration and control. Massey's schematic representation of this form seems to imply that particular production units may be associated with head offices, but this does not imply a privileged status for any particular unit because head office functions may not be associated with any productive unit and are in any event highly mobile.

The offshore industry has tended towards this cloning form, although

Press on Tyneside is close up to the boundary with locationally concentrated structure. Clothing plants are generally clones as is the Formica Plant as part of Formica Inc. and Wilkinson Sword and Lonrho Textiles, even though the latter is a one and only operation, because crucial investment decisions are taken at Lonrho headquarters. The third form is 'part process' in which not only is head office administration spatially separated but the actual production process is split up into discrete bits which are carried out at different spatial locations. This seems to be the position of some of the pharmaceutical plants in the modernizing sector.

Massey agrees that the fate of entities which are part of large spatially diverse enterprises can be related to explicit planning decisions, but considers that it is dangerous to somehow regard such actions as 'worse' than the consequences of the anonymous system forces of capitalism as manifested through market relations. Such an attitude gives 'credence to the market as "natural" [and accepts] . . . one of the fundamental underlying ideological tenets of capitalist social relations' (Massey, 1984: 103). The point is well taken but attention to the planning decisions of 'spatially independent' capitalist organizations does show the character of power relations in capitalist exploitation. It addresses action.

The need for this is revealed by Massey's notion that spatial structures of production succeed one another but with successors shaped and influenced by the character of predecessors. Out of this 'combination' emerges uniqueness and hence determinism is avoided. In other words, Massey generates an account of the relationship between capitalist production and space in which spatial manifestations of capitalist social relations are not the simple one-on-one determined products of the logic of capitalism as a mode of production. Rather, variation can be explained (the object of the new geography) by the interaction of capitalist system logic with a historically generated set of pre-existing structures. This is not wholly asociological. In the hands of Cooke, with his account of 'radical regional cultures', a very similar approach is rooted in action. However, cultural forms themselves are essentially external to human beings as actors. To assign a role to culture is not to resolve the problems of structure versus action because the here and now culture, whatever its foundations in historical action, can be regarded as a component of social structure in a general sense.

Massey provides us with a fascinating and persuasive account of how capitalist production has used space. It is, as all such accounts are, a description of processes of combined and uneven development. At the end of it, is all that is left a kind of residual and outmoded cultural tradition which cannot stand against capital's organizational expertise in confronting labour? The miners after all have lost. As a description this has a lot of force but description must not be confused with prescription. Perhaps this chapter can best be concluded by raising a theme which will recur in this book, the idea of cultural counter-revolution. The power of capital is very great and it was a Tynesider (Jack Common) who pointed out that those who do not admire capitalism will never beat it. However, there is a distinction between admiration for the productive capacity of capitalism, the sense of which has always lain behind working-class hopes for the future because of a realization of the enormous capacity of the forces of production, and a kind of shocked acceptance of the innovative capacity of capital as a social force in creating conditions for its continued reproduction. Sociological studies of actual decision-making processes and power concentrations, of the planning of production, seldom produce such admiration. What is admired (in the old sense of negative awed wonder, an example to be admired rather than imitated), is the apparent role of anonymous system forces seen not as natural but as overweening.

In the introduction to this book industrial culture was identified as a component of base as was the role of the state in terms of 'reacculturation'. That position is maintained. However, we will have to leave this for now with a sense of pessimism, because we will find no way forward until we have got to grips with forces other than production change which, very much in interaction with production change, are constitutive of civil society and of social being. However, we first need to deal with the role of land in relation to production and accumulation.

5

The question of land

Introduction

In the introduction it was suggested that land became important during times of change. Thus land development was important for capital when North Shields was being put together as an industrial town and it seems to be important again when its industrial base is being taken apart. We have got this far and ignored a lot of work regarding issues of land rent and of the nature of capital's relation with land as part of a general accumulation process. And so we will continue. It is not that these issues are being dismissed in terms of their general abstract importance as a way of getting to grips with capitalism as a system. Rather, they are not particularly useful in terms of understanding located historical process. This is partly a matter of the distinction between ways of understanding the abstract character of a system and actual history already identified in a quotation from Gramsci. However, it also reflects the general applicability of a point made by Ball about one of the leading theorists in this area:

> The capital logic of Harvey's work is continually expressed in the functionalism assigned to the built environment. With only a degree of oversimplification, his general conclusion can be summarised as saying that whatever is happening in the built environment will eventually be resolved to the benefit of the undifferentiated interests

of capital in general, even if that resolution generates further problems that have to be resolved in turn.

(Ball, 1986: 452)

Even if things look pretty grim at the moment consideration of twentieth-century housing developments in North Shields shows that capital has by no means always has its own way and that, as Ball indicates above, capital is not undifferentiated in relation to land and what is built on it.

Massey and Catalano (1978) suggest a typology of forms of landownership distinguishing between what they call 'former landed property' (a rather odd term because one of the major contributions of their work is the extent to which they demonstrate the continued importance of this element), 'industrial' landownership and 'financial' landownership. The first is a survival if not of feudalism (although in Northumberland it is exactly that) then of early modern social relations. The next, industrial landownership, involves those who own land as a condition of production. The last describes the relation of finance capital with land as in investment. Massey and Catalano dismiss the importance of land interests as the basis of either fractions or a combined fraction of capital based on all three types.

This seems to be a matter of level of attention. The evidence from North Shields and Cramlington suggests that landed interests have acted as fractions of capital. It may be that at the national political level in the late twentieth century it is harder to identify discrete instrumentalist land interests than it is when looking at specific places, although even at the national level it is easy enough in 1988. Understanding cannot be based on any one level. Events at the local level are not simply subsumed into some larger, general process. Both the local and national matter, and what is going on in history will not be understood without reference to both.

In practice, Ambrose's recent distinction between two routes to capital accumulation through land, has been more useful in dealing with North Shields and Cramlington. Ambrose identifies an investment route in which buildings (shorthand for modification of land by action) are acquired in order to yield a stream of income. In contrast, the production route involves the modification of land and its relatively immediate sale. In the first case, profits depend on having annual incomes which exceed annual outgoings; in the second, the price must be greater than the total cost of production inputs (see Ambrose, 1986: 4).

Both processes are going on in the two locales, sometimes with a single agency carrying out both simultaneously. Both have gone on for a long time. A preliminary account of events up to the mid-1970s has already been given for both locales, which will stand as an account for Cramlington but some elaboration is necessary for North Shields. This will be followed by a consideration of recent developments in relation to the provision of land for housing on the one hand, and conflict over land use between industry and non-industrial uses on the other.

In both localities we are dealing with events subsequent to the formulation and issuing of structure plans. In Cramlington, the intentions of the Northumberland Structure Plan, which in any event reflected existing planning policy, have been more or less observed in practice. This is by no means the case for North Shields and the rest of North Tyneside in relation to the Tyne and Wear Structure Plan. Cramlington seems to be still planned but in the inner city we are now very definitely after the planners. This is primarily a matter of the anti-planning ideological commitment of the present central administration, reflected *interalia* in the out of hand rejection of the Northern Regional Strategy which was an assumption of the Tyne and Wear exercise.

North Shields: from green fields to green fields in three generations

A full account of the development of North Shields is given in North Tyneside CDP (1978a, b) and a summary is given in Chapter 3. Events before 1977 will be considered here in relation to three aspects:

1. The form of industrial development which has two sub-aspects, namely the development of maritime industrial land in the nineteenth century and the development of industrial estates in the twentieth century.
2. The development of land for housing up until the mid-1970s.
3. The saga of North Shields town centre and adjacent housing areas.

Industrial development of the Tyne in the nineteenth century involved conflicts over land, or rather in this instance water, rights. The Corporation of the City of Newcastle had controlled the river, and most of the coast of northern England, under rights allocated by Royal Charter. The merchant capitalists who controlled the City were much opposed to changes in this. Against them were marshalled industrial capital in coal mining, shipping and shipbuilding led by the great radical (Karl Marx's description) Joseph Cowen. Much of 'the surrounding area' of historic North Shields was owned by the Duke of Northumberland. The development of North Shields was clearly in the interests of the ducal estate, both in terms of gains made in North Shields, and in relation to wayleave payments for coal travelling to North Shields by rail for shipment. The estate sold or leased much of the land used for downriver port activities to the Tyne Improvement Commission. The traditional landowner was quite happy to convert land into capital.

Land acquired by the Tyne Improvement Commission came into public ownership and most remains there as the property of the Port of Tyne Authority which replaced the Improvement Commission in 1968. Other riverfront industrial developments, e.g. Smith's Dock, occurred on owner-occupied land or on land leased from the Port Authority. All riverfront industrial land in North Shields is within the designated area of the Tyne and Wear Development Corporation, the Urban Development Corporation, established in 1987.

The developmental history of non-riverfront industrial land is rather different. The most significant sites in North Shields are Chirton Industrial Estate, originally comprising 110 acres, which was acquired by the council and transferred to North East Trading Estates, and Tyne Tunnel Industrial Estate, comprising 132 acres bought from the Duke of Northumberland in the mid-1960s by Property Security Investment Trust Ltd. This company is a clear example of 'financial landholding' in Massey and Catalano's (1978) terms. It is worth recalling the importance of Tynemouth County Borough as a land developer in the inter-war years. Sites acquired included Balkwell Farm (130 acres acquired from the copyholder, with the Duke of Northumberland's interest as Lord of the Manor bought out), the Meadowell Farm (135 acres bought from the Ducal estate in the 1930s) and land at Hunt Hill and Cullercoats. Part of this land was used for council housing but, as North Tyneside CDP (1978a) makes clear, much was made available for the building of private housing. This practice was revived in the 1950s with the sale of land at Marden and elsewhere.

The other source of housing land apart from such acquisition of green field sites on the urban periphery, the development basis of 'suburbanization by addition', was through slum clearance. The bankside land acquired as a result of the clearances of the 1930s has been left as public recreational space but the river top site acquired in the early 1960s with the clearance of Dockwray Square has been redeveloped, twice, first as flatted council housing in the 1960s. When this was in turn cleared in the early 1980s the site was disposed of for private construction. This is closely related to the history of the town centre development.

The history of that development is important because it shows the shift in interests of the development and retail 'industries' over the last 20 years. Accounts of the background in terms of the impact of central area plans on adjacent areas of working-class housing are given in North Tyneside CDP (1976; 1978a, b). The 'property world', 'financial landowners' and finance capital in general, were keenly interested in the development opportunities offered by the reconstruction of the UK's Victorian town centres. Local authorities were involved because it was necessary to use planning powers to assemble land for comprehensive redevelopment. There were a number of false starts for North Shields after 1948 but things really began in 1961. At that time North Shields had a set of Victorian shopping streets. The area to the south of Saville Street which had been the commercial centre for the port was already in a state of decay with banks, etc. moving north towards residential areas. There had been some war damage but this was not on a scale which lent itself to large-scale redevelopment.

In April 1961, Tynemouth CBC's Town Improvement Committee authorized a survey with a view to the declaration of a Comprehensive Development Area. The report was presented in June 1962 by the Town Clerk and Borough Surveyor and indicated the desirability of seeking a partnership between the Corporation and a development company which would regard development as a long-term investment and be interested in the equity. By July 1964, J. G. L. Poulson and Associates had been engaged. There seems to have been no element of corruption in this, despite the involvement of Poulson in a range of corrupt activities in the North East in the 1960s. Poulson and Associates made it clear that they were not a 'financial development company' but that they could locate a suitable such investor for the scheme.

The Poulson Report was presented to committees in 1966 after which it was published. All reports to this date were looking to the development of a large area to the north of Saville Street in North Shields town centre with a view to creating a new shopping centre which would serve a population of some 70 000, although at various times more grandiose claims about potential catchment area were made. Even the earliest report of the Borough Surveyor in 1961 had recognized the impact of population shift:

> The tremendous post war housing development within the Borough has not benefited North Shields nearly as much as it should have done had its position been central. Instead new development has gradually gravitated away from North Shields and is now much nearer to Whitley Bay [then a separate local authority].
> (Tynemouth CBC, Surveyor, 1961: 11)

This problem was identified in all reports on the feasibility of the scheme. If North Shields was to become a viable shopping centre and attract the kind of investment necessary for a scheme on the scale being envisaged in the 1960s and 1970s, then population and purchasing power had to be drawn into the town centre. It was in this connection that 'the land south of Saville Street' became important. This is the area between the southern edge of the shopping area and the top of the bluffs which run down to the river. It contained an area of nineteenth-century by-law housing, the old commercial centre of the town which by this time was in a semi-derelict condition, and the slum-cleared and redeveloped area of Dockwray Square with medium-rise council flats. In practice, it has been this area which has been most significant in relation to land development and planning policies. The immediate effect was on the two housing areas known as East and West Ropery Banks (see North Tyneside CDP, 1976, 1978c). Basically, the local authority suspended improvement grants which had previously been available because it was considered that these areas might be cleared in order to meet 'the necessity for new housing development being provided to the south of Saville Street to contribute to the success of the proposed new shopping centre' (Town Improvement Committee, 8 March 1971). The view that the East Ropery Banks site might be considered for 'high value' housing in order to provide potential consumers for the shopping centre had first been expressed in the Poulson Report of 1965, but it had greater saliency by 1971 because the authority was already dealing with its second property company (Town and City) and it was clear that market conditions made the redevelopment of North Shields centre a highly marginal project.

The CDP was associated with a good deal of unsuccessful community action around this issue. Eventually, West Ropery Banks was cleared. However, East Ropery Banks remains, is now designated as long-life property and seems to have recovered from some 8 years of planning blight through a combination of the re-availability of improvement grants and a strong market demand for small dwellings in central North Shields. The abandonment of grandiose planning intentions was the consequence of market conditions. After a long-running saga of development companies coming into North Shields and withdrawing from a relatively small-scale development (200 000 sq ft overall, 130 000 selling space), development of the town centre was begun on part of the original site in 1977 funded by the Coal Industry Pension Fund. The viability of this centre is now under threat from new shopping developments, which will be dealt with in the next section. For now the point to emphasize is the extent to which planning decisions, including the planning decisions of Labour-controlled North Tyneside Council between 1974 and the early 1980s, regarded working-class residential communities as movable pieces in the development game.

The Structure Plan and after

The Tyne and Wear Structure Plan was prepared in the late 1970s and finalized in 1980. In the *Report of Survey* its nature was defined: 'The Structure Plan is a land use plan, not an instrument of social planning' (Tyne and Wear County Council, 1979a: 15, para. 2.1). It can be argued that this confinement to land-use issues was the basic problem with structure planning and goes far to explain why the exercise has in practice proved so limited in its impact, but in this chapter the focus is precisely on the politics of land use, and structure plan intentions are of considerable importance. There were three related areas of interest to us. These were to do with housing land, with the availability of adequate industrial land in general and of strategic industrial sites in particular, and with the pattern of shopping provision within the county. The objectives in relation to each area were to control urban sprawl and preserve the inner areas as housing locations, to use land availability as part of a programme of economic regeneration and preserve sites suitable for large-scale developments, and to maintain existing shopping centres in a viable condition. Only with regard to the first has there been even limited success.

The planners made much of the growth of the built-up area of Tyne and Wear during the twentieth century. In 1979, they pointed out that what we have called suburbanization by addition had increased this by nine times since 1901, whereas population had increased by only 25%. Since 1945 the built-up area had increased by 2.5 times, whereas population had hardly increased at all. Demographic and migration trends indicated that the rate of new household formation over the period of the structure plan (i.e. until the mid-1990s) was expected to be half of the post-war average levels and total population was likely to fall. The implications of this were discussed almost entirely in relation to the release of land for housing, but it also had considerable implications for the tenure pattern of new housing. Tyne and Wear County was committed to 'conservation of the urban areas, and conservation of land and buildings' (Tyne and Wear County Council, 1979b: 13, para. 2.12).

The main opposition to this came from developer builders who were significant landowners on the urban fringe, but there was a recognized tension between Tyne and Wear's intentions and the Northumberland Structure Plan's continued commitment to the growth of Cramlington on the basis of outmigration from Tyne and Wear. A number of peripheral sites for large-scale housebuilding were designated but the policy commitment to the inner area was explicit:

> Priority in new housebuilding should be given to the inner area, including measures to provide private housebuilding and building to meet special needs.
> (Tyne and Wear County Council, 1979b: 59, Policy H9)

In consultation there was considerable opposition to this from the developer builders as indicated in the *Report of Panel on Examination in Public of the Tyne and Wear Structure Plan*:

> All around the fringe of the urban area there are pockets of land in the ownership of private builders just waiting for the signal to turn from red to amber. Admirable as the desire is to ensure that these builders have the opportunity to construct the dwellings that the public will want to buy, the special position of Tyne and Wear, the real shortage of new land, makes it essential in planning terms that existing urban areas should be scoured for land upon which to build.
> (Tyne and Wear County Council, 1980: 34, para. 5.22)

The discussion of the developers' reluctance to engage in inner urban development centred on problems of smaller sites. In the examination in public, evidence showed that the threshold size of a viable site in the inner areas was about 5 acres. This is important because specific mechanisms have since been developed for subsidizing private operations in the inner area, but it should also be noted that all inner-area housing sites were already designated as housing land and there were no 'change of use' profits to be made on them. In many instances, peripheral sites offered such development gain to large land-holding builders. This factor had considerable importance in engendering urban sprawl.

The response of the Secretary of State for the Environment is interesting. In effect, the housing land policy was modified in detail to such an extent that the County Planners considered it to be contradicted (Tyne and Wear County Council, 1981a: 13). The justification for this interference was that:

> It is considered essential that the effect of both central and local government in fulfilling the aims of the inner city policy should be balanced with the need to enable housebuilders to meet the demand for home ownership.
> (Tyne and Wear County Council, 1981c: 12)

This introduction of tenure as a component of planning policy was not wholly new. The Northern Regional Strategy Team had commented on the relatively small rate of owner-occupation and planners had long whinged about the impact of the shortage of 'executive housing' on industrial development. However, DoE reservations about the structure plan's intentions for housing land were far more explicit. In the first *Structure Plan – Annual Report*, the likely consequences of these changes were indicated:

> In general it is likely that builders will prefer the additional greenfield land to the substantive existing provision within the built-up area. Such sites suit their conventional styles of building and marketing, and at a time of low demand would improve their cash-flow by capitalising on their extensive land holdings of farm land on the fringe.
> (Tyne and Wear County Council 1981b: 19, para. 3.30)

There has been more DoE resistance to peripheral development in relation to planning appeals than might have been anticipated given the nature of the Secretary of State's response to the Structure Plan. However, this has been associated with the development of a massive system of subsidies for private development in the inner urban area, primarily through the operation of Urban Development Grants (UDGs). At the same time there has been virtually no new council house building. This will be discussed in relation to housing developments in and around North Shields. Before dealing with this, it is necessary to document what has happened to industrial land and shopping, two issues not linked at all in the Structure Plan but very much interrelated in subsequent developments.

The objectives for shopping development were stated in Policy S4 (Tyne and Wear County Council, 1979b: 85):

> The development of major shopping facilities outside established shopping centres . . . or in a location or on a scale which would be likely to have an excessive impact on another established shopping centre should not be permitted.

Objections during consultation came from district councils concerned with the relative status given to existing shopping centres. North Tyneside complained about the low status given to North Shields shopping centre. In practice, the real issue has been something quite different: the development of 'warehouses' and shopping malls outside town centres on land originally designated for industrial use. The most important examples of this are in Gateshead at Retail World on the Team Valley (retail warehouses), and at the Metro Centre (Mall). Both occurred outside normal planning controls as they were located within the area of the Newcastle–Gateshead Enterprise Zone (see Anderson, 1983). However, the apparent success of retail development and the much higher land prices and rents which sites developed for out-of-town retail purposes command, has led to continuing pressure on industrial sites in general, including sites in and around North Shields.

Broadly speaking, the land around the Tyne Tunnel approach road to the west of North Shields including Chirton Industrial Estate, the Tyne Tunnel Industrial Estate and surrounding agricultural land, was designated either as first call industrial land or as part of a strategic reserve, although this latter status was modified by the Secretary of State in his revisions. The first large non-industrial development here was the opening of a retail furniture and carpet warehouse in the existing Arborite factory on Chirton Estate in 1983. By 1986, Formica, together with the B and Q do-it-yourself chain, had applied for 150 000 sq. ft of non-food retail development, leisure facilities and a railway museum adjacent to the Moat House Hotel. Tyne Tunnel Trading Estates Ltd. were seeking planning permission for a 360 000 sq. ft retail park on their site. This latter was described as 'a Metrocentre twin for North Tyneside'. North Tyneside MBC opposed both these developments pointing out that the Tyne Tunnel proposal in particular was for more square feet than currently existed in the whole of central North Shields. This opposition was upheld by the DoE with regard to the Tyne Tunnel Estate but the DoE Inspector approved the Formica/B and Q proposal. Thus land originally acquired by a manufacturing company for expansion was now being utilized, contrary to Structure Plan intentions, as a development asset for out-of-town retailing.

Other out-of-town proposals included a 55 000 sq. ft store by the

Newcastle developer's City and Northern Ltd. at Hillheads Industrial Estate, and the local authority's grant of planning permission to itself for a superstore at Red House Farm, both in Whitley Bay. Events at Red House Farm, which was acquired by the local authority in 1979 under the Community Land Act for housing purposes, are closely tied up with North Tyneside MBC's fiscal crisis. The picture is one of industrial land owners, including English Estates, abandoning the development of industrial premises in a frantic search for the supposedly massive profits to be made from retail developments. The basis for such profits, it is argued, are the high disposable incomes of employed Tynesiders given the low level of house prices.

The report prepared by a series of consultants for the DoE in relation to *The Formation of the Tyne and Wear Development Corporation* (DoE, 1987) is a good example of this fashion. In 'realising development potential' the consultants propose that over 10 years some 930 000 sq. ft of additional retail development should be achieved in the area of the UDC; this contrasts with a proposed 240 000 sq. ft of industrial development. Their proposals for 'Port of Tyne North' (the Whitehill Point site of the Port of Tyne Authority) are for an arena, marina, riverside village and exhibition space. In the Structure Plan this was regarded, at least in original proposals, as a strategic site for port-related industry and it remained as industrial land in the final version. The proposals for it by the UDC's consultants are not for retail use, but they are 'consumption-' rather than production-orientated. This is an important point about land use in and around North Shields. In the Structure Plan and in all earlier discussion, land was seen as something which provides a location for industry, for the population employed in and as a consequence of that industry and for the services necessary for that population. The point has already been made that industry here can include nationally or internationally orientated services like DHSS Longbenton. In the UDC proposals land is seen as the basis of a kind of wholly autonomous service sector. This is also the orientation of the 'market' and of DoE 'non-planning' decisions on land-use appeals. This idea of the service city is very well illustrated by recent developments in housing in and around North Shields.

Housing in North Tyneside since 1974

When the North Tyneside District Labour Party drew up a programme of objectives for the new authority in 1973, it placed considerable emphasis on new housebuilding. The party considered that a building programme of 11 000 new dwellings over a 5-year period was required of which 3000 were needed to deal with slum clearance, 2000 to clear the priority waiting lists and a further 6000 for general waiting list applications. At this point there was no conception of 'slum clearance' of purpose-built council dwellings, although since 1980 the authority has in fact demolished dwellings at Dockwray Square, Killingworth Towers, Hunter's Close and elsewhere. The intention was to meet housing need through public sector construction. Unlikely as that seems now, it must be remembered that in the early 1970s the private market was in a very bad condition and many developer builders were only rescued from bankruptcy by 'package deals' under which the DoE gave local authorities special loan sanctions in order to buy in whole estates of unsold private dwellings.

Actual local authority completions in North Tyneside between 1974 and 1986 totalled 5473, of which all but 639 were completed before 1981 and thus reflect pre-1979 capital programmes. In addition, there were 1668 Housing Association dwellings completed between 1974 and 1986. Of these 617 were completed after 1981, which indicates the comparative favouring of housing associations by Tory central government. Private construction since 1974 totals 5315, of which 2531 were completed after 1981. These figures show the effect of central controls on local authority capital spending on housing construction. New housebuilding in North Tyneside is now essentially a private sector activity and the local authority has gone along with this (particularly while under the control of 'Labour against Militant') by engaging in schemes designed to facilitate the access of low-income households to new owner-occupied dwellings.

The first system used was HELP (housing in exchange for land) and the second was 'Partnership'. In HELP schemes the development took place on land formerly owned by the local authority and sold on favourable terms in return for the acquisition of some of the new dwellings by the local authority for its rented stock. In 'Partnership', again local authority-owned land was made available for private development, but the new dwellings were reserved for 12 weeks at a stipulated price for purchasers falling into a restricted set of categories of which the most important were first-time buyers on the housing waiting list and households from slum-cleared areas. These priority households were also entitled to a discount from the land element in the finished dwelling. In 1982 this amounted to £750 on a bungalow costing £16 300.

The decisions on this were taken in August 1981 before the formal emergence of the Labour Party split at a time when the old guard were in control of the Labour Group. The then Chairman of the Housing Committee was to be a leading member of 'Labour against Militant' and crucial decisions, including this one, were usually remitted from the full Housing Committee to a smaller Housing Committee Working Group which met privately and was given the task of disposing of 25 sites which had originally been reserved for council house or Housing Association use, but were to be sold, used for Partnership or HELP schemes, or used for equity shares. The justification of this shift was both the unlikelihood of any massive programme of public sector housebuilding being permitted by Tory central government and the usefulness to the authority of capital receipts for land.

Most of these schemes were completed and sold in 1982–3. In all, Partnership and HELP produced about 360 dwellings which in the early 1980s were selling at prices of between £14 000 and £24 000, with most fetching below £20 000. At these prices the stock was certainly accessible to average income households. In addition, some 90 'equity share' dwellings were developed on sites owned originally by the local authority by the Enterprise 5 and Cheviot Housing Associations. These 450 dwellings were an important part of the 2500 private sector dwellings built after 1981 and correspond to the subsidized private sector construction of the 1920s. However, the bulk of new housing has been built on a straightforward commercial basis and corresponds to the developments of the 1930s. It is accessible because it is affordable *for those with average and reliable household incomes*.

One interesting aspect of all this has been the series of developments in 'maritime' North Shields by housing associations in advance of similar activity by the Urban Development Corporation. Schemes include Enterprise 5's transformation of the Old Customs House and Sailor's Home on the New Quay into *yuppie* flats and, something which is quite bizarre, the redevelopment of the old Bell St Tenements on the fish quay, originally built for the poorest of the poor in the 1920s, as posh flats. The total number of dwellings involved is not large, but the significance of the gentrification of what was industrial areas is considerable.

Another example of gentrification is the Yuill's development of 'St John's Green' between Percy Main and the Meadowell Estate using an Urban Development Grant. An account of this scheme is given in Munday and Mallinson (1983) and in Cameron's (1987) study of build and refurbish for sale in the North East (I am grateful to Stuart Cameron of Newcastle University for his generous provision of materials). Basically, this scheme uses half the point blocks built by the local authority in the early 1950s in this location. All the rest, save one, have been demolished and that block is now used as a neighbourhood local authority services centre (housing management, social services, etc.) rather than for housing. The scheme was expensive, with in effect £8000 of public money being spent on each dwelling, since the local authority contribution to UDG almost exactly cancelled out the price it received for the land. The total costs were in excess of £2.4 million, whereas receipts only totalled about £1.6 million. This gearing ratio of some 34% of costs born by subsidies was well outside the original UDG guidelines. Cameron shows that this scheme was not one of structural reconstruction but of altering appearance and apparent location in a very clever marketing exercise. The scheme has been associated with the former mining and railway village of Percy Main and with the Cricket Club (historically a pretty proletarian league institution) by reorganizing the road layout. Most of the refurbishment has gone into making the blocks look as unlike traditional council developments as possible.

Cameron's study indicates that the first-time residents in this scheme were largely young, white-collar, first-time buyers. Mortgage facilities were generous and, although prices were low in national terms in 1982 – between £10 000 for single studio flats and £16 500 for maisonettes – they were not low for Tyneside. Turnover has been high and several households have been rehoused in local authority stock after experiencing difficulties maintaining payments. There has been conflict about access from the Meadowell through this development to Percy Main and, remarkably, the Labour-controlled authority have agreed to this being blocked off. St John's Green was again a Labour against Militant faction-initiated scheme.

The other real piece of gentrification relates to the development of the Dockwray Square site in the east end of North Shields, a dramatic location looking over Shields harbour. The medium-rise deck access maisonettes and flats built here on a slum clearance site in the 1960s were very unpopular and by the late 1970s had become difficult to let. The residents campaigned for demolition and rehousing and achieved this in 1982. On 5 July 1984, the *Evening Chronicle* reported that North Tyneside Council was looking for 'imaginative designs' for the 12-acre site. By October 1984 the Housing Committee Working Group had accepted a scheme prepared by Gordon Durham Homes Ltd. for the development of the site as high-value housing. The housing built on the site is expensive terrace dwellings of pseudo-Georgian design, selling at £50 000 and over. Clearly, these prices are beyond the range of low- or medium-income, first-time purchasers from North Shields.

The final aspect of housing which merits attention is the condition of the older housing stock. A local authority report on changes between 1979 and 1987 indicates that of the 16 600 pre-1919 dwelling in North Tyneside, the number without amenities had fallen from 2800 in 1979 to 262 in 1987. The number considered below fully standard remained constant at about 8200, and the number considered to be fully standard increased from 5500 to 8100. By 1987 48% of the pre-1919 stock had been brought up to full standard. The 1986 Housing Investment Programme submission by the local authority showed 24 297 private sector dwellings in need of renovation, nearly 50% of the total private stock. Absence of amenity is no longer of real significance in housing in North Shields but the ageing stock may have considerable problems regarding structural repair. Between 1979 and 1987 more than 7000 improvement grants were paid out in North Tyneside. In the early 1980s, the shift towards repair grants was apparent but a shortage of resources has led to a cutback. However, as much of this stock has not become owner-occupied, it may well be that increases in market values will cope with the disrepair problem. The Tyneside experience seems to be that in 'gentrified' areas this will happen, but in areas which retain their original working-class population as owners rather than tenants, then grant aid is necessary if the stock is not to deteriorate beyond redemption. This issue is closely related to the form of socio-tenurial polarization in the Northern Tyneside area.

Developments in Cramlington

It is clear that there have been profound changes in North Shields since the mid-1970s. This is not true of Cramlington, where the basic development programme laid down in the early 1960s has continued, with only two significant changes relating to the use of industrial land and the role of the shopping centre development. Since 1974, some 6600 dwellings have been completed in Blyth Valley, the bulk of which are in the private sector (4400). In contrast with North Tyneside, all sectors have seen a downturn since 1981. Thus 266 of 961 Housing Association houses have been completed since that date, 141 of 1201 local authority dwellings and 737 of 4395 private dwellings. Local authority housebuilding has virtually ceased, whereas private sector development has simply slowed down. The only conflict about housing land in Cramlington during the preparation and revision of the Northumberland Structure Plan was about releases in relation to total numbers. At the behest of the developers the Secretary of State increased this from 5750 to 6500 sites in his *Decision Letter*. This was an issue of detail rather than principle.

The original intention was that Cramlington would be a free-standing new town with a full range of shopping services. However, this has never really come off. A report of the Director of Planning in June 1987 indicated the nature of the problem. Basically, much of Cramlington's population commuted to Newcastle to work and continued to shop there. The development of the Metro Centre in Gateshead (which is readily accessible from Cramlington) posed an additional problem. At this time there were some 23 500 sq. ft of shopping space in Cramlington Centre. This has since been complemented by a Co-op super-store with 40 000 sq. ft, which makes Cramlington one of the major peripheral retail developments in Tyneside but does not produce the kind of balanced traditional shopping centre originally intended.

Originally, some 424 acres (170 hectares) of land in Cramlington had been designated for industrial development. By the time of the first review of the Northumberland Structure Plan in 1984, 64 hectares of this were still available. Since the beginning of the Structure Plan period, 42.5 hectares had been developed. As has already been indicated this considerable additional development of land was happening while manufacturing employment was falling. Some land had been transferred to environmental uses.

The only real conflict over industrial land relates to the South

Cramlington Strategic Reserve Site. In the review of the Structure Plan the County wanted to redesignate this for warehousing and transport services and had some preliminary negotiations with a large tyre and exhaust fitting company with a view to that company taking over the development. Blyth Valley objected to this, not on the grounds that industrial land was being used for non-manufacturing purposes, but because it wanted the site retained as a green belt. Both local authorities seem to have accepted that some service development of this sort was a desirable addition to the Cramlington employment base.

The limited attention paid to developments in Cramlington since 1974 is not a matter of those developments being unimportant. Rather, it is that the processes described in the previous chapter have continued during the more recent period. Land is important in Cramlington but there has been no recent radical change in its ownership or development pattern.

Conclusion

The two themes which need to be addressed here are 'market' and 'consumption'. The present government's urban policies have emphasized the role of market forces as opposed to any sort of systematic planning. As it happens, the Tyne and Wear Urban Development Corporation, headed by a DoE civil servant on secondment, has not adopted an aggressively ideological assertion of market rationales, which is in marked contrast to the public performances of the head of its Teesside equivalent. None the less, the UDC has to show gains in the short term. To this extent it is bound by market forces and its operations are broadly equivalent to and supportive of private capital's interventions. What the review of developments in North Shields and Cramlington shows is that markets in land are essentially markets in planning permissions. This is true even when formal requirements for planning permission are removed, as in the Enterprise Zones, because the absence of a requirement for permission in a context where most land is subject to planning controls, is a planning permission of a very general kind.

The relation of the developers to the planning system is a combination of cooperation and conflict. Cramlington is an example of an almost entirely cooperative relationship. Disputes between planners and private sector developers have been over matters of detail. There has been no serious conflict about the designation of land for particular uses. Housing has been built on housing land and industrial land has either been retained for industrial purposes or is being redesignated by the planning process itself. Both of Ambrose's (1986) mechanisms of capital accumulation have operated in a straightforward fashion. The private developers have pursued the investment route with regard to the shopping centre, and to smaller sector shopping centres on particular estates. Owner-occupied housing has been developed with a view to derived profits via the production route. Cramlington illustrates real issues, in particular the extensive development gains made by the private developers on land they owned at the beginning of the whole process. The generally cooperative partnership between the local states and the developers did break down over the distribution of investment profits from central shopping development. However, things have largely gone as intended.

With regard to housing development in, as opposed to around, North Shields, the same is true with one qualification. In formal terms, the Labour Party in North Tyneside was committed to the central role of council housing in urban development after 1974. It was not actively hostile to the construction of owner-occupied stock, but its own intended programme was so large that the potential demand for such stock would have been much reduced. Once the constraints on local authority capital expenditure began to bite it cooperated with private housing development on inner-area sites. This was entirely in accordance with the intentions of the Structure Plan which had imposed virtually no constraints on such development. Until the creation of the UDC, there was no sense of competition in the inner area between housing and industrial uses for land. The conflict over housing land has been on the edge of the conurbation with a still undecided battle being fought over suburbanization by addition on a site-by-site basis.

The real conflict has been over the development of industrial land for retail purposes. Retail has not had a high profile in Marxist discussions of these issues. Basically, the tradition has been for financial landowners to pursue the investment route by building shopping centres as a long-term project, e.g. the Coal Industry Pension fund in North Shields. However, entrepreneurial developers have adopted a production route at least in part. Thus Cameron Hall Developments, who built the Gateshead Metro Centre, seem to have done so on borrowed money and to have sold out to the Church Commissioners, although they remain in charge of operations. This means that both production and investment accumulation is involved. No development on former industrial land in North Shields is yet this far along, but possibilities exist and intentions have been declared.

Conflict over designation is symptomatic of something already referred to in this chapter – the transformation of the city from a locale of production to one of consumption–reproduction. Cramlington is the most intensively industrialized locale in Northumberland, but the great majority of those who live there have minimal connection with that industry. In North Shields the river, the literal reason for the place, is now being seen as a consumption goodie rather than a production possibility. This is most evident in the gentrified housing developments on the quays and in Dockwray Square (now River View, because although Dockwray

Square was originally a very posh Georgian development, its pseudo-Georgian replacement has to shed the image of a public sector slum). A good deal of money has been made tarting up riverside and banktop pubs to take account of the new ambiance and to cater to the non-industrial affluent. The location is no longer industrial but, instead, is a zone of consumption where artefacts from its productive past are used to give colour to its present. The 'Tall Ships' race which started from Tyneside in the summer of 1986 was perhaps the best indicator of this. If the river had still been working with any serious use of its productive capacity, this presentation of delightful monuments would not have been possible.

Historically, Newcastle as the regional capital was always governed with a concern for style and consumption (see Byrne, forthcoming), but this is now crucial in what were totally industrial locations. The relevance of this to the concerns of a chapter on land lies in the way in which location and style are the core of much of the development process. The inner city is now chic, and this in the Low Street in North Shields. Let us turn to social implications.

6

Socio-spatial segregation in Northern Tyneside

Introduction

In this chapter an old procedure will be used as the basis of an empirical examination of contemporary social reality in Northern Tyneside. Castells (1977), in his effort to expunge the spatial, was particularly scathing about the tradition of social ecology which as formal social science goes back to the Chicago school but can be recognized in Engels' (1968) *The Condition of the Working Class in England in 1844*. The rejection of the positivist quasi-biological determinism which underlay much of the work of the Chicago school was appropriate but, as Engels, if not Castells, appreciated, exploratory mappings of the arrangements of social differentiated populations in residential locales are important in describing the nature of life in urban industrial cities and have significance because the spatially ordered experience of differentiated reproduction is an important source of social action.

This chapter deals with a consequence of the development of Northern Tyneside through organized capitalism into disorganized capitalism. Socio-spatial differentiation is the result of the interaction of market forces and state action, including planning and housing development/management policies. The issues of land use discussed in Chapter 5 are clearly important for developments here. How has the use of land for residential purposes interacted with the labour market positions and the impact of state policies to produce a spatially as well as socially differentiated working class? What are the implications of this? We will proceed from quantitative description based on census-derived social indicators to an account of everyday life derived from specific surveys, some interviews with significant informants and newspaper-based recent history.

The debate over the sources of social differentiation forms the background to what is being described and will be reconsidered in the conclusion to this chapter which will be concerned with the broad implications of socio-spatial differentiation for social action.

North Shields: A quantitative profile of a social area

One of the first tasks undertaken by the CDP was the preparation of a 'quantitative profile' of the CDP area in comparison with the rest of North Tyneside MBC. The original objective was to generate a baseline for a study of 'spatial social income distributions' within North Tyneside which could then be compared with the distribution at the end of the Project's work. We had grandiose notions of generating a quantitative basis for the evaluation of the effectiveness of the Project's interventions, although we never adopted the methodological premises associated with positivist conceptions of the role of experiments in social action (see Marris and Rein, 1967; Lees and Smith, 1974).

The combination of the change in direction of our work and the cancellation of the 1976 census which would have provided us with the database necessary for inter-temporal comparisons meant, that our quantitative work was not used in evaluation. None the less, we found it a useful exercise. The understanding of the relative positions of localities within the project area, of the project area as a whole and of North Shields in general were important elements in the development of our perspective and the data-based descriptions were continually used by us both in action work and in analysis. The availability of small area data from the 1981 census coupled with some rather more limited data of more recent vintage means that a reanalysis is now possible.

1971 and 1981
Comparisons between locales within the area of North Tyneside MBC can be made by comparing the results of a cluster analysis of the 1971 Enumeration Districts (EDs) within the area with an equivalent exercise for North Tyneside in 1981. Tables 6.1 and 6.2 show the character of clusters generated by simple exploratory procedures from index sets for each point in time. The 1971 and 1981 Small Area Census Statistics were rather different. However, a rough and useful comparison can still be made.

Table 6.1 Social deprivation in North Tyneside in 1971

Index	Cl 1	Cl 2	Cl 3	Cl 4	Cl 5
Population 0–16 (%)	38.5	19.2	27.2	25.0	26.7
Population, pensioners (%)	8.4	21.7	13.7	16.3	13.6
Fertility rate	3.53	2.1	2.7	2.1	2.0
Male unemployment (%)	15.9	4.9	8.4	8.0	2.4
Female unemployment (%)	8.9	4.7	5.4	6.1	3.7
Owner-occupation (%)	0.1	43.8	8.6	23.2	80.6
Council tenants (%)	94.4	30.5	79.9	12.2	12.6
Other tenures (%)	5.6	25.7	11.5	65.6	6.8
Households with three basic amenities (%)	92.0	87.3	92.6	35.8	98.0
Households with 6 or more persons (%)	18.8	3.4	9.0	3.8	4.0
Households without car (%)	85.9	62.2	73.0	76.3	30.3
Households headed by single-parent female (%)	3.1	1.0	1.6	2.5	1.4
Economically active and retired males, professional and managerial (%)	1.3	13.7	5.5	5.4	34.9
Economically active and retired males, other non-manual (%)	4.0	19.1	11.8	9.8	28.7
Economically active and retired males, skilled (%)	40.4	41.5	46.2	41.9	22.7
Economically active and retired males, semi- and unskilled (%)	48.8	20.0	30.0	36.0	7.5
Economically active and retired males, other (%)	4.5	4.6	5.4	6.8	5.0

In 1971 a 'social deprivation' analysis showed that a significant typology existed at five cluster levels when a simple combination of Ward's method of fusion and relocation was employed for the data set of indices for the 468 ordinary (i.e. neither special nor restricted) EDs in North Tyneside (see Everitt, 1974, for a description of terminology). 'Social Deprivation Cluster 1' contained the most deprived EDs in 1971: male unemployment was twice that for North Tyneside as a whole; there was a very high proportion of children in the population; overcrowding was five times the all North Tyneside average; and car ownership figures were very low. Only on the possession of amenities did this cluster score highly, which was not surprising as 94% of households lived in purpose-built council housing. The general impression of household structure was of largish households living in smallish dwellings. Fertility was high. Occupational profiles for men showed a predominance of semi- and unskilled backgrounds. Female employment was slightly lower than the North Tyneside average. The EDs in this cluster had a total population of approximately 11 300 or 6% of North Tyneside's population, and they were located on the Meadowell in North Shields, in Dockwray Square, in Wallsend and on the Newcastle Estate in Longbenton, although only the South Meadowell and Dockwray Square were homogeneous in membership of this cluster. All the areas were 'slum clearance replacement'.

Social Deprivation Cluster 2 contained 148 EDs and 28% of the total population of North Tyneside. Its general character was slightly better than average in relation to social deprivation indices, tenure characteristics and occupational characteristics. The demarcating factor was the high proportion of pensioners and correspondingly low proportion of households with children and scores on fertility indices.

Social Deprivation Cluster 3 comprised 109 EDs containing 52 000 people or 25% of the population of North Tyneside. Nearly 50% of the households were council tenants. Otherwise, it was close to the North Tyneside mean but a bit below it regarding the social deprivation indices and it contained an above average proportion of children and below average proportion of pensioners. Clusters 2 and 3 basically amalgamated at the next stage in the fusion process and together represent the average of the area in 1971. The EDs in both clusters were broadly distributed throughout North Tyneside and included most of the good 'general needs' council housing, cheaper owner-occupied housing and the better pre-1914 terraced stock.

Social Deprivation Cluster 4 followed the river and included the bulk of the inner-city older housing. The 79 EDs contained nearly 30 000 people or 14% of the North Tyneside population. Amenities were poor, with only 36% of households having the three basics, i.e. fixed bath, inside WC and hot water supply, compared with over 80% for North Tyneside as a whole. There was also a high level of overcrowding and a lot of children under the age of 4. The dominant tenure (63%) was private renting. The socio-economic profile was overwhelmingly manual working class and the demographic profile supports an impression of the importance of privately rented dwellings in the inner area as an important stage in household career in the early 1970s. Young families rented before becoming council tenants (their undoubted intention and aspiration in the late 1960s and early 1970s) through slum clearance or point rehousing, or becoming owner-occupiers through access to cheap, newly built or tenure-transferred stock. In practice, this latter route has been of far greater importance than anyone would have anticipated in the mid-1970s.

Social Deprivation Cluster 5 was the affluent locale. It comprised 111 EDs containing 55 000 people or 26% of the North Tyneside population: over 80% of households were owner-occupiers; unemployment was half the North Tyneside average; car ownership rates were very high; dwellings were large and possessed all amenities; 35% of males were

Table 6.2 Social deprivation in North Tyneside in 1981

Index	Cl 1	Cl 2	Cl 3	Cl 4
Population, 0–16 (%)	18	23	21	24
Population, pensioners (%)	24	14	18	14
Fertility rate	18	23	23	37
Male unemployment (%)	16	5	10	28
Female unemployment (%)	8	4	5	14
Economically active (%)	57	64	61	61
Households, owner-occupied (%)	22	92	59	6
Households, local authority tenants (%)	58	3	25	83
Households, other tenants (%)	19	5	16	13
Households with more than 1 per room (%)	4	1	3	7
Households with 6 or more people (%)	3	2	2	5
Households without a car (%)	67	20	46	79
Households with 5 or more rooms (%)	41	76	62	39
Households with children (%)	25	38	33	37
Households with single-parent head (%)	5	3	4	12
Adults migrant in last year (%)	10	8	9	14
Married women working full-time (%)	19	27	24	16
Married women working part-time (%)	24	24	25	25
Dwellings, flats (%)	14	3	4	37
Working outside district (%)	36	54	43	32
Economically active heads of households, social class I (%)	2	4	5	0
As above, social class II (%)	13	24	26	5
As above, social class III non-manual (%)	13	15	16	10
As above, social class III manual (%)	45	33	36	42
As above, social class IV (%)	20	13	14	27
As above, social class V (%)	9	4	4	17
Heads of households economically inactive (%)	44	25	30	40

professional managerial and a further 30% were routine white collar or semi-professional. Most EDs in this cluster were in suburban Whitley Bay, Forest Hall and Tynemouth.

One general point to make before proceeding to the results of a similar cluster analysis for 1981 relates to the position of women. The analysis carried out in 1976 on the 1971 data neglected the significance of women's employment in detailed terms, which is an indication of the gender blindness of our work at that time, although some redress was made in the final volume of the CDP report. However, female employment rates were calculated and found to be remarkably even across the five clusters (range=36–42%). The other point relates to working rates for both men and women. In the most socially deprived cluster, 80% of economically active men and 90% of economically active women were in work. This was a work-dominated society for most households.

Table 6.2 shows the results of a similar cluster analysis carried out on an index set generated for the 419 'ordinary' EDs in North Tyneside in 1981. Again the classificatory variables were 'social deprivation' in form. The four cluster levels appear interesting. Cluster 4 was a severely deprived cluster which contained nearly 30 000 people or 15% of North Tyneside's population. Nearly 30% of men and 15% of women were unemployed. The population was young, fertility was high and nearly a third of households containing children were headed by single parents. Almost all of the households in this cluster lived in council dwellings, many of which were flats. The number of married women in full-time employment was low, but the part-time rate was much the same as for the other clusters. Few households owned a car and dwelling sizes were small. The EDs in this cluster were located in North Tyneside's 'difficult to let' estates in North Shields, Wallsend and Longbenton, including Killingworth.

The next most deprived cluster was Cluster 1, containing 63 000 people or 32% of North Tyneside's population. Male unemployment stood at 16% and female unemployment at 8%. The population was older with more pensioners and fewer households containing children. This cluster had a mixed tenure pattern but a small majority lived in council housing. Again, car ownership figures were low and dwelling sizes were smaller. As with Cluster 4, economically active heads of households were overwhelmingly manual workers. The EDs in this cluster were widely dispersed throughout North Tyneside including much of inner North Shields, Wallsend and the former pit villages of Shiremoor and Backworth.

Cluster 3, with 62 000 people, contained 31% of the district's population. This was a mirror image of Cluster 1 with lower than average unemployment, the majority of dwellings being owner-occupied and higher levels of car ownership. Economically active heads of households in this cluster were equally divided between manual and non-manual occupations. The EDs were widely dispersed in the Borough including the best council estates, much recently constructed cheaper owner-occupied housing and a good deal of pre-1914 terraced housing.

Cluster 2, with 43 000 people or 22% of the population of North Tyneside, was the really affluent cluster. A total of 80% of households had cars, dwelling sizes were large and almost all were owner-occupied, and unemployment was low. A majority of the economically active married women were working full-time, and a large majority of the

Table 6.3 Social deprivation in North Tyneside in 1981

Index	Cl 1	Cl 2	Cl 3
Population, 0–16 (%)	22	23	19
Population, pensioners (%)	18	15	22
Fertility rate	30	23	20
Male unemployment (%)	25	6	13
Female unemployment (%)	12	4	6
Economically active (%)	59	63	59
Households, owner-occupied (%)	8	85	37
Households, local authority tenants (%)	80	9	41
Households, other tenants (%)	13	6	19
Households with more than 1 per room (%)	6	1	3
Households with 6 or more people (%)	4	2	2
Households without a car (%)	77	27	59
Households with 5 or more rooms (%)	32	74	48
Households with children (%)	32	37	28
Households with single-parent head (%)	10	3	5
Adults migrant in last year (%)	13	8	9
Married women working full-time (%)	16	26	21
Married women working part-time (%)	25	24	24
Dwellings, flats (%)	31	3	8
Working outside district (%)	36	51	37
Economically active heads of households, social class I (%)	0	8	3
As above, social class II (%)	4	37	16
As above, social class III non-manual (%)	11	20	15
As above, social class III manual (%)	45	25	41
As above, social class IV (%)	25	8	18
As above, social class V (%)	15	1	7
Heads of households economically inactive (%)	45	29	39

economically active heads of households were in non-manual occupations. The majority of those employed in this cluster worked outside North Tyneside. This cluster's EDs were concentrated in the more prosperous parts of Whitley Bay and Tynemouth, although there were some in Forest Hall.

The pattern of fusion to the levels of three and two clusters was interesting. Fusion with relocation produced the three clusters described in Table 6.3. Cluster 1 was a relatively deprived cluster which was close to Cluster 4 in Table 6.2 and contained 47 000 people or 25% of North Tyneside's population. Cluster 2 had a population of 82 000 or 41% of North Tyneside's population, and was similar to Cluster 1 in Table 6.2. Cluster 3 the affluent group, contained 68 000 people or 34% of the population, and was closest to Cluster 2 in Table 6.2. At the two-cluster level, Cluster 1 contained 110 000 people or 56% of North Tyneside's population, and male unemployment averaged 18%. Cluster 2 with 87 000 people or 44% of North Tyneside's population, had a male unemployment rate of 7%. Actually, the three-fold division into deprived, average and affluent corresponds most closely to perceived socio-spatial division but it is worth noting from the clustering pattern that the majority of the middle areas are closer to the deprived than to the affluent.

There are differences between the 1971 and 1981 patterns. First, there were more areas and people in the very deprived category in 1981. In 1971, this included 11 000 people. At its strictest 1981 definition, it included 30 000 people and a good case can be made for assigning areas with a total population of 45 000 to this group. Secondly, in 1981 there was no social deprivation cluster which corresponded with older housing areas. It was possible to produce an inner-area cluster of older housing by using tenure as a classificatory principle, but the lack of amenities no longer had any significance and this tenure-generated cluster was middle in character. The very poor almost all live in council housing now and the worst old private housing has been either cleared or improved, but in both cases the poor no longer live there.

Another crucial set of differences relate to economic activity. In 1971 the worst cluster had a male unemployment rate of 16% and the next worst was 8%. By 1981 the equivalent figures were 28 and 16%. The relative distribution of male unemployment, however, remained the same between the two dates. This was not true in relation to the patterns of economic activity by women. In 1981 this ranged from 45% in the more deprived clusters to 51% in the most affluent. This was a reverse of 1971 when the most affluent area had the lowest rate. The major reason for this difference was the pattern of full-time work by married women in 1981. The pattern of part-time work was similar across clusters, but in the most deprived cluster only 16% of married women worked full-time, whereas in the most affluent 27% did so.

The clear indication of this analysis for North Tyneside is that socio-spatial differentiation in 1981 was much greater than in 1971.

Cramlington: polarization comes with you
There is no point in carrying out a 1971 ED-based cluster analysis for Cramlington because that was too early in the New Town's development. However, the results of an analysis for 1981 are presented in Table 6.4. Here, it was interesting when there were three clusters. Cluster 3, with 53% of Cramlington's population in 27 EDs consisted of owner-occupied households (97%) with a low rate of unemployment, high levels of female employment, high rates of car ownership and a high proportion of white collar heads of households. The workers from this locale predominantly worked outside Blyth Valley (74%). Figures for the proportion of children

Table 6.4 Social deprivation in Cramlington in 1981

Index	Cl 1	Cl 2	Cl 3
Population, 0–16 (%)	22	39	31
Population, pensioners (%)	19	5	3
Fertility rate	19	61	40
Male unemployment (%)	14	24	4
Female unemployment (%)	9	14	5
Economically active (%)	59	65	77
Households, owner-occupied (%)	18	2	97
Households, local authority tenants (%)	68	62	0
Households, other tenants (%)	13	36	3
Households with more than 1 per room (%)	3	5	0
Households with 6 or more people (%)	6	6	1
Households without a car (%)	52	52	13
Households with 5 or more rooms (%)	52	71	66
Households with children (%)	34	68	52
Households with single-parent head (%)	5	13	2
Adults migrant in last year (%)	7	14	16
Married women working full-time (%)	21	17	38
Married women working part-time (%)	24	20	21
Dwellings, flats (%)	4	0	3
Working outside district (%)	38	46	74
Economically active heads of households, social class I (%)	2	6	8
As above, social class II (%)	6	16	30
As above, social class III non-manual (%)	11	11	20
As above, social class III manual (%)	41	43	33
As above, social class IV (%)	27	21	9
As above, social class V (%)	13	9	6
Heads of households economically inactive (%)	37	26	7

in the population and for the proportion of all households containing children show that the population of this area in 1981 was comparatively young. There were certainly very few pensioners.

Cluster 2, with 6 EDs contained 14% of Cramlington's population. In this cluster, there were also young households, many of which contained children. However, they lived in social housing, with 62% as council tenants and 36% as tenants of housing associations (which have built a good deal of the social housing stock in Cramlington), there was high unemployment and households were often headed by single parents. Employment for married women stood at only 37% compared with 59% for Cluster 3.

Cluster 1 comprised 16 EDs and contained 32% of the New Town's population in 1981. This was a council-housing cluster with an older population, an intermediate rate of unemployment and workers predominantly working in Blyth Valley. These EDs were in the pre-New Town council-housing areas and in the oldest of the New Town social housing, together with what remained of pre-New Town pit housing. The deprived locals were in the very recent New Town council estate of Shankhouse and the housing association stock in Beacon Hill.

The way in which recent industrial developments in Cramlington have generated this situation, and in particular the way in which a population was assembled for manufacturing work which has disappeared, is more fully documented in Byrne (forthcoming). What is interesting is the degree of correspondence between the form of social polarization in North Tyneside and in Cramlington in 1981. The latter is just as polarized as the Metropolitan Borough with its inner-city locales.

The 1971–81 change clusters
The availability of information for both 1971 and 1981 on a census tract basis (i.e. for the smallest grouping of EDs which has the same boundary in 1981 as the grouping had in 1971, which may be a single unaltered ED), makes possible some interesting but more restricted comparisons for the whole of 'Northern Tyneside', comprising the metropolitan districts of Newcastle and North Tyneside and the Shire Districts of Blyth Valley and Castle Morpeth. This has already been extensively employed in this study as the northern half of the Tyneside conurbation.

There were 848 tracts and these were classified using the same clustering procedure as before. This sort of cluster analysis is, as Openshaw (1983) puts it, a version of exploratory data analysis, and the actual indices used for classification are more important than the particular classificatory algorithm. A total of 26 indices were constructed from the 1971 to 1981 change files for both 1971 and 1981. A combination of economic activity, material possession and housing conditions indicators were used as classificatory variables. Table 6.5 indicates the nature of clusters generated at the level of five clusters using 1971 indices for the classification. Table 6.6 shows a level of three clusters using 1981 indices. Full pen-pictures will not be given here, but readers will be able to see from the tables that the 'all Northern Tyneside picture' using change tract data is very like that generated using the 1971 and 1981 data for North Tyneside alone. Again with the change tract data we see the disappearance of a specific 'older housing without amenity' cluster between 1971 and 1981.

The other value of the change tract data is that it enables a direct comparison between the North Shields and Cramlington sub-localities, at least for 1981. The important thing to note here is that Shankhouse in Cramlington was in the same deprived cluster as most of the Meadowell Estate and that both North Shields and Cramlington contained tracts from every cluster.

Table 6.5 Census tract clusters, 1971

Index	Cl 1	Cl 2	Cl 3	Cl 4	Cl 5
Population, 0–15 (%)	32	23	21	22	27
Population, pensioners (%)	14	18	21	21	10
Male unemployment (%)	21	8	10	3	4
Female unemployment (%)	11	5	6	4	4
Male economic activity (%)	80	80	78	75	87
Female economic activity (%)	34	40	40	33	46
Households without a car (%)	85	66	75	32	36
Households with 5 or more rooms (%)	30	50	24	78	65
Households, owner-occupiers (%)	4	27	19	77	66
Households, public tenants (%)	86	53	36	4	27
Households, other tenants (%)	9	20	44	17	7
Households with all amenities (%)	91	92	59	95	98
Households with more than 1 per room (%)	23	8	9	2	4
Households, no children (%)	57	67	72	67	57

Table 6.6 Census tract clusters, 1981

Index	Cl 1	Cl 2	Cl 3
Population, 0–15 (%)	19	19	20
Population, pensioners (%)	23	20	19
Male unemployment (%)	31	18	7
Female unemployment (%)	15	8	7
Male economic activity (%)	72	76	76
Female economic activity (%)	55	66	68
Households without a car (%)	80	62	33
Households with 5 or more rooms (%)	25	45	74
Households, owner-occupiers (%)	7	32	81
Households, public tenants (%)	79	44	11
Households, other tenants (%)	13	22	8
Households with all amenities (%)	97	95	99
Households with more than 1 per room (%)	8	4	1
Households, no children (%)	71	70	67

The consequences of social differentiation

Kirk Mann (1987) has commented on the re-emergence of debates about an underclass in British society which employ a vocabularly decidedly reminiscent of that of Victorian concerns with the residuum. Reference has already been made to the way in which the identification of such an underclass (e.g. Dahrendorf, 1987; Bauman, 1987) is characteristic of 'post-modern' commentary on the nature of social developments in the late twentieth-century in this country. Certainly, the position of the population in the most deprived locales identified in the foregoing analyses seems to correspond to that described in such work as 'below the working class'.

An example is provided by the South Meadowell Estate in the former CDP area in North Shields. In 1971 male unemployment in this locale stood at 22% and female unemployment at 12%. By 1981 these figures had increased to 48 and 32% respectively. By 1981, 17% of households were headed by a single parent and 13% contained only pensioners. It is clear that the majority of households in this area did not contain anyone in waged work and were likely to be dependent on state benefits. Shankhouse in Cramlington had a similar but less extreme profile. Male unemployment in 1981 was just under 30% and female unemployment just under 20%. The census showed that 15% of households were headed by a single parent. A more recent review of the conditions on this estate (Byrne, 1987) found that nearly 70% of households were in receipt of housing benefit and only 42% of household heads were in employment of any kind (full-time, part-time or self-employed). This was in an area where 93% of household heads were aged less than 50 and 88% were aged less than 40. Similar detailed recent figures for the South Meadowell show that over 85% of households are in receipt of housing benefit, 47% of households are headed by single parents and the unemployment rate is over 80%. The use of housing benefit receipts as an indicator of low income is appropriate but it should only be used with caution in relation to the identification of the 'sub-working class', because means-tested supplements to low wages on the Speenhamland model are crucial for the working poor.

Characteristically, there has been a good deal of social investigation of these 'locales in space of the stagnant reserve army of labour' (Byrne and Parson, 1983). This has been a consequence of the 'social problems' manifested in such locales, particularly the emergence of 'difficult to let' public sector housing stock or, rather, as the Department of the Environment Housing Development Group (1980) have correctly pointed out, the emergence of a significant component of the stock which is difficult to let to anyone who has any real choice in the matter. Certainly, turnover and consequent management problems have been a real issue in both the South Meadowell and Shankhouse.

However, the concentration of very seriously deprived people who lack any organic connection with organized work has consequences over and above the real problems generated by housing voids. There is a potential for social disintegration, anomic crime and violence, and the breakdown of social order. Interviews with housing managers, social workers, community workers, elected representatives and residents in various areas in Northern Tyneside, but particularly in North Shields and Cramlington, all give a picture of a considerable degree of survival of traditional community institutions and values in severely deprived locales. Only in two areas has there been an apparent breakdown of such systems. One is in Killingworth Towers prior to demolition, although it is probable that never in Killingworth Towers' brief history was any real system of social organization established apart from a residents' organization dedicated to demolition. This is not to disparage the importance and worth of that organization which was both effective and coherent. Rather, the point relates to the more nebulous institutions of civil society in working-class areas. Crime, and particularly burglary, is a major perceived social problem for inner-city working-class people on Tyneside. However, statements on these lines are not usual: 'Here they rob their own – people who have nothing to start with' (Killingworth resident quoted in *Evening Chronicle*, 27 June 1985). A good deal of 'robbing of your own' goes on in most deprived localities. However, it is (quite rightly) regarded as particularly contemptible and suppressed by community pressure. The impression from press coverage of Killingworth Towers towards the end of its existence is that the hoods were then in charge in a way that would never have been possible in a stable but tough locale like the North Meadowell.

The interesting thing about the South Meadowell is that the historical record shows that these two versions of what a place should be like have actually been fought out on the ground. In the summer of 1985 a group of residents were identified with police attempts to introduce a 'Neighbourhood Watch' scheme into the area. This attracted considerable and expressed resentment (in marked contrast to the introduction of Neighbourhood Watch in most other inner area locales), which came to a head when local youths attacked the homes of figures associated with the scheme and one man was assaulted with a burning traffic cone. Press commentary referred to barricades and petrol bombs. A subsequent article in the local weekly paper dealt with the situation 'after the petrol bombs' and commented on the development of a more stable situation. However, the Neighbourhood Watch scheme collapsed and the area is now scattered with graffiti (summer of 1988) denouncing a local 'grass' and threatening his life if he does not leave Tyneside. Local sources consider that the level of crime on the South Meadowell is much higher than on the North Meadowell and that there is now a significant drug problem. There is also extensive evidence of loan sharking.

Interestingly, the boundary between the estates is not precise. Historically, the railway (now Metro) line did form a sharp boundary although the social implications of this were mainly a function of differential treatment in improvement programmes (see North Tyneside CDP, 1978b). However, local housing managers consider that many of the lettings and management problems of the South Meadowell are now spilling over into that part of the North Meadowell which is south of Waterville Road and are applying for a large-scale Estate Action programme in an effort to hold ground here. There is evidence that much of the problem lies with the general lettings policy of the local authority since 1974 but, more particularly, in the 1980s, which has resulted in a concentration of 'difficult' households (including many very young single parents) in the area from all over North Tyneside.

Another indication was the establishment in 1984 of a detached youth work project in the area in response to a paper entitled *Proposed Initiative to Positively Counter Vandalism in the Inner Riverside Area of North Tyneside* (North Tyneside MBC, 1984). This was stimulated by the level of vandalism and theft at the Smith's Park Metro Station. The workers published an interesting report entitled *Streetwise – Meadowell Detached Project* (North Tyneside MBC, 1985), which was remarkably reminiscent of the experiences of the CDP in youth and play work some 10 years earlier.

The level of 'apparent criminality' is not reminiscent of previous experience. During the period of the CDP (1973–8) I always thought that the reputation of 'the Ridges' was greatly exaggerated. The area had significant problems with regard to housing and poverty and an impending problem derived from deindustrialization. However, it was a lot more pleasant as a place than its reputation held it to be and the local people could not have been friendlier, more helpful and just plain downright nice. I am reluctant returning as an outsider to accept accounts of social disorganization at face value but these accounts are confirmed by workers for whom I have a great deal of respect. These workers did not present a universally gloomy picture. Social problems were not at all on the same scale on the North Meadowell. On the South Meadowell successful initiatives were underway, notably a food co-op. All local sources presented structural accounts of developments. None the less the picture was depressing.

Clearly, the immediate problems of the South Meadowell are in large part derived from allocation policies and the experience of rehousing. The modernization of the Meadowell as a whole involved the converting of flats into houses and a reduction in dwelling units. On the South Meadowell the original 700 plus units have been reduced to 503. When this was done many people were decanted and remained in their new dwellings. The population of the South Meadowell in 1971 was over 2200, but by 1981 it had fallen below 1000. This was during the period of modernization which involved decanting, and the present-day population is higher. Current estimates for both estates are some 5200 compared with 7300 in 1971. Many of the residents of the pre-modernized South Meadowell now live on the North Meadowell and many residents of both localities now live elsewhere in North Tyneside. The modernized

Table 6.7 South Meadowell and Parkside

Index	South Meadowell	Parkside
Population, 0–15 (%)	36	33
Population, pensioners (%)	10	6
Male unemployment (%)	48	3
Female unemployment (%)	32	6
Male economic activity (%)	83	96
Female economic activity (%)	51	72
Households without a car (%)	84	9
Households with 5 or more rooms (%)	42	77
Households, owner-occupiers (%)	0	99
Households, public tenants (%)	89	0
Households, other tenants (%)	10	0
Households with all amenities (%)	100	100
Households with more than 1 per room (%)	11	1
Households, no children (%)	45	44

South Meadowell experienced something of the 'generational shock' which produced Shankhouse. It became available for re-letting when many of the households needing council housing were the young poor. In the larger context of the Metropolitan District with a more varied housing stock, it acquired a disproportionate number of non-conventional households with serious social difficulties. However, as always, it is important to make it clear that such households are in a minority.

The South Meadowell deserves particular attention because of the severity of social deprivation in this locale. It figured as an example of an 'urban priority area' in *Faith in the City* (Commission on Urban Priority Areas, 1984). However, that very useful 'Arch-Episcopal Commission' Report did tend to assert the radical distinctiveness of the worst locales. The value of the cluster analyses reported here is that they show no such sharp distinctions. Severe relative deprivation is much more widespread than is generally recognized. A total of 32% of North Tyneside's population lived in locales where male unemployment was over 30%. Change cluster analyses suggested that this large proportion of relatively deprived locales included a minority of severely deprived locales including the South Meadowell, but the impact of deindustrialization was clear on a much more general scale.

A vivid contrast with the South Meadowell is provided by Parkside in Cramlington. This Ward contains Shankhouse, but Table 6.7 gives social indicator figures for that part which is owner-occupied. This is by no means the most affluent area in Northern Tyneside; rather, it is an area of mixed recent development which contains a range of housing types of varying standards. The majority of the stock was originally marketed in the middle of the price range for such housing. There were not many cheap 'starter home' type developments but the bulk were certainly not priced above the equivalent of £30 000 on 1988 values. Parkside's ordinariness is indicated by the fact that the most common social class of household heads was Registrar General's Social Class 3, i.e. manual. Over 90% of households owned a car and 80% had five or more rooms (although almost all households in Cramlington lived in dwellings of this size). Unemployment in 1981 was minimal with rates of 3% for men and 6% for women. This higher rate for women – compared with men – was most unusual in Northern Tyneside locales, but what it reflected was the very high rate of economic activity by women in this locale. Of those persons over age 16, 80% were economically active and this included over 60% of married females of whom two-thirds worked full-time.

Demographically, Parkside was not unlike the South Meadowell with very few pensioners and with most households containing children, and it was almost identical to Shankhouse which was Cramlington's most deprived locale. The only real difference was the comparative absence of households headed by single parents. Thus it seems the crucial difference between the two sorts of locales was in terms of access to work. Most South Meadowell households had no employed workers resident within them. Most Parkside households had two and the most common situation was for both to be employed full-time. This lends support to Pahl's (1984: 314) previously quoted contention that:

> A process of polarization is developing, with households busily engaged in all forms of work at one pole and households unable to do a wide range of work at the other. . . . The division between the more affluent home-owning households of ordinary working people and the less advantaged under-class households is coming to be more significant than conventional divisions based on manual/non-manual distinctions.

Pahl's statement does have to be taken carefully in relation to the Northern Tyneside evidence. The crucial distinction in these localities is between households with more than one wage-earner and those which are benefit-dependent. This is not a matter of access to 'black-economy' supplements. All the ethnographic evidence suggests that this is differentially a matter for the poor in Cramlington (see Byrne, forthcoming). Neither are the effects of ownership of assets separate from labour market effects, as Saunders (1984) would have it in relation to consumption cleavages. They are quite simply a product of income differentials which reflect the gap between the benefit-dependent and multi-earner household. We have no direct evidence on income levels for Parkside but most of the dwellings would, in 1988, be perfectly accessible to households with a total gross income of £12 000 on a conservative 2.5 times income basis for total mortgage lending. These people are not rich, but they are for the moment comfortable.

What about the in-between areas? If we look at the tables describing the cluster analyses we see something very interesting. These intermediate areas contain the highest proportion of households without dependent children. This confirms the impression of a generational effect in operation and squares very well with the history of the interaction of labour market entry effects and housing development, the origin of the patterns of socio-spatial differentiation being described. Those that live in these areas are middle-aged manual workers and their wives who entered the labour market during full-employment in the affluent 1940s and 1950s. They are often council tenants, because at the time they established their households this was the normal way of achieving reasonable housing conditions. Many of the women are employed, but they tend to work part-time rather than full-time. What we are seeing here is the reproduction of time in space. The cohorting of different localities is a function of the survival in them of the populations who occupied them when they were first built and who continue to display the labour market characteristics which they acquired through their generation's experience of access to employment. The middle-aged are relatively homogeneous, at least as far as the working class are concerned. The young are very much divided.

On the face of it, this material seems to support the notion of a post-industrial under-class. However, a different interpretation is necessary when it is considered in relation to the account of developments in the industrial base as described in Chapter 4. After all, a crucial element in Bauman's (1987) conception of the place of an underclass in contemporary British society is the assertion that the poor no longer play the role of a reserve army of labour. The exact content of this idea is discussed in some detail in Byrne and Parson (1983). Here we need to take notice of two components of the function of such a reserve. First, it is a mechanism for the disciplining of employed labour and in particular for eroding the capacity of employed labour to resist 'restructuring in the interests of capital' (see O'Connor, 1982). The creation of a large reserve army of the unemployed weakens the capacity of employed workers to resist the reorganization of production and the erosion of their wages.

All this is part of the move from full-employment. It seems patently obvious that mass unemployment in the early 1980s was important in facilitating the major changes in working practices and employment levels in marine manufacturing in Northern Tyneside. There have been a number of local examples of the direct disciplining effect of the availability of unemployed substitutes, most recently at HFW Plastics Ltd in Gateshead where a unionized workforce (predominantly female) was locked out over a wage claim and replaced by non-unionized labour recruited from the dole queue. The original workforce was quite young but the replacements were almost all under 25. The ability of the management to bust the union was based on the impact of Tory legislation outlawing secondary picketing and the maintenance of a large police presence to render direct picketing ineffective. This dispute dragged on for some 6 months, but in the end the management won hands down.

Direct confrontations are by no means uncommon but the main impact of the elimination of trade unionism has been in new start ups. HFW Plastics was in severe competition with a new non-union plant (these are plants ancillary to the printing industry which has a history of strong union organization), but the best example is provided by the opening of a Nissan Plant on what is effectively a non-union basis (see Tyne and Wear County Association of Trades Council, 1988; Garrahan, 1986).

A very useful corrective to post-Gorzian efforts at handling the implications of the supposed disappearance forever of full male employment (the emphasis on male employment is, I suppose, a way of making concern for full-employment sexist and hence disreputable. This is garbage in its own terms but is particularly ridiculous given the impact of industrial restructuring on full-time employment for women.) is provided by Therborn's (1986) *Why Some Peoples are More Unemployed Than Others*, which debunks the contention that mass unemployment in the contemporary West is an inevitable consequence of anonymous system forces. Instead, it is identified as the product of particular political strategies pursued in particular states (the implications of this theme will be taken up again in Chapters 9 and 10). What is immediately useful, in the context of a discussion of the background to socio-spatial differentiation, is the scenario of the *Brazilianization of advanced capitalism*. Therborn considers that if mass unemployment is maintained in advanced capitalist societies what will emerge is a kind of:

> richer and somewhat more humane Brazil, with increasing trichotomous socio-economic divisions. At the bottom will be the permanently and marginally unemployed with certain welfare entitlements which are almost certain to be reduced over time. Some of these people will make a living in the black economy. . . . In the middle will be the stably employed, or those with the possibility of re-employment, who will be increasingly divided according to enterprise, sector and hierarchical position. They will make a fairly decent living, no more, but will be able to congratulate themselves on the widening distance between themselves and the unemployed. . . . The marginalization of a significant part of the former and the potential working class has already gone hand in hand, in the first half of the 1980s, with increasing wealth and incomes of capitalists and top business managers. They constitute the third layer of mass unemployment societies. . . . Politically this ruling class will appeal to the bulk of employees as guarantors of the latter not falling into the abyss of unemployment and they will invite the citizenry at

large to a vicarious enjoyment of the success of the wealthy and beautiful.

(Therborn, 1986: 32–3)

Therborn describes this as 'not only a nightmare. It is a society which is being envisaged and designed' (ibid.). The notion of a trichotomous division of society seems to fit very well with the products of the cluster analyses of Northern Tyneside. However, the three-fold division is somewhat different from that which, at first sight, Therborn seems to be proposing. In particular, the 'affluent cluster' is not a locale of a capitalist ruling class, although it is perfectly clear that those members of the capitalist ruling class who do live in Northern Tyneside do live in the locales contained in this cluster. There are plenty of senior managers, very highly remunerated professionals and indeed capitalists, in Ponteland, Gosforth, Morpeth, Jesmond and the posher parts of Whitley Bay and Tynemouth. However, there are lots of people who are rather closer to being 'plain employed folk'. None the less, the importance of Registrar General's Social Class 2 among heads of households in this locale is interesting. The Registrar General's categories are notoriously inappropriate for the measurement of relationally defined class (see Nichols, 1979), but this category does have something of the intermediate-authority exercising about it. Certainly, it has been a beneficiary of tax cuts, although the bulk of the benefits have gone to the really rich.

The point is that the trichotomous division is not hard but rather consists of fuzzy sets. This is important in terms of the relationship between the marginalized and the middle group. Not only are the former of vital significance for the latter in their role as a disciplined reserve army, the boundaries are imprecise in general and are likely to be crossed in the course of a working life by individuals. Perhaps even more important, particularly in an area like Northern Tyneside where there is a minimal basis for racial or sectarian differentiation, is the likelihood of family members of the stably employed belonging to the marginalized. The significance of differential generational experiences of the impact of mass unemployment is very great here.

This fuzziness is reinforced by the other role of a reserve army, i.e. the basis of especially exploitative branches of accumulation, the aspect of restructuring which has been described by Cleaver (1977) in terms of the under-development of the working class. Examples in Northern Tyneside include the replacement of full-time industrial employment for women by part-time service employment, the casualization of almost all labour in marine manufacturing and the location of a very substantial part of construction employment in the black economy. Indeed, that oldest and worst of all forms of capitalist production, home work, is making a major comeback. It is of course the poor who are differentially exposed to this.

Evidence on the operation of the black economy is not easily come by. However, 80% of respondents to the Shankhouse household survey of 1986 felt that a substantial number of those people dependent on state benefits were 'on the fiddle' in construction, cleaning and catering, and 53% said that they personally knew someone who was so engaged. There is no survey evidence from North Shields but the author's informants are convinced of the significance of such employment, including factory employment for women, and much of this anecdotal evidence is first hand.

This does not discount the importance of a barrier between the regularly employed and the marginalized. However, as the best known formulation of this distinction made clear (Friedman's, 1979, differentiation between 'central' and 'peripheral' workers) the boundary is shifting and permeable. The turnover in Shankhouse in Cramlington was examined with some care (see Byrne, forthcoming), and it seems to confirm the impression of housing management staff that people fall out of owner-occupation in periods of prolonged unemployment and scramble back into it when they get something resembling a steady job. For these groups, tenure is certainly not a principle of stratification independent of production relations.

Yet ownership of assets does have some significance. After all, the cluster-derived socio-tenurial maps of Northern Tyneside correspond almost exactly to estate agents' pricing patterns and, despite the absence of tenure as a classificatory variable set, a mapping of social deprivation is (with divisions within both owner-occupation and council housing recognized) also a mapping of tenure. Again this seems to be a matter of fuzziness of boundaries *and* of generation. The household which crosses tenures as a consequence of immediate employment change will be manual or routine white collar or a mixture of both. It will also be young. The household of two 50-year-olds who bought their first house 25 years ago for £3000 and now have accumulated £40 000 equity is in a different position from the two 25-year-olds plus child in a starter home with a negative equity (worth less than they owe on it because of the depreciation of the included consumer durables). It is often the case that the latter are the children of the former. What will be the impact of inheritance, assuming that this becomes important, rather than owner-occupiers mobilizing their assets to support themselves during prolonged retirement? For the moment the one action consequence of socio-tenurial polarization which we can examine directly is voting patterns. What are these and what do they suggest?

Table 6.8 shows the correlation matrix derived by correlating the percentage of votes cast for each of the three major parties in each North Tyneside Ward in both 1982 and 1988 with the percentage of EDs within that ward lying in each of Clusters 1, 2 and 3 at the three-cluster level and in each of Clusters 1 and 2 at the two-cluster level. Before commenting on

Table 6.8 Cluster – vote correlations

1981 Cluster	82Lab	82SLD	82Tory	88Lab	88SLD	88Tory
3C11	0.5	0.0	−0.5	0.4	0.2	−0.6
3C12	−0.6	0.0	0.6	−0.6	−0.1	0.7
3C13	0.2	−0.0	−0.2	0.2	−0.1	−0.2
2C11	0.7	−0.0	−0.7	0.7	−0.1	−0.7
2C12	−0.7	−0.0	0.7	−0.7	−0.1	0.7

the results, some general points need to be made. In 1982 there were three vacancies in each ward following a boundary revision. The highest vote cast for each party's candidate has been used as the vote in that year. In 1982 Labour received 22 881 votes on this principle. The Tory vote was 21 102 and the Alliance vote was 18 320. Despite this, Labour won 11 of the 20 seats contested to the Tory's 7 and the Alliance's 2, largely because the Tories piled up big majorities on high turnouts in safe seats. In 1988 when there was only one candidate in each ward the Labour vote totalled 35 005, the Tory vote 18 439 and the Alliance (taking SLD and SDP together) 12 752. The background to these shifts will be discussed in the next chapter. In 1988 Labour won 13 seats, the Alliance 1 and the Tories 6. North Tyneside has the largest proportionate Tory representation of any Tyne and Wear Metropolitan District and contains the only Conservative parliamentary seat, Tynemouth.

The matrix shows a very similar pattern of relationships between the proportionate make up of votes and cluster membership in both the years selected, despite the very different total number of votes cast. The total Labour vote is strongly positively correlated with the proportion of EDs in the most deprived cluster at the three-cluster level ($r^2=0.20$) and strongly negatively correlated with the proportion of EDs in the most affluent cluster ($r^2=0.39$). The correlation between the Labour vote and the percentage of EDs in the middle cluster is positive but weak. All the correlations of the SLD vote with locale make up are too weak to be substantively significant. The Tory vote is strongly negatively correlated with the proportion of deprived EDs ($r^2 = 0.24$) and strongly positively correlated with the affluent cluster ($r^2 = 0.39$). At the two-cluster level, the proportion of EDs in the larger, poorer cluster is positively correlated with the Labour vote and negatively with the Tory vote, and vice versa for the more prosperous cluster. The r^2s are all of the order of 0.5 or more which indicates a very strong relationship.

These relationships between locale characteristics and vote are very predictable. They can be explained in terms of a composition of class effect (the poor vote Labour everywhere in the UK), and regional effect (the ordinary working class vote Labour in the North of England although they do not do so in the South East). For now all we need to note is that socio-tenurial polarization has political consequences.

7

The state and civil society in Northern Tyneside

Introduction

This chapter reviews the nature of the political sphere in the locales under study, including both the formal arrangements of administration and control – the state in its various aspects – and that part of the arena of civil society which is concerned with social action relevant to politics. Boundaries are not precise. Political parties exist both in relation to the state and as part of civil society, as do other organized groupings. The state itself enters into civil society through the operations of administrative mechanisms concerned with reproduction. Both state and civil society intersect with the economic sphere. Nevertheless, with the fuzziness of boundaries recognized, it makes sense to discuss the state and civil society in turn before attempting a synthesizing overview.

There is one major disadvantage to beginning with *the state*. Recent considerations of the nature of the state have been more or less functionalist and very much dominated by capital logic. Even when some consideration has been given to class action there has been a tendency to see things in terms of the requirements of capital for order and accumulation, despite the possibility of conflict between these. Empirical studies are far more likely to be concerned with action and its consequences. The importance of the location of the state within capitalist social relations is not to be discounted. The identification of the state as essentially capitalist seems fine and much to be preferred to accounts which emphasize its autonomy. However, rejection of 'relative autonomy' is very different from elimination of the possibility of transformation. The best way to put this is to explain a personal response. I find it quite easy to admire capitalist production. It is fascinating, complex and enormously fruitful. It seems to me that a lot of Marxist writers have the same kind of admiring fascination for the state. I do not. At best it is a means to collective ends and the only thing I find to admire is the struggle for democracy and the consequences of democratic action.

The state has a number of components which need consideration: there are the consequences of national state action expressed through the impact of legislation and policy; directly controlled agencies of the national state, like the local offices of the DHSS; nominee bodies of the national state which combine local membership with national direction, including the Health Authorities and the Urban Development Corporation; and there is a residual regional state. Originally, this was only partially a creature of the national state and owed more to corporatist collaboration between regional capital, trade unions and local government. Finally, there is the democratic component of the local state in the form of the local authorities. We will begin with the regional state because of the significance of its focus on economic restructuring, go on to look at the democratic local state and conclude with a consideration of the role of nominee local state agencies. The role of the national state will be dealt with in terms of its implications for the other three levels.

The regional state

This term is being used here to describe the institutions which are or have been the product of a regionalist form of corporatism dating back to the 1930s. This is a more narrowly focused sense of the idea of a regional state than that employed by Saunders (1983), for example, and it is very different from what Duncan and Goodwin (1988: 250) mean by the 'regionalization' of local autonomy through 'regional-scale corporatist bodies heavily subject to central direction'. Much of it is being replaced by centrally nominated local/regional agencies. However, that is a fundamental change because the crucial characteristic of the agencies of the old regional state, in my narrow sense, was that they were the product of regionally organized political forces rather than of central imposition. Of course, they have always overlapped with the centrally created regional agencies, particularly in terms of membership, and the centrally created agencies have been regionalist in form precisely so that local pressures and political realities could be to some extent accommodated.

These regional institutions had one objective – modernization, primarily of the productive base but also of reproduction, particularly housing and urban environment. The élites which met within them were of two kinds. There was a strong representation of capital through the CBI and various employers' federations, particularly in engineering. The other élite was of Labour/Trade Union origin in the form of council leaders and trade union regional secretaries. I do not propose to attempt a full account of the history of regionalist institutions which drew on these cooperating élites; rather, I want to pay particular attention to an abortive effort at the development of strategic regional planning beginning with the regional representation of Labour's National Plan in the mid-1960s and culminating in the rejection of the recommendations of the Northern Regional Strategy Team (NRST) in 1979.

The origins of this phase lie with Hailsham's intervention as Minister for the North East in 1963. The restructuring of coal mining had led to a steep rise in regional unemployment to 5%. Extraordinary as it may seem today, this was regarded as a crisis for political stability, threatening as it did the core of the post-war Keynes-Beveridge settlement. The resulting White Paper (Hailsham, 1963) was about modernization in order to create employment, particularly by the inward attraction of large manufacturing enterprises. The White Paper recreated a regionalist sense in the North and when a system of Regional Economic Planning Boards (consisting of civil servants) and Economic Planning Councils was established, there was a considerable enthusiasm for this form of intervention. The Northern Economic Planning Council (NEPC) comprised 9 local authority members (legally not representatives but simply ministerial nominees), 11 industrialists, 4 trade unionists, the Earl of Lonsdale to represent the landed interest, the Vice Chancellor of Durham University and the Director of the North East Development Council. Two of the local authority members were later gaoled for corruption.

Saunders (1983) gives a neat account of the gelding of the Economic Planning Councils as a backwash of the disappearance of any national plan, but the NEPC remained more active than most and was one of the sponsors of the Northern Regional Strategy Team established in 1974 with a brief of producing a strategic plan to take the North into the 1990s. The other sponsors were the DoE and the northern local authorities organized as the Northern Regional Planning Committee. The NRST represented their brief assertively:

> the emphasis of the Strategy will be on economic development, and the improvement of social and environmental conditions, rather than on the 'land-use' issues which have been predominant in some other regional strategies.
>
> (1976: 1, para. 1.2)

> We use the term 'strategy' to mean the same as a 'plan'. That is to say, the Regional Strategy will be a set of consistent policy and action recommendations; and guidelines for future policy determination, based on an assessment of the Region's economic, social and

locational problems, needs, and agreed objectives. The Regional Strategy might equally well be called the Regional Development Plan.

(ibid.)

The scope of the Plan is broad, embracing policies directed towards the economy, housing and social questions, the quality of the environment, the pattern of physical and transport development, and also towards inter-sectoral allocation of public expenditure. This is the kind of broad look at public policy which is not usually possible outside the Cabinet room or the political parties' policy committees.

(1977: Vol. 1, p. 2, para. 1.6 (i))

This amounts to a programme for major social change. However, it was only an indicative plan. The Durham Regional Research Unit (1977: 53) pointed out that there were no recommendations for the legislative and administrative changes which might be necessary for its implementation. The Strategy was the product of the team that wrote it. It was a professional product from a group behaving as if they were ENArques (products of the élite Ecole Nationale d'Administration) working for a Commissariat du Plan. They were not, however, and the fate of the strategy was to be dumped by the incoming Conservative Government of 1979 which also abolished the Economic Planning Councils as an economy measure.

The question of how an ambitious strategy for modernization could be so summarily abandoned with minimal protest bears careful examination because there are really only two sorts of ways to get *beyond the inner city* — market solutions and planning solutions. The latter can be subdivided into democratic planning and corporatist planning and the Northern Regional Strategy Team was very much the latter. This is illustrated by an examination of its central objective. In every document produced by the NRST this was stated to be a strong regional economy. However, the meaning of this term does change over time. Thus in 1976 we find reference to 'a healthy and stable economy capable of providing work for all who seek it, a range of employment opportunities and incomes comparable to those found elsewhere in Britain' (NRST, 1976). By the time the final report was produced, definitions had changed:

In the context of the UK, a strong regional economy may be defined as one that, over the longer term, is not continually dependent on a special resource transfer from the rest of the country in order (i) to sustain a level of prosperity no less than the national average and (ii) to generate new job opportunities such that the rate of unemployment and balance of migration are acceptable from a national point of view.

(1977: Vol. 1, p. 4, para 2.4)

THE STATE AND CIVIL SOCIETY 125

As the Durham Regional Research Unit (1977: 17) said:

It is . . . simply not clear whether in a strong economy, as envisaged by the Team, there will be full employment of labour or whether there will be a considerable volume of permanently unemployed labour. . . . At the same time the Team admit that in the short-term measures to produce a 'strong economy' will lead to job losses. In addition . . . the Team quite plainly say that their proposed strategy does not directly seek or imply the attainment of particular levels of population or employment.

This is a fair assessment but the change between the second interim report with its very clear commitment to full-employment and the final report is fascinating. The involvement of figures from the hegemonic labour movement in Northern Regional planning was always justified in terms of the maintenance of full-employment, and there is every reason to think that they did indeed subscribe to this central political commitment of the class forces for which they stood. Thus the whole programme of modernization was identified as employment generating and the first version of a regional strategy endorsed this. However, the national government of Harold Wilson had already abandoned a commitment to full-employment in the interests of modernization. After the IMF intervention in the British economy in 1975 this was no longer the central economic objective. The technocrats responsible for the Northern Regional Strategy moved with the times.

The politicians could not. Even now it would be political suicide for any northern regional Labour figure to declare that full-employment as an objective should be abandoned, even temporarily, in the interests of economic restructuring. The leading lights of the 1960s and 1970s had bought a version of 'one region' politics and were quite prepared to collaborate with regional capital by co-opting protest against change. Witness the minimal opposition to Robens' colliery closures. However, the price for this collaboration was real job creation, a price which was paid in the late 1960s and early 1970s with a considerable amount of in-migrant manufacturing attracted by regional aid. When the technocrats accepted that a sound regional economy for capital could be one with a high level of unemployment, then their strategy could not be presented as a public political commitment of the left. This is an interesting point about the nature of political civil society in the Northern Region and I will return to it.

The technocrats were planning for capital through a state-managed process of capitalist development. However, their plan was presented to a radical new government with very different conceptions. All the NRST documents identify three policy options. These can be summarized as:

1. Leave things as they are with extensive inward subsidy and let things slowly and gently decline.

2. The preferred option – managed change in accordance with a strategic plan.
3. Let the forces of the market prevail.

Since 1979, by the elimination of any, even corporatist, regional power, the state has imposed option 3 on the Northern Region and hence on the locales dealt with in this study. There is no longer any real regional focus for change. The Northern Development Company is a very feeble version of a regional development agency. Corporatist regionalism survives as a kind of élitist nostalgia. Thus there was a recent effort at the establishment of a 'Northern Regional Executive', as described in Northern Trade Union Labour Left (1984). The desire of leading trade unionists to sit down with 'regional notables' is very great. Perhaps Northern Trade Union Labour Left underestimated the desire of the regional notables to sit down with the Labour Party and trade unionists. There seems to be an entirely genuine, and given the interests of the personages involved entirely comprehendible, desire for a kind of regionalist state capitalism on lines more familiar with Europe than with Thatcherite Britain. Northern industrial capital is not radical free-market in its approach and its interests are ill-served by the economic consequences of such policies. The political programme of corporatist 'one regionalism' propounded for more than 50 years by northern political élites now lacks real significance, but it was of great importance for a long time.

The local state

By local state is meant the democratically elected local authorities – North Tyneside MBC for North Shields and Blyth Valley DC and Northumberland CC for Cramlington. Duncan and Goodwin (1988) make a general point about local states which applies just as much to the regional state and to appointed regional and local elements: 'that these local agencies *exist* [their emphasis] at all is due to the need for states to manage the uneven development of society' (1988: xv). These authors are somewhat uneasy disciples of the realist position and this kind of modified functionalism is characteristic of that approach. However, that does not make it wrong. Functionalist accounts are always in danger of being teleological but it is hard to see how any national state can operate without at least some administrative autonomy at lower levels so as to take account of variation. This is true even of an almost ideal bureaucracy, such as the administration of Social Security. However, Duncan and Goodwin also want to bring in action, in particular the collective action of the working class in achieving and using mass franchises. Here they draw on a useful insight of Miliband's (1969):

national representation cannot always deal adequately with local differentiation, and so local electoral politics was clearly a necessary part of representative democracy. But adding a democratic or popular element to some local state institutions also strengthens and legitimize the role of representing local interests *to* the centre. This may increasingly contradict the role of dealing with local situations *for* the centre . . . local state became both obstacle and agent for the national state.

(Duncan and Goodwin, 1988: 45–6)

Thus the democratic local state has to operate within capitalism in a way which takes account of local variation while also being affected by democratic political action. The task is reproduction. The direct ancestor of the modern local authority was the mid-nineteenth century sanitary authority without which urban physical reproduction would literally have been impossible. Other elements of reproduction were also local, notably poor relief, health care and education. Income maintenance had finally been nationalized by a Labour government in 1948. Most health care was removed from the democratic to the nominated state in 1945 and the rest in 1974. What remains is education, housing provision, local planning, provision of social services, parks and recreation, libraries and arts, environmental health and highways functions. The present central government is engaged in a major attack on the role of local government as the provider of much of this, through increased pressure for privatization of a range of functions, through opting out and alternative provision in education, and through the replacement of local authority management in housing by Housing Action Trusts, etc. However, much of the relevant legislation is either very recent or at the time of writing still in passage through Parliament. Although the implications are profound, they have still to be seen in practice. In the localities under study, the only actual replacement of local authority powers takes the form of the Urban Development Corporation in North Shields.

None the less, the attack on local government already has force and focus. Cochrane (1986) pointed out that much of this was properly interpreted as part of the attack on the conditions and terms of reproduction represented by the Welfare State because local government was a major delivery system for welfare. The main attack has been financial through constraints on local authority resources and budgets (see Duncan and Goodwin, 1988). In the locales under study here the source of conflict both between national and local state and within the local state has not seen a serious development of 'radical alternative policies' at the local level, but rather efforts to maintain and expand employment and service provision in traditional local services. The serious politics of the three local states have been about budgets, expressed through conflict within the Labour group in North Tyneside and through conflict between Labour and the opposition (primarily Alliance/SLD) in Blyth Valley and Northumberland.

The Labour Group which took control of the new North Tyneside authority in 1974 was very traditionalist and conformist. It was dominated by ex-working-class and relatively elderly councillors with little political commitment. Under their regime, which ran unchallenged until the late 1970s, North Tyneside was a moderate spending authority with no particular political focus.

From the late 1970s on, the Labour Party and the Labour Group began to change. There was recruitment both of the 'new urban left', i.e. white-collar, public service workers who had experienced higher education, and of younger working-class people. Some of the latter were trade unionists, taking more interest in local politics as industrial politics became more difficult. Some were drawn from community action groups, particularly in the area of the CDP in North Shields. The Labour Group became factionalized around the election of its Leader. In 1984, one of the 'new left' displaced the old leader. This had been preceded by a purge of sitting councillors through deselection by their ward Labour parties or removal from the panel of eligible nominees by the District Labour Party. Not all went quietly. Some ran against the official candidate in elections, particularly in Longbenton where there was a record of irregularities in the running of the ward party by the old guard. All those who did received humiliatingly small votes.

During 1984–5 the Labour Group was dominated by the new left but the old right still held important positions as committee chairs and on the powerful Policy and Resources Committee. The left enrolled North Tyneside in the battle against public expenditure cuts and were one of a number of controlling Labour groups who delayed setting a budget in the run up to the financial year 1985–6. Things came to a head in March 1985 when at a special council meeting called by the Tory group, 12 Labour rebels proposed that a budget be set which would result in a 15% rise in rates. The Tories had been proposing a 5% cut and the Alliance had wanted a budget with a 10% rise in the rates. The official Labour line was that North Tyneside needed £93 million for the year 1985–6 if services and employment were to be maintained, but the actual budget proposed by the rebels was £83 million. This was passed with Tory and Alliance support.

The rebels were then disciplined by the Labour Group under the terms of the standing orders for the Group as fixed by the National Executive Committee of the Labour Party. The penalties imposed were mild by usual standards for such a severe offence against party discipline. Nine councillors were required to apologize and three were suspended from the Group for varying periods. One of those who had voted for the rebel budget henceforth returned to the official fold but at the Annual Meeting of North Tyneside Council the other 11, who had been stripped of Labour nominations for committee chairs, etc., put up their own candidates for Leader and committee chairs. These were elected against the official Labour nominees with Tory support and with the Alliance abstaining.

This rebel group (who subsequently described themselves as Labour against Militant) ran the authority in 1985–6. All but one who returned to the official Labour Group were expelled from the Labour Party in September 1985, much to the disgust of the Newcastle Press who saw them as martyrs in a battle against 'Liverpool style politics in North Tyneside' and who hoped that their stand would be endorsed by the voters. There were some supporters of the Militant Tendency in the official Labour Group but the vast majority of it, including the Leader and Deputy Leader, were simply mainstream left of centre. During their year in office the rebel group maintained local authority expenditure by drawing heavily on balances. Indeed, it was their expenditure in 1985–6 which led to North Tyneside being rate-capped in 1986–7.

In the May elections in 1986 Labour against Militant lost every seat they contested gaining only derisory votes against official Labour candidates, although one of the seats did go to the SDP. This left Labour as the largest party in the council with 27 seats with Labour against Militant 6, Tories 18, Alliance 7 and 'Independent Labour' 1 (a former Labour councillor who had earlier been expelled from the Group for buying her council house). The Alliance remained neutral in the leadership elections and official Labour took over the authority as a minority administration. Labour returned to majority power with further election victories over Labour against Militant and the opposition in 1987 and consolidated their hold in 1988.

After the year of the rate-capped budget Labour were very keen to maintain services and employment but had abandoned any notion of overt defiance of central government powers. Instead, they sought to use creative accounting and prepared a budget for 1987–8 based on a lease and leaseback scheme involving £48.5 million worth of the local authorities properties. However, such schemes were rendered illegal by special legislation and the Labour Group were forced to create a new budget virtually overnight. Since then their major task has been the management of cuts. The only innovation was the sale of a site at Red House Farm to Sainsbury's for a mega-store.

North Tyneside's post-1987 politics are best described as liberal new realism in terms of the way the Labour Group has managed cuts. There have been some innovations, notably the appointment of a women's officer and an officer for the unemployed, but their main efforts have been directed at maintaining employment, with most cuts achieved by natural wastage as a consequence of falling school rolls and through rent increases. North Tyneside is the most left-wing of the Tyne and Wear districts but its behaviour is not radically different from that of the other two rate-capped MBCs, Newcastle and Gateshead, which have not had anything like the same degree of open political conflict within the ruling group. The form is different with, for example, trade union advisory representatives sitting on 67 council committees and sub-committees, but in the present state of central–local relations it is difficult to see what difference this ultimately makes.

There have been no really radical innovations in North Tyneside, in contrast with say Sheffield City's employment department, although it is likely that such a department would have been created if Labour had been in control throughout the 1980s. However, the authority has a high public profile regarding job-creating alternatives in economic policy, most notably due to the publication of *The Plan for Jobs* (North Tyneside MBC, 1987) in 1987 in the run up to the General Election. This was a claim for a Keynsian public sector intervention in job creation coupled with some private sector industrial planning. The detailed content of this will be examined in Chapter 9, because it does represent a radical local alternative version of the future. However, it was a plan for a Labour General Election victory which did not occur and, while not abandoned in principle, had had little practical impact.

Thus we have had a period of serious political conflict within the Labour Party in North Tyneside about the quality and quantity of traditional services and jobs. In Cramlington, the conflict was between Labour and its new rival, the Alliance. At the district level, Blyth Valley, this has been entirely a matter of political conflict in elections because Labour has, with one brief period due to a lost ballot box, managed to hang on to overall control of the council. Generally, Blyth Valley Labour Group has been very conventional in its politics. For example, it makes no contribution to the Housing Revenue Account from the General Rate Fund. The Alliance (now SLD), which forms the effective opposition, originated from the Independent Labour Group which began as the supporters of Eddie Milne when he lost his Labour nomination after accusing prominent Northern Labour and Trade Union figures of corruption. This is a bizarre development because Milne was on the left of the party and his opponents within the Labour hierarchy were very much figures of the right. However, the Alliance in Blyth Valley seems to have no particularly distinctive policies and is most assertive about very small-scale local issues.

On Northumberland County Council things are rather more open. Labour lost overall control in 1985 and ruled as a minority administration until March 1988 when the Tories and Alliance combined to vote down Labour's budget for 1988–9 which would have resulted in an 18% rate increase. The opposition wanted to make cuts of some £2 million. Labour refused to administer a budget they did not make and, as of May 1988, they refused to take any offices. The Alliance now provide the Leader and Deputy Leader of the Council and the Tories provide the Chair and Vice-Chair. The dispute was entirely about the volume of the budget. The cuts proposed and now implemented by the opposition were simply reductions in traditional services. Thus the democratic local state in Cramlington is, despite the apparent much greater radicalism of the North Tyneside Labour Group, really dealing with very much the same issues of the amount of resources to be devoted to mainstream local government services.

The appointed state

Duncan and Goodwin (1988) argue that Britain is moving towards decentralized administration of centrally determined policies by an appointed regional state under central control. I am not convinced that there is anything distinctive about regional bodies of this form. They are important but the most obvious examples of direct replacement of elected local authorities in recent years – Urban Development Corporations and Housing Action Trusts – operate at a different level. However, the appointed state is of increasing importance. By far the most important example of it in both Cramlington and North Shields is represented by the mechanisms of control over the Health Service. Health is highly political at the national level and particular decisions on patterns of provision are very much part of the political process at the local level. However, the NHS, since its foundation, has had an administrative structure which operates against significant political discretion about the level of resources to be devoted to reproductive expenditures in any given locality.

This is most obviously because it is for all practical purposes centrally funded and the level of resources is determined by a national formula. Currently, this is the RAWP formula which seeks to relate funding to the need for health care provision and which has been beneficial to the Northern Health Region and to most districts within it. However, there used to be some scope for variation and this has been progressively reduced. First, all health services were finally concentrated in the NHS with the removal of remaining health care functions from local authorities in 1974. However, there remains the massive issue of 'community care', which is a rubric for transferring long-term dependents to local authority social services, their families and their female relatives, but that is beyond the scope of this book. Secondly, direct local authority representation as of right has been much reduced. Local authorities were never represented by their own nominees on the strategic planning Regional Authorities, but they did have a third of the membership of the now abolished Area Health Authorities. They now have only one-fifth of the District Health Authorities. With the increasing transfer of power to General Managers these have little practical significance. Many local authorities have established health issues committees as a source of pressure on their District Health Authorities. These are useful propaganda devices but they just amount to a formalizing of the local authority's role as a health pressure group.

There is ample evidence that the present government is packing health authorities with its supporters, e.g. in Labour-dominated North Tyneside the Chair of the Health Authority is a Tory Councillor. Health is important for local politics but at the moment it is mainly a focus for trade union representation in relation to privatization and broadly based community pressure in relation to highly specific and identifiable services. Consideration of the latter is better dealt with in relation to civil society.

The other nominated body is much more directly and obviously a replacement for the local authority. Mention has already been made of the Tyne Wear Development Corporation in discussion of maritime industry and land. The notorious example of a UDC is the London Docklands Development Corporation, of whose operations Ambrose (1986: 251–2) has written:

> The area has been 'taken into care' by central government because its natural parents, the local boroughs, were too leftish, too committed to local needs and too sensitive to local feelings to carry out the kind of private sector led redevelopment strategy that the Thatcher government had in mind. The pattern of redevelopment, the opportunistic philosophy and the divergence from democratically produced plans in almost every important respect has been demonstrated. However well or badly the crude rate of development between 1980 and 1985 may compare to the rate that would have occurred without the LDDC (and this is not knowable), there is no doubt that the *content* of development does not suit the generality of local housing and employment needs. There is no doubt either that the corporation had engineered a huge public subsidy to the private development industry. The link has been virtually cut between a powerful planning agency and the local people who have a vital and legitimate interest in the workings of the agency.

The situation in Tyne and Wear is different. In a review of the proposals made by the consultants appointed in advance of the TWDC by the DoE (Byrne, 1987), I concluded that, given the absence of radical alternative proposals by the local authorities and their record of using the established planning system in support of the development industry, it was difficult to see what need there was for a UDC, even in capital's terms. So it has proved with the major conflicts around UDC operations involving a site in Newcastle, which the UDC wanted to use for an industrial park (a good idea in my view) and which the local authority wanted to sell for commercial development in retail, and a dispute between the UDC and the Port of Tyne Authority where the PTA, true to its industrial origins, has attempted to emphasize maritime industrial development at Whitehill Point in North Shields while the UDC has a lulu scheme for marina, arena and yet more houses. The UDC has proved reluctant to employ its compulsory purchase powers. Instead, Tynemouth's Tory MP, Neville Trotter, has brought pressure to bear by blocking the passage of a private bill promoted by the Port Authority to widen its development powers. Remarkably, North Tyneside's Labour Leader has endorsed the UDC Whitehill Point scheme.

The operations of TWDC do not involve the displacement of occupational communities, which is the major source of conflict in Docklands. Neither is there serious competition for housing land. Instead, traditional maritime industrial sites which are currently not operating are being permanently sterilized. Indeed, the proposals for Whitehill Point involve the removal of currently active operations although there is an alternative location proposed at Tyne Dock/Jarrow Slack on the opposite bank.

The Board of the TWDC includes a local brewer from a company with traditional Tory connections (although he has also been a supporter of regional initiatives and is very much part of regional capital), a banker, an accountant, a director of the Northern Region's largest private sector company, Northern Engineering Industries, a director of Cookson Group which has always been important as a representative of regional capital, John Hall of Cameron-Hall, the Metro Centre developers, two Labour councillors from the conformist right-wing of the party, a former Tory councillor who lost his seat in May 1988, and the Regional Secretary of the TGWU. Thus its composition is very like that of the traditional regional corporatist bodies described in the section on the regional state. However, the TWDC is a creature of central government and works to its priorities. The Labour figures are not representatives but members in a personal capacity, although it is clearly intended that their presence should act to defuse organized opposition to proposals. This sort of system has been described as 'authoritarian corporatism' and has to be distinguished from traditional tripartite corporatism (see Panitch, 1980), because that delivered some goodies which corresponded with traditional labourist objectives, particularly in terms of support for full-employment.

The TWDC is not about employment, although employment glosses are sometimes offered. No long-term employment plan would convert shipyards into housing estates when perfectly suitable housing sites which could be developed without subsidy to the private sector are readily available within 2 miles. It is rather a kind of ideological device with money which represents the future as non-industrial. As such, it is intervening in civil society.

The workerist place in the world

Frankel (1987) has trenchantly criticized the tendency in modern Marxist-derived political theory to identify a sharp division between civil society and the state. He points out the extent to which such boundaries are disappearing under the impact of social change and rejects proponents of civil society's dismissal of the importance of state planning as an essential part of socialist transformation. I very much agree with him and will return to these issues in Chapter 9. However, with the interpenetration of the state and civil society recognized there is still some value in treating the two as poles on a continuum. And that continuum has to be at least three-dimensional because the economic sphere has been of such profound importance in the formation of the cultural components of civil society.

This is recognized by the present Tory Government in its efforts to promote an 'enterprise culture'. A Tory Minister on the radio in August 1988 identified the North East as the most difficult region for the promulgation of Thatcher's message because of the tradition of employment in large enterprises. There is an interesting contradiction about the word enterprise here, but what he was getting at is the strongly collectivist tradition which has emerged from one of the longest and most intense industrial experiences in the world. Lash and Urry (1987) noted that the UK as a whole was not the most developed example of organized capitalism. This is surely correct, but if we look below the national to the regional level then parts of the UK, particularly West Central Scotland and the North East coast, were indeed the most developed examples of organized capitalist regions which could be identified on a world scale. Only the Ruhr or the industrial mid-West would be comparable in degree of industrial intensity and capital organization.

The importance of this in political terms is represented both by voting behaviour, with the Tory vote on industrial Tyneside declining dramatically in local and parliamentary elections at a time when nationally that party has become dominant, and by important cultural themes. Traditional Toryism in the North East was by no means anti-collectivist but rather emphasized a traditional deferential paternalistic version of collectivism in contrast to Labour.

Some of the swing from the Tories has gone to the Alliance, particularly in Blyth Valley. There are particular historical reasons for Labour's decline in this seat but the development of Cramlington is also important. Local politicians consider that the owner-occupied areas of Cramlington vote Alliance because their residents have abandoned the Labour Party with their change in status represented by their move from inner-Tyneside, but are not prepared to endorse anti-collectivist policies. Given the importance of public sector employment to owner-occupying households in Cramlington, this is entirely rational. Thus the suburbanization which has been of great importance in expanding the Tory vote in the South East has different consequences in this area.

Voting behaviour is not the sum of political action in civil society. Ardagh (1979) commented on the enormous significance of voluntary bodies on Tyneside in contrast with his other European locales. These were recreational and service in kind and produced a contrary situation in which, in a highly collectivized society, people did not rely on the state to resolve problems. This indicates that the simplistic dichotomy proposed by the new right between state collectivism and privatized individualism is wrong as a description of the forms of political orientation. Tyneside displays a very high degree of collectivism in civil society through an extraordinary range of organizations. Many of these are simultaneously complementary to the Welfare State and represent pressures on it. Thus almost all the 'condition' societies (e.g. leukaemia, cystic fibrosis, schizophrenia, etc.) both raise funds which complement state resources in the Health Service *and* demand a higher level of state commitment to care and prevention provision. Of particular interest in the context of this study are 'community' bodies, organized representations in civil society of that very society, the existence of which have been explicitly denied by Thatcher in contrast with traditional Toryism which proposed the interests of a unitary community against class division as proposed by socialism.

Socio-tenurial polarization has led to a distinct partitioning of community groups. Working-class groups located in public sector estates tend to be very task-specific, although an examination of present groups in North Shields shows that some people have had a kind of serial membership of consecutive groups since the mid-1970s. Thus the Meadowell Estate has had a series of 'improvement groups', which were concerned with obtaining resources for the modernization of housing, and currently has 'service' groups in the form of a credit union and food co-op. Despite considerable efforts, in particular by Churches, to promote 'community' in Cramlington, there is no Cramlington-wide community organization. Instead, there are a range of very local pressure groups on planning and development issues and a large number of service and youth groups.

The division between community groups as an aspect of civil society and the state is almost non-existent. There are a range of community organizations which depend almost entirely for their funding on the local state and there are a number of workers directly employed by the state as supports to community organizations. The People's Centre, established as a community and educational resource in central North Shields, is almost entirely funded by the local authority. The Meadowell groups are heavily dependent for organizational support and services on employees of North Tyneside's Housing and Social Services Departments. These relationships with the state are complex and will be explored further in Chapter 10. Here, it is only necessary to say that they amount to more than the simple incorporation described by Piven and Cloward (1979) in *Poor People's Movements – How They Succeed and Why They Fail*. The relationship between community organizations and the state involves the former in claims on the resources represented by the latter and has profound implications for forms of political action.

The permeation of collectivism into North Eastern civil society has produced something very odd. The national state in association with particular figures from non-industrial regional capital is promoting individualism against a collectivist civil culture. The formal objectives of the UDCs form part of this project. Another example is provided by the claims made for John Hall's Metro Centre in government and other propaganda (see the Coleman interview with Hall in *The Guardian*, 8 August 1988). The Metro Centre is almost wholly a product of fiscally orientated central incentives to private development (see Byrne, forthcoming). Its job impact has been through displacement from existing shopping centres, although interestingly the Enterprise Zone package which sustains it has never been subject to the tests for potential displacement which are now routinely applied to applications from manufacturing industry for selective regional assistance from the DTI. Yet it is presented both as a symbol of the post-industrial North and as a solution to employment problems.

There is little evidence of success in any of this. Community business is developing in the most deprived areas but this is neither more nor less than a reinvention of a highly collectivist and most encouraging form of consumer cooperation. Despite claims that the North is about to be made safe for Thatcher, the electoral evidence from Tyneside in particular is that the Tory Party is being wiped out at both the parliamentary and local level. This leaves the state with the problem of administering an antagonistic civil society. As the powers of the local state are progressively eliminated and as genuine regional corporatism becomes reduced to authoritarian agency on behalf of an alien central government, then the relationship between state and civil society progressively becomes one of the *occupation* of the second by the first. This has profound implications for social change. It means that there is a crisis of legitimation which is not simply resolvable by appeals to parliamentary mandate. This ought not to be exaggerated. There is, thankfully, little immediate prospect of armed regionalist insurgence in the North East on the lines of ETA or the Corsican nationalists. However, with the increasing disjunction between collectivist political commitment by voters and anti-collectivist policies by government, then the conflict between regional political culture and the national state is of very great importance.

8

The inner city and beyond in 1988

What can be made of the situation in Northern Tyneside in the light of the developments described in the empirical chapters of this book as they might be interpreted in relation to the sorts of theoretical approaches outlined in Chapter 2? There are two possible ways of seeing things. One, which corresponds with the views of writers like Saunders, is to see the late twentieth century as a period in which a new post-modern social order has been established in the developed West. This order has its planes of cleavage but they are not, simply, those of the old industrial society. Rather, there are separate planes of cleavage around production, and around what is usually referred to as consumption, although it might better be described in terms of asset ownership. Although there are serious divisions in this new order, and certain deprived social groups have been excluded from participation in major parts of it, it is stable with long-term prospects of survival as it is. In these terms the social changes of the 1970s and 1980s have produced a new equilibrium which has replaced the post-war equilibrium based on the Keynes-Beveridge consensus.

Sociologically, this sort of approach is reminiscent of the 'functional conflict' line advanced by Coser (1956), in that it sees the presence of cross-cutting divisions, instead of one big division on class lines, as producing stability. This is despite claims for validation in terms of Weberian action theory. Politically, it is the background to the 'new realism' as advanced by journalists like Lloyd and Leadbeater, post-modernist social theorists like Bauman and politicians like Gould in the UK.

The alternative position is that things have not settled down for another long period of comparative stability but that we are still in the throws of a crisis. Crisis means turning point. Things can go in different ways. In O'Connor's trenchant phraseology of 1982, it is not a matter of which way they will go, but of which way they are made to go. In other words, instead of seeing a crisis resolved on capital's terms, proponents of the alternative position see a crisis which still has to be resolved and where the political options are still open. This emphasis on politics is crucial – it means that what will happen will be determined by conscious collective action.

I contend that the evidence from Northern Tyneside, from the inner city and beyond, shows that in this place there is still an unresolved crisis. The emphasis on place is quite deliberate. If we are going to understand what can happen in history we have to, in terms of a quotation from Gramsci already employed in this book, distinguish between general concepts which allow us to establish the nature of classes and their relationships in the abstract and those which allow us to analyse specific historical situations in order to identify the potential within them. If the debate about locality has any value, it is in that it identifies some sort of spatial specificity for the working out of history in the way in which base and social being add up to produce the potential for action. Revolutions did not happen in abstract social systems. They happened in Paris, Petrograd, Morales, and so on. Neither was the foundation of general, more gradual transformation abstract and aspatial. Specific historical experiences were crucial in the formation and working out in action of the social forces which produced such changes. This is not an endorsement of space as some component of a grand, general social theory on the lines of Giddens's structuration, it is an assertion of the need to look at particular *places* because history happens, and can be made to happen, in places.

If we look at Northern Tyneside we see a very profound and unresolved crisis in production. In 1988 Swan Hunter's lost an order for a frigate which placed the whole future of shipbuilding on the Tyne in jeopardy. No element in marine manufacturing can be regarded as safe and very little of the skilled labour necessary for the maintenance of this sector in the twenty-first century has been replaced. Recent initiatives for retraining long-term unemployed adults under a system of workfare on the job are no substitute for the properly organized formation of human capital.

Marine manufacturing may be a sector on the way out. Non-traditional manufacturing in Northern Tyneside is not on the way out but it offers little in terms of employment prospects. It is true that job placement prospects for school leavers have recently improved in line with demographic trends which mean that there are far fewer of them, but there remains a chronic problem of long-term unemployment among that age group, now in its early 20s, in which demographic bulge corresponded with minimal industrial recruitment – the lost generation selected by age cohort as a sacrifice on the altar of free-market ideology and sentenced to reserve army status for a lifetime.

National government is vigorously asserting that all will be resolved by growth in the service sector and is underwriting this assertion with massive subsidization of land development through Urban Development Corporations, etc. However, service sector employment growth seems to have simply reinforced social divisions by offering in the main part-time female employment which is primarily attractive to married women who are members of households already connected with employment. Such full-time jobs as are created in the service industry offer very low wages (e.g. £1.80 per hour for security guards working a 72-hour week). Members of benefit-dependent households gain minimal advantage by taking up such job opportunities which simply create a class of working poor. At the same time, full-time male and female employment has declined dramatically. There is another contradiction in government's emphasis on service sector solutions. Only if real wages in production were to expand so that the total production wage bill was at least as large with much reduced employment as it had been previously, would there be the resources available locally to purchase the services and thereby create employment. The prospects of the external purchase of north-eastern services, other than of existing public sector head offices which are more properly counted as part of production, is minimal. In these circumstances it is appropriate to remember that no community can survive if all its members have to do is take in each other's washing.

The Northern Tyneside evidence suggests that not only is the government 'free-market', service-orientated policy misguided, but that it is positively damaging by its emphasis on land development. Irreplaceable industrial sites are being sterilized so that short-term profits can be achieved through the provision of services and housing. This construction–development boom is displaying its own contradictions. Already there is a major shortage of skilled building labour and of building materials in the UK as the government pours more resources into this sector in an almost totally unplanned fashion. Thus investment in construction, which traditionally has been an effective mechanism for stimulating regional economies (e.g. under Heath in 1972), is now far less effective because even the building industry is dependent on imports for growth.

This is a crisis at the base but its severity is by no means the product of anonymous system forces. As Therborn (1986: 16) points out, these forces have a name and sometimes also a face, faces which can be recognized in the Cabinet. In other words, the particular form of the crisis at the base with its employment effects, has political origins. This means that the relative emmisaration of much of Northern Tyneside's population has not been caused by anonymous *natural* market forces which no political system can affect. Something can be done. The emmisaration already has politico-structural consequences, in terms of problems for order and integration, but these illustrations of division are of far less significance that the remarkable resilience of a collectivist political culture in civil society.

This is where place seems particularly significant. There is a very considerable force in the ideas represented in summary form by a notion of disorganized capitalism and it is clear that in the North East in general and Northern Tyneside in particular labour is disorganized at the point of production. Yet at the same time the world view produced by a common cultural experience of organized capitalism and a history of organized opposition to it, is profoundly antagonistic to the character of recent developments and to proposals that the only possible solutions are market-driven.

If backing the market is not the solution, and the likely outcome of market force developments seems to have little to offer Northern Tyneside in the medium and longer term, then the only alternative is some sort of planning for managed change. Our historical consideration has documented the collapse of regional economic planning and county-level land-use based structure planning, but we must recognize that the failure of both of these systems was not a failure to achieve results: one was never allowed to operate at all and the other was implemented under difficult conditions for a far shorter period of time than was intended. The failure of planning was a political failure. This political failure had two dimensions. First, regional planning never had an agency of implementation and structure planning's agency (at least in Tyne and Wear) was abolished during the life of the plan. Secondly, and more fundamental, the plans presented were corporatist at best. Indeed, both the Northern Regional Strategy and the Tyne and Wear Structure Plan – but perhaps the former in particular once the commitment to full-employment was abandoned – are more properly regarded as technocratic attempts to plan for a particular kind of capitalist restructuring. In essence, they (and particularly the Regional Strategy) were 'regionalist state capital' projects on the lines of 'national state capitalist' support for organized capital, in contrast to the *laissez-faire* approach of early nineteenth-century and contemporary Britain.

A kind of awful parallel might be drawn between the last pre-famine effort to propose an interventionist solution for Ireland's problems, the Report of the Irish Commissioners on the Poor Law before 1837, and the Northern Regional Strategy. The Irish Commissioners proposed a national capitalist strategy of agricultural and industrial development which would be at the expense of the rural poor but which offered some prospects of protection against the worst excesses of market forces. Market forces were what the Irish got. Things are perhaps more complex in the North East in the 1980s. Certainly, the economy is wide open to real market forces with the least subsidized shipbuilding industry in the world and a complete absence of exchange controls. However, we have market forces of a real kind plus state assertion of market change by subsidizing things the market would not do if left to itself. This might be regarded as the worst of both worlds.

What is needed in this labourist region is a labourist plan based in, and derived from, working-class political support. The remaining two chapters of this book will be about the political prerequisites of such a plan in terms of state form and popular organization in order to achieve that state form. Before proceeding to them it is necessary to review what we have found out about the inner city and beyond and to specify what is particular about this inner city and what lies beyond it (and beyond here has as much a temporal as a spatial meaning).

So far this chapter has dealt almost entirely with base and with the cultural products of base. 'Consumption cleavage' theory's applicability to Northern Tyneside has been dismissed but not refuted. Almost no attention has been given, either in summary or in the developed account in the empirical chapters, to 'inner-city' policies as such other than those represented by subsidies to land development through Urban Development Grants and the Urban Development Corporation. In particular, little attention has been paid to 'community work' as a complex and contradictory method of integrating the disorganized and marginalized in the interests of order (see Byrne, 1986). This neglect of community work, so far as North Shields and Cramlington are concerned, is partly justifiable because there is relatively little of it. Certainly, in Cramlington there is minimal community development intervention and in North Shields much of the intervention takes the form of service provision, e.g. Welfare Rights. In both locales the most important form of integrative community work is probably that done under the rubric of decentralized housing management. However, these state interventions have not, in my judgement, been fundamental in shaping the nature of the places or the consciousness of the people. They are very important in relation to potential for change but are not crucial in setting context, and are therefore appropriately dealt with in Chapter 10.

The refutation of the significance of consumption cleavages is another matter. There are two aspects to this, the specific and the general. The first deals with the significance of such cleavages in Northern Tyneside, the second with what the situation in Northern Tyneside tells us about the general applicability of such notions and the political implications which are drawn from them. First, let us agree that there are very real cleavages in Northern Tyneside. The difference in life chances between the South Meadowell and Parkside is enormous. However, what determines these differences? It is location within a labour market which is derived from the conditions of basal production. Here the possession of material assets separate from work are not of great significance. What matters is the possession of a job. This is not to say that owning a dwelling is not relevant to life chances, but that in this region such ownership is dependent on employment location and immediately accessible to most of the employed. It does not have fundamental independence.

That really gets rid of the idea that cleavages can be constructed around 'consumption', but it does not dispose of the importance of 'assets'. After all, what determines employment status? Why are some people unemployed in benefit-dependent households when others have jobs in multiple-earner households? This can certainly be explained in terms of employment-relevant assets, i.e. skills, qualifications and experience. There is no problem with looking to this sort of thing to explain an individual's location. The issue is whether the differential distribution of employment-related assets (which distribution is determinant of differential distributions of consumption) forms a basis for distinct and antagonistic social collectivities? What we are dealing with here is fractions within the working class (because the overwhelming majority of households are dependent on wages and/or benefits) and the significance of the divisions among fractions. If one was looking for an alternative to Marxism for handling this issue, then Parkin's (1979) conception of 'double closure' is far more impressive than consumption cleavage, precisely because it does put work and its consequences as central.

However, the question is not whether there are fractions within the working class, because there undoubtedly are, but what political implications flow from this? All the evidence from Northern Tyneside suggests that in this place with its distinctive civil society the existence of class fractions does not produce a fundamental political division within the working class, and hence and excluded and marginalized underclass. The dominance of collectivist perspectives derived from a specific historical experience is amply strong enough to be maintained through great social changes in the form of production *and* (which may be even more important) in the organization of reproduction in urban life. This is a culturalist explanation which is closely related to Cooke's (1982) conception of the formation of civil society in his radical regions.

Fair enough as an explanation of the specific. This seems to me entirely adequate as the Northern Tyneside contribution to an explanation of the background to the increasing regionalization of voting patterns in the UK. However, proponents of the importance of 'asset ownership' could use the same voting behaviour patterns to dismiss this as a 'merely specific' explanation. Different histories are producing different civil societies in different places. What holds in Northern Tyneside does not hold in South London.

To which the response must be yes and no. Yes to the extent that the historical experience of capitalism and its social relations has been different and has produced a different form of social being with profound consequences for the nature of civil society and political action. No to the extent that we are still dealing with a situation in which base is determinant. Reference has already been made to the necessity of using the word 'determine' in the sense of setting limits. This allows for a lot of variation but it also means that in the last instance [E. P. Thompson (1978: 288) reminds us that the lonely hour of the last instance has a disconcerting habit of arriving], there are boundaries which cannot be transcended without fundamental transformation.

Here Bauman (1987) is far more formidable than theorists of consumption cleavage because he recognizes very clearly that we can only talk in any meaningful way of an underclass if all the traditional functions of a reserve army have been dispensed with. Evidence from Northern Tyneside suggests that this is not the case. More generally:

> in the last seven years labour productivity growth in manufacturing has averaged almost 6% a year, more than double the rate achieved in the previous twenty years. The reformation in industrial relations is paramount in explaining this transformation in economic performance. The climate of industrial relations has been altered by fear, competition and decentralization of collective bargaining.
> (Metcalf, 1988 quoted in *The Guardian*, 27/7/88: 15)

So long as the benefit-dependent are a reserve army then the long-term real interest of the employed working class is in abolishing them through a policy of full-employment. While they continue to exist the employed have a real interest in maintaining the conditions of reproduction of the non-employed through benefit systems. A clear understanding of this is part of the cultural equipment in Northern Tyneside. In areas where it is not we can see a dominance of 'momentary interest' over long-term interest. This dominance has to be explained in terms of the way that cultural equipment has been formed in those places and here I would suggest that the role of institutional racism, when much of the reserve army is black, is of very great importance. This becomes a matter for political struggle, for active political intervention of a highly workerist kind to reconstruct the notions of general collective long-term interest. That struggle is not necessary in Northern Tyneside.

However, the question remains of what can we make of that cultural advantage in political terms? Recent experience suggests that the traditional mechanism, labourist support for regionalist corporatism, has minimal potential. The last two chapters of this book will consist of my suggestions for an alternative and for mobilizing support for that alternative. This has to begin with what Therborn (1986: 35) has called a '*labour comeback* scenario'. I am perhaps rather more optimistic than Therborn about the possibilities of developing such a scenario quite quickly towards socialism but I agree absolutely that it is a necessary precondition of any positive moves.

This ends up being very dismissive of 'social movements' *but not of the social proletariat*. If I have any criticism of Therborn's very valuable analysis, it is that he somewhat neglects the welfare component which historically has been a concomitant of demands for full-employment. This is important because it leads us towards ideas of social planning (in the sense that Walker, 1984, uses that term) rather than mere economic planning. And that means that the active, not constituency which is far too passive a term, but (using a good aggressive Northumbrian word) muster of support is far wider than if we construct demands in terms of work alone. The significance of the social proletariat means that women and black people have a very important role in these sorts of struggle, although the latter group is not of practical significance in Northern Tyneside in the 1980s. Indeed, a good deal of the potential for change derives precisely from the role of women in production and reproduction and the way in which the contradictions between these are so much more apparent in the 1980s *because of the massively increased participation of women in waged work*. However, emphasis on the role of the social proletariat is diametrically opposed to the kind of post-industrial strategies with which such emphasis is often confused (see Byrne, 1984).

I want to conclude this chapter with a brief discussion of the potential for the generalization of the analytical description so far presented, and hence of the prescription to come. I will simply assert that anything which goes for Northern Tyneside goes for Southern Tyneside, Wearside and the present and past Durham and South Northumberland coalfields with knobs on. This detailed account has been focused so as to make it manageable, but those other places are 'more so'. I am less confident of generalizing this account to all the industrial North. Teesside and West Cumbria do have different post-war industrial histories. Certainly, the cultural elimination of the Tories has not yet been achieved in Teesside, which suggests that this different history has generated a different civil society, and the civil society of West Cumbria has been much changed by the role of the nuclear industry. However, what this implies is the development of similar contextual research-based accounts as a basis for the planning of action, which take account of differences (and that is CDP talk indeed).

More generally, I am struck by the potential applicability to Clydeside of much of what I have found. This may be because my contacts on Clydeside are people whose political line is very much like mine, but I think that their line, and the applicability of description and analysis, is in fact a product of a very similar industrial history. What this begins to come down to is a claim for the generalizability of the account to city regions whose 'industrial culture' has been shaped by a dominance of large enterprise-based skilled employment and whose political culture has consequent labourist elements. This is particularly the case if sectarian and racial division has either not existed as a significant political force (as on Tyneside in the twentieth century) or has been overcome by very well-handled political action (as the Independent Labour Party and Communist Party transcended the Orange Green division in industrial politics on Clydeside).

The only other place I know well enough to make specific comments about is Belfast. Again this is a great estuarine shipbuilding city and I know that much of the analysis already holds for its industrial base, and will hold entirely with the privatization of Shorts and the shipyard. However, sectarianism is so central as a base for politics that it is difficult to see how an industrial-welfare labourist politics can ever take hold. If it does not, the outlook for Belfast's working class is appalling.

I do not want to make too much of these claims for generalization. They are suggestions to others (with particular people in mind) for them to take note of as they see fit. There is no claim for grand theory or master plan here. This is not a dismissal of the applicability of the Marxist analytical framework. It is a taking note of Gramsci's guidance on how to use it.

PART III

Towards 2000 – strategies and tactics for change

9

Beyond the inner city: planning for a future

At first view the title of this work may be found surprising. Can the social democracy be against reforms? Can we contrapose the social revolution, the transformation of the existing social order, our final goal, to social reforms? Certainly not. The daily struggle for reforms, for the amelioration of the conditions of the workers within the framework of the existing social order, and for democratic institutions, offers to the Social Democracy the only means of engaging in the proletarian class war and working in the direction of the final goal – the conquest of political power and the suppression of wage labour. Between social reforms and revolution there exists for the social democracy an indissoluble tie. The struggle for reforms is its means: the social revolution its aim.

(Luxemburg, 1972: vii)

Therborn's (1986: 35) *'labour comeback scenario'* has already been mentioned in this book. It is a *national* road to full-employment. Therborn places a good deal of emphasis on this because he considers the prospects for international cooperation as demanded by Stuart Holland's (1983) *Project for European Recovery* as minimal given the poor record of internationalism by labour parties in office. Fair enough, and undeniably true: but for socialists in member states of the EEC it is necessary to look beyond 1992. Even in advance of a single European market, the EEC Commission is placing limitations on the scope of member states' industrial policies. For example, it is clear that the Commission wants to reduce EEC shipbuilding capacity and would obstruct new programmes of subsidies to this crucial sector. Thus there has to be some element of international cooperation to handle this aspect at least.

The emphasis on the national level would also seem to reduce the significance of regional policies as they could be generated and developed in a centralized society like the UK. It may well be that in the next millenium, the national level in Europe will wither away (or be eliminated) leaving a European state relating to regions. There is actually a good deal to be said for this if what is created is a federal democracy. However, in the years up to A.D. 2000, this is not going to happen. The national level will be of enormous importance.

It may seem odd to start a chapter which is going to be largely about the content and implementation of a regional plan with such qualifications of its scope and potential. However, they are not introduced here to reduce the importance of regional and local planning, but rather to identify problems which the development of democratic planning will have to contend with, and which can be contended with only by constitutional reform. Offe (1984: 246) has remarked that 'Socialism in industrially advanced societies cannot be built *without* state power and it cannot be built *on* state power' (original emphasis). This, as it stands, is merely a clever and pessimistic paradox but his expansion of the theme does allow for possibilities:

> The decisive theoretical and political problem for all modern socialist politics . . . is this: given the unavoidability of the fact that in the process of transformation, one has to rely on the institutions, opportunities and progressive and constraining traditions of the system that is to *be* transformed, how can those links of continuity, and the *forms* and instruments of change be prevented from turning *against* the purpose and content of the transformation itself?
> (Offe, 1984: 241–2, original emphasis)

It is not that hard to specify the content of a plan for full-employment, just as it was not that hard for the Northern Regional Strategy Team to specify the content for a capitalist-planned modernization of the region's economy. The problem is one of implementation, and specifically of the development of institutional mechanisms for implementation.

This is the point of the quotation from Rosa Luxemburg. It indicates the *potential* of reform but the content of the notion of reform has to be carefully identified. This was not just a matter for the social *democracy* of welfare provision and better conditions for reproduction, although that was important; it also included struggles for democracy, for changes in the form of the state's decision-making and administrative processes. This struggle for democracy was certainly not completed with the achievement of a mass adult franchise, although conventional socialist (but not *Liberal*) politics generally seems to accept that it was. Surely part of the project of transformation involves the transformation of the state. The record of recent attempts to move in a progressive direction, which have confined themselves to the use of existing central UK state agencies *or* the existing form of local government, has been disastrous. In proposing *what* is to be done we must also make constitutional proposals about *how* it is to be done, and done in the world in which we are and in specific places in that world.

This chapter will continue by identifying the components of a *structural social policy* for the Northern Region and how this would relate to the needs of the people in the two locales which have been the subject of investigation. It will conclude by a consideration of what agencies would be necessary for the implementation of any such policy.

Full-employment, a decent environment, welfare for all

Alan Walker's conception of structural social planning has already been cited. Zusa Ferge has described the same process which she calls by a different name, i.e. Societal Policy. This:

> encompasses the sphere of *social policy* (the organization of social services, or the redistribution of incomes), but also includes systematic social interventions at all points of the reproduction of social life with the aim of changing the structure of society.
>
> (Ferge, 1979: 13, her emphasis)

Ferge goes on to warn us that:

> Societal policy is deliberate social action, both short-term and long-term. If it neglects the immediate problems for the sake of the distant future, it may easily become utopian. If it does not strive to do more than solve visible problems without having a coherent image of what the future should be, its results will be fragmentary. And, in the absence of a firm system of priorities, current problems may reproduce themselves in the future, possibly in a more serious form. An effective societal policy presupposes then, an awareness of the present situation and at least a broad outline of the future.
>
> (Ferge, 1979: 19)

Walker and Ferge are proposing a contemporary version of radical transformational reform. This has to be distinguished on the one hand from insurrectionary notions of sudden revolutionary overthrow, now abandoned in advanced Western societies by all except sectarian lunatics, and on the other from that version of reform which is designed simply to permit the amelioration of capitalism so as to ensure the survival of a system of wage labour. There are problems with their approach, not least as Deacon (1983) has noted, the absence of any conception of agency in Ferge's work. She has no notion of class struggle and the same is true for Walker. However, they do provide a very useful way of conceptualizing what is to be done, a way of getting to tomorrow which starts today.

This suggests that Therborn's (1986) distinction between labourist and socialist strategies may be too precise. Therborn is surely right to identify the re-achievement of full-employment as a basis for progress. As he says, people on the dole do not make revolutions. But put this baldly his programme could amount to merely a restoration of the Keynes-Beveridge settlement and then starting again. The point is that the institutional mechanisms which we need to achieve the labourist objectives are different from those which already exist. The challenges to state forms, and in particular to the processes of decision making, are the basis for going beyond a labourist to a socialist programme.

Thus it is not hard to identify the immediate components of a regional derivative of a national labourist strategy in terms of policy objectives. Therborn lays down the national parameters in terms of a reflationary strategy geared to prioritizing investment, both private and public, above consumption. This should be associated with an active labour market policy of retraining public sector employment. Finance capital has to be subordinated to productive industrial capital. The tax structure has to be changed to shift the burden from wages to taxes on capital assets and value added. Finally, given full-employment and rising real wages, the labour movement has to be committed to innovatory change and agreed moderation on money wages. Easy!

North Tyneside's *Plan for Jobs* in (North Tyneside MBC) 1987 was very much a local derivative of such an approach. This was designed to halve unemployment in North Tyneside MBC by creating 10 500 jobs or real training places over a period of 2 years. The Plan's authors specified the nature of the central government programme needed for its implementation in terms essentially identical to those of Therborn. The 10 500 jobs to be created would be made up of 2000 in manufacturing, 2000 in construction (including the public sector), 2750 in local government services, 500 in other public services and 3250 training places. The public sector jobs would be spread over a range of services, primarily personal social services and health care in the community, although environmental works, leisure, education and housing would also supply a significant element. A total of 75 posts were to be in economic development. The construction programme included the development of the infra-structure and housing repairs and maintenance with the local authority building 800 new dwellings a year. The location of private sector employment growth is worth specifying in detail – 500 in shipbuilding, 100 in ship-repair, 100 offshore, 50 in fishing, 225 in power engineering, 100 in coal-related work, 200 in clothing, 80 in cultural work, 175 in private housing insulation, 75 in co-ops and 395 general jobs. This is a very sensible reflection of the local industrial structure and involves a major commitment to the traditional base. Of the training posts, 2150 would be in the local authority, including much construction training, and 1100 would be private sector.

The main author of this plan found that the response of the private sector manufacturers to it was complex. His contacts in production and training all agreed that the basic idea was sound – good economic sense in their terms – but they were cynical about the prospects of the introduction of any such scheme under any government, but particularly by Thatcher. Certainly, any such plan would seem to be in the interests of manufacturing capital in Northern Tyneside.

This was explicitly a plan for jobs, but it was implicitly a plan for better services to be provided by those who worked in the public sector – improved community care, house repairs, environment, and so on. The one element that was missing related to the conditions of reproduction of the non-employed. In *Full Employment in a Free Society* (1944), Beveridge identified a national programme which was identical to that proposed 43 years later by Therborn. However, the old Liberal went further by reminding his readers of the content of his 1942 report which had specified adequacy in state benefits. This was right in itself and a part of any counter-cyclical economic strategy. Adequate state benefits are properly a national matter. In the only example of devolution in the modern UK, Northern Ireland 1922–72, parity of state benefits with Britain was maintained. This is a subsidy to consumption but it is also a vital part of removing the capacity of capital in abstract, and capitalists in reality, for using a reserve army against employed labour.

Fine, we have an immediate plan for Northern Tyneside because North Tyneside's approach is immediately applicable in Cramlington, etc. What about the longer view towards 2000? What about strategy? Here the objective of the NRST can be agreed with. What is needed is a strong economy, but that means a strong economy for labour and the working class. And that means a revival of a *modernized* version of marine manufacturing. The approach here must involve something like that of Japan's Ministry of International Trade and Industry (MITI), the organizing body of Japan PLC. We have had a major paradox in the UK. Nationalized industries competing on a world scale, and in particular shipbuilding, have been run with less positive direction from the central state than private capitalist production in Japan. There has been plenty of direction of late, almost all negative and destructive. This is the essence of *The Peculiarities of the British Economy* (Fine and Harris, 1985). How can capital goods production, always more amenable to political planning than the production of consumption goods – indeed it cannot properly function without it – be planned in places like Northern Tyneside today? Nationalization is certainly one approach, but it is politically discredited because the fraction of capital controlling contemporary Toryism, finance and rentier capitalism, has used central control of nationalized mining and shipbuilding to destroy the employment base of antagonistic regions. How to plan remains an issue to be addressed later in this chapter.

What to plan for is easier, although what follows has to be taken for what it is worth – as the tentative suggestions of someone with an interest in marine manufacturing but no practical experience of it. Essentially, UK marine manufacturing in general and the north east coast in particular (i.e. about half of all UK capacity), must plan to have a large proportion of world high value-added production in the first decade of the new millenium. High value-added production includes naval vessels, complex merchant vessels (e.g. chemical tankers, cruise liners, safe ferries, etc.) and offshore fabrication, particularly wave-energy facilities. Such developments would require an R and D commitment now and an immediate programme of skills training. Marine manufacturing in Northern Tyneside has still just about enough capacity to get this sort of programme underway, but it will not have it for long.

The approach being suggested here is not one which involves getting production right and hoping that reproduction – the provision of services as part of welfare – will follow. Walker, in particular, is very insistent that social planning cannot be subordinated to economic planning with the latter having to be got right before we can afford the former and its consequences. I agree absolutely that the two have to be taken together. Resources must be devoted to health care, better housing and proper social services. However, as has been reiterated in this book, I remain convinced that we must get an economic base in manufacturing as the basis of a just and equal society in places like Northern Tyneside. Reproduction cannot be left until production has been got right, but decency in reproduction cannot be achieved without production being sorted out.

Traditionally, marine manufacturing has employed men, with the important exception of the Second World War when large numbers of women were employed in the shipyards. Certainly, any publicly supported expansion of this sector ought to involve efforts to break down gender stereotyping in recruitment, which would be most easily achieved by the control over recruitment to training programmes. This is a proper objective and should be vigorously pursued, but in the shorter term women's employment opportunities are probably best improved in Northern Tyneside by systematic support for the clothing industry, which does offer industrial jobs and the prospect of trade union organization, together with an expansion of employment opportunities in the public sector.

How to plan for a decent future

The crucial issues of what forms of state intervention are appropriate for achieving such goals immediately arises. Geddes (1988) has recently reviewed the efforts at radical innovation by 'municipal socialism' and has criticized both the content of such proposals and the general direction of consideration of them, for an almost total neglect of the issue of what needs to be done to the state in order to achieve objectives. He also identifies the peculiar way in which new innovations were 'added on' to the local state rather than there being any transformation of the content of existing central areas of activity, other than through moves towards the decentralization of service provision. For me, one of the most remarkable absences in the 'red enclaves' of the 1980s was a serious confrontation with issues related to land. This was not wholly neglected (see GLC, 1985), but it was much less high-profile than efforts at direct intervention where the local authorities had far less resources and power. Yet the first attack on local democracy as a process of determination was precisely on land-use planning powers through the introduction of Urban Development Corporations.

Land-use planning cannot lead structural social planning as a whole, but it must be an important part of it, and it has particular importance in the short term because it has a recent history of democratic control. The cultural reasons for this are worth thinking about. Those who make profits out of land speculation are not highly regarded by the population at large. This is an entirely appropriate and accurate survival of the very general nineteenth-century hostility to rentier landlords in contrast with productive and innovative industrial capitalists. Land is there. The charge on it derives entirely from the existence of private ownership. One of the original intentions of planning legislation in this country was to nationalize all development value, not just as a 100% tax on rent in the best Ricardian tradition, but also to prevent speculators shaping the development process (see Ambrose, 1986). Landholders do not possess the power of financiers to make war on transformation by a flight of capital. It is not possible to transfer Whitehill Point out of the UK by electronic devices. Neither can it be withheld from use if the state wants it. Compulsory purchase exists and, in any event, this site, like so many others crucial to inner-city industrial revival, is already in public ownership. The immediate issue is to prevent its privatization and sterilization.

Traditionally, land-use planning has followed on from the specification of wider economic objectives in the way in which the Tyne and Wear Structure Plan followed the Northern Regional Strategy. This is the correct ordering in the longer term but demands for the revival of positive land-use planning are again an important short-term part of any serious strategy. It has to be recognized that in the short term, i.e. until the agencies for structural social planning are established, the positive approach to most land-use issues in the inner city is to do nothing if that can be done, and to agitate and organize against private speculators' pre-emptive activities. Positive intervention by local authorities in the use of land for industrial development is nothing new in the North East. Witness the Tyne Improvement Commission and the development of industrial estates in the 1930s. What is new is the proposal that local authorities should take an aggressive negative stance against 'consumption' development on the grounds that here something is worse than nothing.

The best way to change the form of the state and attack centralism in the UK is the development of a powerful level of elected regional government. In the 1970s, devolution was considered only in relation to Scotland and Wales and was complicated by questions of nationalism. What is needed now is a programme of devolution for all regions in Britain. A constitutional programme for such change is laid out in Tyne and Wear 2000 (1987). The central principle is effective and powerful regional government and the method of achieving this is by the generalization of what the minority of the Kilbrandon Commission (1974) called the interlocking principle. It is no good introducing devolved regional government into the UK if, as was envisaged for Scotland and Wales in the Government White Paper of 1976, the actions of the assemblies are subject to easy reversal by central government and if central government retains the power to abolish the regional level. Indeed, Labour's proposals of the 1970s would have given Scottish and Welsh Secretaries of State powers identical to the Viceroy of India. Lost colonies indeed! Under the interlocking principle, the second chamber of the central legislature would be retained with increased powers over that which it already possesses but its members would be elected, as are the members of the West German Senate, by regional assemblies. Regional senates would be drawn in a similar fashion from local authorities with similar appropriate powers at that level. The more general proportional representation then was in elected bodies the better, but the regional assemblies should certainly be elected on this basis.

Regional assemblies would have considerable administrative powers including control over the NHS, energy, water, transport and tertiary education and training. We also proposed that they control the police and locally raised militias on the lines of the US national guard. However, their central function would be economic planning – hence the need for control over post-school education and training so that workforce planning could be easily achieved. A regional structure plan would be prepared and would be related to a national plan which would be formulated in consultation with regional governments. Regions would have powers to establish regional investment banks and to develop wage-earner funds on Swedish lines to give them considerable financial powers. Democratic control over land, training and much of investment capital would provide a considerable capacity for directive planning. Trade unions in a context of full-employment and legally guaranteed rights to strike and picket would be able to enforce planning agreements with private capital in production. Things would not be automatically easy. Offe (1984) has reminded us of capital's ability to engage in investment strikes, and the dismantling of exchange controls makes this much easier in the UK, but proper social control of pensions funds alone would provide considerable financial power as a counterweight.

To be effective, regional government would have to have financial independence. Tyne and Wear 2000 (1987) proposed the adoption of a version of the West German basic law which allows central government to determine the overall volume of its tax collection but allocates a fixed proportion of this to the regions. The amount would be adjusted on a 'resources' basis because the regions would have a form of rates based on capital values for domestic property and a land tax equivalent to the old schedule A. Rates would be shared with local authorities but schedule A (a tax on the notional income derived by owner-occupiers) would be the region's alone. Regions with high resources from this tax would receive less from central taxation than those with less.

Full details of all this are given in the Tyne and Wear booklet. This was produced avowedly as a 'green paper', i.e. a discussion document. However, the central principle remains – to change the economy we need to change the state. Moves towards regionalism in the UK seem to be the best way of doing that. Certainly, public opinion in the Northern Region is almost entirely behind such a shift and devolution for the regions of England would remove the major source of opposition to Scottish and Welsh devolution. It is important to remember that the SLD is committed to a devolution programme and that constitutional changes of this kind would form a useful part of the programme of any Labour–SLD pact or coalition in central government.

Devolution is not a panacea but it has the effect of democratizing the process of taking decisions about how the future will be constructed. Anderson (1980: 20) makes a point of great significance:

It is the modern labour movement that has really given birth to this quite new conception of historical change; and it is with the advent of what its founders called scientific socialism that, in effect, for the first time collective projects of social transformation were married to systematic efforts to understand the processes of past and present in order to produce a premeditated future.

There is no need to adopt Anderson's élitist and mechanical version of what constitutes scientific socialism for this to matter. O'Connor (1982), in a discussion of crisis, suggested that what matters is not what will happen but what will be *made* to happen. Therborn tells us that we are faced with alternatives – Brazilianization or a move towards equality. We can specify what we want to happen – that is planning. What we have to do is push forward the democratic revolution so that it can and will happen. The last chapter of this book is about who will be there when push comes to shove.

10

The sources of collective action for change

Introduction

The starting point of any serious analysis of the nature of the social forces likely to support a transformational societal policy must be an examination of the interests of existing and potential collectivities. The word 'interest' has to be considered carefully. Far too often it has been interpreted as short-term and material and that only – an importation into the real social world of the abstract psychology of economic 'man'. The Leninist alternative of a distinction between 'momentary' and 'real' interests is not much more satisfactory. It distinguishes between the conception of interest developed by a materialist analysis in the tradition of 'scientific socialism' and the bloody mindedness of actual social action in relation to apparently immediate issues.

Historical analysis has to take account of more than the immediately material or the longer-term real material interest. People's interests are also constituted in terms of their cultures and the survival of those cultures may form part of their material interests. We also have to look carefully at the boundaries of personal interests. Contrary to the individualistic psychology of economic 'man', people take account of others when they construct a sense of what matters to them. Sometimes this is straight material interest. In the modern UK the significant unit of consumption is not the individual but the partnership household. Members of couples look to each others' interests in employment at least in part because they determine both lives. Wives have always had a real material interest in the conditions of wage-earning men. Things are getting more symmetrical.

Households are units of consumption as a basis for reproduction. Families are units of affectivity. There is considerable evidence of intergenerational and cross-sibling transfer of material resources in modern UK life but there are also bonds of care and attention which may have far greater significance for social action. The employment locations of children, parents and siblings all matter and in a relatively ethnically homogeneous community (that word again) with a high level of residential stability, familial and quasi-familial bonds matter a good deal for social action. An example of a quasi-familial bond is that constituted in terms of a common North Eastern phrase by 'the lads (or lasses, or if young enough, both) I went to school with'; in other words, the members of your own generation who shared formative experiences in your own place. This 'collectivity of formation' is extended to shared work experience – the lasses from Dukes and Marcus, the lads from Parsons – not least because work is often the basis of the organization of a good deal of social life. There is clearly some significance in the employment of the term for adolescents by people of all ages to describe themselves and those with whom they share such experiences.

These 'extended interests' are very important in considering the contemporary basis of social action in Northern Tyneside because the account of industrial and consequent social development has been one of *divergence* from a very even set of social circumstances established under conditions of full-employment. Siblings, schoolfellows and workmates have gone in different directions. Perhaps even more importantly many of the generation now in their early and mid-20s were unable to establish the skill base of their parents (a very common experience of the Afro-Carribean community elsewhere in the UK) and occupy much more vulnerable positions in the labour market. This matters because over and above the vital real interest of the employed in general in the reduction of the reserve army, employed and relatively prosperous individuals have crucial social bonds with those who are deprived through benefit-dependency or low wages.

Transcending all this is the common culture with its origins in industrial experience and urban pit-village life. Ardagh's (1979) point about the dominance of working class values on Tyneside has been cited before but is worth repeating here. Tyneside's culture remains that of highly paid proletarians in a world of organized capitalism. Today, those values are most easily expressed by the non-poor, but they always were values of the non-poor. Cramlington's white-collar workers are usually the descendants of skilled workers and miners (see Banim, 1987) and they are almost invariably the cultural descendants. The other explanation offered for the region's consumption boom apart from low house prices in relation to nationally determined wage scales, is a tradition of immediate hedonistic expenditure derived from the transient status of working-class prosperity. The point is that this culture is *inclusive*. It is based on a unitary non-exclusionary conception of communal interest which traditionally was closed only above to capital and not below to an ethnically or religiously distinctive excluded group. That this is the case is, as with contemporary mass unemployment, not so much the product of anonymous forces as of the acts of specific personalities like the leadership of the miners' union in the 1840s and of the Seamen's Minority Movement in the 1930s. It also derives in considerable part from the absence of much post-1920 immigration, but historical action always deserves favourable notice.

What follows is underpinned by the specific local possibility of the formation of union around real immediate and extended interests including the maintenance of common inclusive cultural values. Not everywhere is like this, but the North East, and Northern Tyneside, is. This is a programme for a place. The chapter will proceed with a consideration of the possibilities for organization among the emmiserated poor with particular reference to the role of community work. This will be followed by a consideration of how the non-poor can be organized around common interests with the poor. The final section will consider the relationship between such organization and a regional programme.

Organizing the disorganized: The potential of contradiction

This book has documented the movement from organized to disorganized capitalism on Northern Tyneside and the consequent disorganization of the area's working class. A consequence of that disorganization has been the peripheralization of a large part of the working class in residentially segregated ghettoes. Some of the social consequences of that process have been delineated. One way of viewing what has happened is represented by pessimistic post-modernism. Capital has broken through into a war of movement, dismembered working-class unity and created a broken residuum. Commentators like Bauman take it that far and stop. It is not that simple. Even if the role of the peripheralized as a reserve army of labour is ignored or forgotten, the existence of a massive residuum poses a serious threat to social order. This comes not from the organized and orderly resistance of a working class whose experiences are formed in disciplined production, but in the form of inchoate and disorganized violence, crime and occasional riot. It is anomic rather than alienated. Nineteenth-century social commentators were perfectly aware of the distinction between the powerful and respectable factory proletariat of the late nineteenth-century northern industrial towns and the disorganized residuum of East London. The former were more powerful but assimilable into the general social order through concessionary reform. The latter were outsiders who were in fact only assimilated through the creation of general workers' unions under skilled worker leadership and Labour Party organization.

There is ample evidence of anomic disorganization in Northern Tyneside and of the problems for the maintenance of order which this poses. A peripheralized and disorganized reserve army is both a weapon of, and a problem for, capital. If we continue with the analogy of the war of movement, capital needs to maintain its lines of communication. To do this it has to maintain order and in addition to overt order maintenance by the police there is a need for some form of conditional reorganization of the disorganized on a controlled and minimal level. Indeed, given some evidence that the relationship of the police to the new ghettoes is largely one of containment of problems within them – a literal ghettoization – then the organizers of the disorganized can be regarded as the major security component of the occupying forces.

This is a one-sided position because the personnel of the state have a contradictory potential. To take the title if not the structuralist content of a review of this, they are both *In and Against the State* (London Edinburgh Weekend Return Group, 1980). However, one aspect of community work, and of the decentralized housing management using community work techniques, which is of very great importance in what are almost invariably social housing ghettoes, is the management and control of the poor. Hence the fairly common use of a collective term to describe those engaged in this – social workers, community workers, housing managers, etc. – poverty professionals.

Thomas has described *The Making of Community Work* (1983). In particular, he chronicles the role of ex-colonial administrators in suggesting the application of techniques and procedures developed in the Empire to social issues in the metropolitan power. For Thomas, this bringing back home of the techniques developed by imperialism for the maintenance of order among conquered populations, was wholly uncontentious. In effect, Colonial Office community development was a procedure applied where Britain ruled directly after eliminating traditional sources of authority as opposed to ruling through them. It was indeed a response to disorganization. Thomas' book is dedicated to a version of community work which is created by the miscegenation of colonial dominance with the élitist social concern which informed the settlement movement. It is worth noting that, traditionally, the latter has never been of much significance on Tyneside. One of the benefits of being part of the organized working class was that you did not have to put up with it. Although efforts were made at its introduction in the 1930s it never could contend with the capacity of the National Unemployed Workers Movement as the organizing force among the unemployed. There is a Church-based initiative on the South Meadowell and the abuse

THE SOURCES OF COLLECTIVE ACTION FOR CHANGE   163

directed here at the principle of such interventions is not intended for the personnel of that project who seem at worst to have been harmless.

Thomas' version of community work is at the very best ameliorative and not transformational. The people who work in and around community work in Northern Tyneside (in Cramlington this means housing managers) have a rather different view, precisely because they too share the inclusive labourist collectivist culture of the North East. This is reinforced by a professional self-identity which includes a coherent and relatively well-developed analytical understanding of the structural origins of the situations and immediate problems with which they are contending. If I have no time at all for Thomas' version of community work, I have a lot of time for most of the community work practitioners and decentralized housing managers in Northern Tyneside.

The issue for community work is the nature of the objective of collective action. If community work is to have any value as a way of maintaining order through a process of legitimation it must have some potential for producing real resources for the groups who are integrated through it. Miller (1981) has described how, in Newcastle, a sophisticated procedure for the allocation of relatively limited resources through Priority Area Teams has served to defuse the potential of community action by enmeshing community groups in a competition for the allocation of a predetermined level of resources:

> The authority has retained its ability to control the terms, the forms and the content of local political debate and action, thereby removing important issues about unequal distribution of scarce resources from local politics and redefining public issues, private troubles and political issues as technical concerns.
>
> (Miller, 1981: 108)

This has not happened in North Tyneside and the reason why it has not happened involves a reconsideration of the role of left politicians in the local state *as they relate to organizations around social reproduction*. In Chapter 7 I was somewhat dismissive of the scope for significantly different action by North Tyneside's left Labour Council in contrast with more conventional authorities without a history of political change. I have quite deliberately left that error of judgement in the text in order to reinforce the importance of what follows.

There are a number of 'reproductive organizations' in North Shields which exist around a variety of issues. These include locale-based tenants' organizations concerned with the quality of housing provision and housing services, women's groups concerned particularly with health services, local consumer co-ops in the form of a credit union and food co-op, and youth and childcare provision organizations. In North Shields town centre, a building has been made over as The People's Centre which provides a meeting place, cafe, childcare facilities and a range of adult education opportunities. One of the organizations in this centre is a group of unemployed people who come together to campaign around benefits and related issues, around the conditions of reproduction of the front-line reserve army of labour just as the NUWM did in the 1930s.

One of the major political problems of the 1980s in contrast with the 1930s has been the absence of any organization on an equivalent scale to the NUWM. There are a number of possible reasons for this but one factor is certainly the removal of any significant powers over the levels and conditions of receipt of income maintenance from democratic local authorities. There is no local target with power. The new Employment Training Scheme (ETS) is a nationally arranged and controlled development but it did present local authorities with a choice – they could refuse to participate in it. The North Tyneside Unemployed Workers Group campaigned strongly for a refusal to participate by the Labour Group, and the Labour Group did refuse to become involved with what is in effect a scheme of workfare.

However, the decision was not simply a negative one. North Tyneside MBC has initiated its own training scheme based on the proposals contained in the *Plan for Jobs* and intends to provide some 600 training places of a kind which represents good practice and is acceptable to the TUC. The poor organized, lobbied and succeeded in getting elected representatives to endorse their position. This really is very important because it represents a constructive example of resistance which depends on the existence of a local democratic system, precisely what recent changes in the relationship between central government, local government and appointed bodies are designed to prevent. Clearly, it was important that the nature of the Labour Group had changed but the existence of organized pressure against the logic of conformity with pressure from above matters at least as much.

Interestingly, Blyth Valley Council has also refused to participate in ETS as has neighbouring Wansbeck. Here National Union of Mineworkers members and ex-miners allied with the left in the Labour Group to resist workfare, although it is important to note that sources indicate they had little political opposition. In these former mining localities the cultural values of labourism alone were almost enough to produce this sort of opposition. Again these district councils are devising their own training provision. No other authorities in greater Tyne and Wear or County Durham have taken a similar position. In Gateshead, there was resistance to the acceptance of ETS and it is only fair to say that nobody regarded participation in the scheme as anything other than making the best of a very bad situation. However, opposition did not prevail, not least because of the absence of organized representation of the kind achieved in North Tyneside.

What happened in North Tyneside was that community organizations sustained by the democratic local state were an important source of pressure on it. The relationship in Gateshead between the Labour Group and such organizations is not at all unfriendly and has led to significant innovations, particularly in terms of a very good scheme for the management and control of houses in multiple occupation, but it is not as formal and direct. The North Tyneside opponents of ETS 'seized the time' in a way in which their equivalents in Gateshead, including the present author – so this is a self-criticism – did not, but the existence of a focus for action was crucial to developments.

This suggests that a vital tactic on the part of left-controlled democratic local states is the funding of critical organization by poor people. This is a relatively cheap activity. The budget of North Shields' People's Centre is quite small, and in addition to a focus for organization the Centre provides a range of direct community services. However, at least as important as such direct support for community action, is the role adopted by directly employed state workers who are, in the American phrase, street-level professionals.

One recent innovation in community work is the notion of training 'indigenous workers' (the Colonial Office lives) who are more representative of those with whom they work. In white, poor working-class locales like much of North Shields and Cramlington most state-employed 'poverty professionals' are already indigenous in terms of ethnic background and social origins but their comparatively high wages and security of employment mean that they are insulated in their personal lives from the conditions of life of the poor with whom they work. Those who work, for example, on decentralized housing management, almost always have a sense of social identity, of extended interest as defined above, with their client communities. Their personal political commitments are, not at all surprising given their social origins and work location, collectivist. However, their job is much more *inherently* contradictory than that of community workers involved in direct community organization. This is not to say that the work of the latter is not contradictory. Under the terms and focus of employment existing for community workers in Newcastle the role is deeply contradictory because much of the effort goes into diverting working-class reproductive organizations from fundamental power struggles. However, straightforward community work is not *necessarily* like that.

Housing management is different: rents have to be collected; voids have to be filled; stock and tenants have to be managed and, despite innovations in decentralized consultation, the poor residents of social housing have never acquired direct control of either their dwellings or those who provide housing services. People in these sorts of jobs have two ways to go. One is to become like the bureaucrats who run the system in places like Soweto. The other is to identify with those whom they serve. The experience of this research is that the latter is the option chosen by the great majority of poverty professionals in Northern Tyneside who relate to collectivities of poor people. Social workers without a community work role do not relate to collectivities and are largely irrelevant to this discussion, although it is worth noting that models of 'community social work' are being asserted which return to what most social scientists would regard as utterly discredited explanations in terms of collective pathology. In this crisis practice is also at a turning point.

What is being suggested here is a set of tactics for organizing the poor in relation to reproduction which are applicable in, against and around the state (the last being autonomous collective activities like credit unions). The tactical objectives are frequently defensive but examples like that of the resistance to Employment Training in North Shields show that they do not need to be confined to this but can go forward beyond the assertion of alternatives towards the practical development of new systems. This applies equally to autonomous cooperation and constructive use of local state power, however limited. North Tyneside CDP devoted a lot of research effort into documenting the way in which working-class people had shaped the character of their reproduction through political pressure on state systems from below. Liberals masquerading as anarchists and those who have attempted history in a capital logic tradition of Marxism have been equally blind to this component of significant reform. It is nice to see that it is still going on.

In fact it is more than nice, it is vital. The problem in organizing poor proletarians in a campaign for social change is very seldom one of their ignorance of the nature and origins of the problems which confront them. It is far more often a sense of hopelessness about the possibilities of significant achievement. This point is well recognized by Piven and Cloward (1979), but their account of the inevitable failure through incorporation of poor people's movements is one written in relation to a particular sort of political culture – one in which labourist political traditions scarcely exist let alone be they socialist – and yet presented as if it were universally applicable. Northern Tyneside is very different, fortunately.

The role of the comfortable

The interest of the poor in transformational social change is obvious. However, in the collective journey beyond the inner city a good part of those who belong to the Northern Tyneside working class of today have arrived at a reasonably desirable destination. Very little of the source of their comparative comfort and decency of life-style should be assigned to the voodoo economic policies of Thatcherism. It is both directly and indirectly far more the product of a combination of welfarism and planning, e.g. in terms of the development of the owner-occupied areas of Cramlington which let it be said again are pleasant and desirable places to live. None the less, here they are now. What interest have they in changing things?

The anwser given by some elements on the left, including some community work theoreticians, is none. There are really few more objectionable facets of contemporary politics than that to be found at left conferences where public school-educated 'radicals' denounce the aristocracy of labour as irredeemably bought off by material prosperity. If there is a more sickening sight it is new realists agreeing with them and proposing that the organized labour movement should abandon any vestigial remnant of left politics because it puts the newly affluent off. Both approaches make two fundamental errors. First, they ignore what is meant by the term 'extended interests' as introduced earlier in this chapter. Secondly, they take an extraordinarily short-term view of likely developments and of their implications for political action. Indeed, they take a much shorter-term view than affluent working-class people do without any political prompting.

Urry (1983: 46) in criticizing the notion of a politics of consumption makes the very pertinent point that:

> It is surely not the case that local struggles necessarily revolve around the politics of consumption. The deindustrialization of an economy effects a substantial restructuring of the politics of production. This is partly because production is put back on the political agenda (if ever it went off) but in a manner in which struggles revolve around the recapitalization of localities.

During the time I have been carrying out research for this book I have had a number of conversations with local authority officers, journalists, industrial managers, small-scale capitalists (especially small builders) and similar people. In addition, I have been involved in a general election canvass in some of the most affluent areas of Northern Tyneside and have had extensive discussion with others so involved. The concerns of the affluent which emerge from this are very interesting. There is a general and profound sense of pessimism about the industrial future of the North East. This is despite some real signs of recent industrial revival as represented by a fall in unemployment which is at least in part genuine, a developing skill shortage and increased demand for, and rents charged on, industrial premises.

Perhaps the key to understanding is represented by the skill shortage. Over the past year, a number of unemployed skilled manual and white-collar workers over the age of 55 on Tyneside who thought that their working lives in industrial employment had finished with redundancy have been drawn back into work in marine manufacturing and its subcontractors. This may well be a temporary phase, particularly with the prospective loss of over 2000 jobs at North Eastern Shipbuilders on the

Wear, but it has happened. All comment on the age of their fellow workers – there is scarcely a skilled tradesman under 30. Manufacturing has not trained to replace skills as they have disappeared with retirement. This erodes the potential for revival and there is virtually universal agreement that ETS will not provide the level of training development necessary to cope with the problem. This is something which is part of the experience of affluent employed workers in industrial production and even more of junior and middle management.

This is a direct reinforcement of the sense of the importance of industrial base but this belief remains central to most peoples' world view, despite efforts by the UDC and other bodies at promoting the 'consumption' city. The problem is mobilizing the cultural commitment for change. In a simple sense, it is already mobilized. The very high Labour vote in the Northern Region, and even more the erosion of the Tory vote, represents the translation of the culture into voting behaviour, but that will not produce real results given the contemporary nature of the UK political system. Unfortunately, this is not generally recognized in the Labour Party where Westminister politics and MPs still dominate to such an extent that the self-interest of existing MPs was allowed to cost the Labour Party an extra Tyne-Wear seat in the revision of parliamentary boundaries prior to 1983. What the North East needs here is a campaign for decentralization which will reinforce the sense of hostility of its prosperous working class to the present character of central politics. Regionalism is an ideology for these groups and should be the basis of organization in relation to them. This will involve a rather traditional form of political campaign, but it will be a campaign with *new* objectives which are about how to *achieve* significant changes. Regionalism is not a panacea but it is a good deal, precisely because of the nature of the place for which it is being proposed.

The Labour Party has a vital role in all of this because of its hegemonic status and association with a regionalist and labourist culture. Or rather, it is more accurate to say that individual members of the Labour Party have such a role. In Northern Tyneside the majority of the members of the Labour Party come from the prosperous working class and live in the areas inhabited by it. Traditionally, the Northern Regional Party has been dominated by big union interests, particularly in recent years by the General, Municipal and Boilermakers Union, but this dominance is increasingly unrepresentative of its individual membership who are certainly union members but are as likely to be in NALGO or the NUT as in the GMBTU. Indeed, an increasing proportion of the individual membership which still works in industrial production is in unions like MSF which recruit what French sociology calls 'cadres'.

The promotion of a transformational strategy predicated on the development of democratically controlled regional administration is far more likely to come from this political class than from the trade union bosses who dominate formal Labour Party machinery through the exercise of block votes. This is not to write off the manual unions. One of the more refreshing aspects of north-eastern politics in recent years has been the tendency of rank-and-file members and lay-elected representative of the GMBTU to develop some independence of judgement and action, but theirs is still an uphill struggle. The Northumberland and Durham Miners and the Durham Mechanics have, since the miners strike, been absolutely associated with progressive and forward-looking ideas. However, the craft unions in engineering have not, largely because of the erosion of shopstewards' power and of the 'workers control' objectives associated with it.

What is being proposed is of course a cultural revolution and cultural practices matter a great deal here. Scotland's advantage over the Northern Region is that a distinctive civil society has obvious institutional existence. The disadvantage is that the social forces controlling much of that institutional framework are not natural allies of the working class, particularly in the legal establishment. Likewise, genuine class/regional interests can become confounded with nationalism. The North lacks the institutional framework but is also free of Writers to the Signet and Tartan fascists. Here regionalism is an unequivocally class-based phenomenon and practice. There is a lot of work to be done but there is also a lot of scope for it.

Bibliography

Addison, P. (1975). *The Road to 1945*. London: Cape.
Ambrose, P. (1986). *Whatever Happened to Planning?* London: Methuen.
Ambrose, P. and Colenutt B. (1975). *The Property Machine*. Harmondsworth: Penguin.
Anderson, G. and Friedland R. (1975). Class structure, class politics and the capitalist state. *Kapitalistate*.
Anderson, J. (1983). Geography as ideology and the politics of crisis. In J. Anderson, S. Duncan and R. Hudson (eds), *Redundant Spaces in Cities and Regions*. London and San Diego: Academic Press, pp. 313-50.
Anderson, J., Duncan, S. and Hudson, R. (eds) (1983). *Redundant Spaces in Cities and Regions*. London and San Diego: Academic Press.
Anderson, P. (1980). *Arguments within English Marxism*. London: Verso.
Ardagh, J. (1979). *A Tale of Five Cities*. London: Secker and Warburg.
Avineri, S. (1965). *The Social and Political Thought of Karl Marx*. Oxford: Oxford University Press.
Ball, M. (1986). The built environment and the urban question. *Society and Space*, 4, 449-64.
Banim, M. (1987). *Occupying Houses - The Social Relations of Tenure*. Unpublished Ph.D. Thesis, University of Durham.
Bauman, Z. (1987). From here to modernity. *New Statesman*, 25 September.
Benwell, CDP (1978). *The Making of a Ruling Class*. Newcastle: Benwell CDP.
Beveridge, W. (1944). *Full Employment in a Free Society*. London: Allen and Unwin.
Beynon, H. (1982). *Global Outpost*. Durham: University of Durham.
Blackman, T. (1987). *Housing Policy and Community Action in County Durham and County Armagh*. Unpublished Ph.D. Thesis, University of Durham.
Blyth Valley District Council (1973). *Minutes of 15/10/1973*. Seaton Delaval: BVOC.

BIBLIOGRAPHY 171

Braverman, H. (1974). *Labour and Monopoly Capital*. New York: Monthly Review Press.
Byrne, D. S. (1980). The decline in the quality of council housing in inter-war North Shields. In J. Melling (ed.), *Housing, Social Policy and the State*. London: Croom Helm, pp. 168–93.
Byrne, D. S. (1984). Just hold on a minute there: A rejection of Andre Gorz's 'Farewell to the Working Class'. *Capital and Class*, **24**, 75–98.
Byrne, D. S. (1986). State sponsored control – managers, poverty professionals and the inner city working class. In K. Hoggart and E. Kofman (eds), *Politics, Geography and Social Stratification*. London: Croom Helm.
Byrne, D. S. (1987). What is the point of a UDC for Tyne and Wear? *Northern Economic Review*, **15**, 63–75.
Byrne, D. S. (forthcoming). Socio-tenurial polarization: Issues of production and consumption in a locality. *International Journal of Urban and Regional Research*.
Byrne, D. S. and Parson, D. (1983). The state and the reserve army: The management of class relations in space. In J. Anderson, S. Duncan and R. Hudson (eds), *Redundant Spaces in Cities and Regions*. London and San Diego: Academic Press.
Cameron, S. (1987). *Recent Approaches to Problem Council Housing in Tyneside*. Newcastle: Department of Town and Country Planning, University of Newcastle.
Castells, M. (1977). *The Urban Question*. London: Arnold.
Centre for Environmental Studies (1983). *Outer Estates in Britain*. London: CES.
Chaplin, S. (1962). *The Watchers and the Watched*. London: Eyre and Spottiswoode.
Chapman, R. (ed.) (1985). *Public Policy Studies – The North East of England*, Edinburgh: University of Edinburgh Press.
Cleaver, H. (1977). Malaria, the politics of public health and the international crisis. *Review of Radical Political Economics*, **9**, 51–103.
Cleaver, H. (1979). *Reading Capital Politically*. Brighton: Harvester.
Cochrane, A. (1986). The attack on local government: What it is and what it isn't. *Critical Social Policy*, **12**, 44–62.
Cockburn, C. (1976). *The Local State*. London: Pluto.
Commission on Urban Priority Areas (1984). *Faith in the City*. Commission set up for the Archbishop of Canterbury. London: Church Publishing House.
Common, J. (1975). *Kiddar's Luck*. Newcastle: Frank Graham.
Cooke, P. (1982). Class interests, regional restructuring, and state formations in Wales. *International Journal of Urban and Regional Research*, **6**, 187–204.
Cooke, P. (1985). Class practices as regional markers. In D. Gregory and J. Urry (eds), *Social Relations and Spatial Structures*. London: Macmillan, pp. 213–41.
Coser, L. (1956). *The Functions of Social Conflict*. New York: Random House.
Dahrendorf, R. (1987). The erosion of citizenship. *New Statesman*, 12 June.
Dawes, A. (1970). The two sociologies. *British Journal of Sociology*, **21**, 207–18.
Deacon, B. (1983). *Social Policy and Socialism*. London: Pluto.
Department of the Environment (1987). *The Formation of Tyne Wear Development Corporation*. London: HMSO.
Department of the Environment Housing Development Group (1980). *An Investigation of Difficult to Let Housing*. London: HMSO.
Dickens, P., Duncan, S., Goodwin, M. and Gray, F. (1985). *Housing, States and Localities*. London: Methuen.
Duncan, S. (1982). Urban research and the methodology of levels – the case of Castells. *International Journal of Urban and Regional Research*, **5**, 231–54.
Duncan, S. (1986). *What is Locality?* Working Papers in Urban and Regional Studies, 51. Brighton: University of Sussex.

Duncan, S. and Goodwin, M. (1988). *The Local State and Uneven Development*. Oxford: Blackwell.

Dunleavy, P. (1981). *The Politics of Mass Housing in Britain*. Oxford: Clarendon Press.

Durham Regional Research Unit (1977). *Prospects for the Northern Region – A Study of NRST's Analyses*. Durham: DRRU.

Elphick, P. (1965). Cramlington – some problems encountered in building a New Town. *Town Planning Review*, **35**, 59–72.

Engels, F. (1968). *The Condition of the Working Class in England in 1844*. London: Allen and Unwin.

Everitt, B. (1974). *Cluster Analysis*. London: Heinemann.

Ferge, Z. (1979). *A Society in the Making*. Harmondsworth: Penguin.

Fine, B. and Harris, L. (1985). *The Peculiarities of the British Economy*. London: Lawrence and Wishart.

Forrest, R. and Murie, A. (1986). Marginalization and subsidized individualism. *International Journal of Urban and Regional Research*, **10**, 46–73.

Foster, J. (1979). How imperial London preserved its slums. *International Journal of Urban and Regional Research*, **3**, 93–113.

Frankel, B. (1987). *The Post Industrial Utopians*. Oxford: Blackwell.

Friedman, A. (1979). *Industry and Labour*. London: Heinemann.

Garrahan, P. (1986). Nissan in the North East of England. *Capital and Class*, **27**, 5–13.

Geddes, M. (1988). The capitalist state and the local economy: Restructuring for labour and beyond. *Capital and Class*, **35**, 85–120.

Giddens, A. (1981). *A Contemporary Critique of Historical Materialism*. London: Macmillan.

GLC (1985). *Planning for Land*. London: GLC.

Goodwin, M. (1986). *Locality and the Local State: Sheffield's Economic Policy*. Working Papers in Urban and Regional Studies, 52. Brighton: University of Sussex.

Gorz, A. (1982). *Farewell to the Working Class*. London: Pluto.

Gough, I. (1979). *The Political Economy of the Welfare State*. London: Macmillan.

Gramsci, A. (1971). *Prison Notebooks*. London: Lawrence and Wishart.

Gregory, D. and Urry, J. (eds) (1985). *Social Relations and Spatial Structures*. London: Macmillan.

Gregson, N. (1987). *The Meaning of Locality*. Working Paper 87, Centre for Urban and Regional Studies, Newcastle: University of Newcastle.

Hailsham, Lord (1963). *The North East: A Programme for Regional Development and Growth*. Cmnd 2206. London: HMSO.

Harloe, M. (1984). Sector and class: A critical comment. *International Journal of Urban and Regional Research*, **8**, 202–7.

Harloe, M. and Lebas E. (1981). *City, Class and Capital*. London: Arnold.

Harris, L. (1980). The state and the economy – Some theoretical problems. *Socialist Register*, London: Merlin.

Held, D. and Krieger, J. (1983). Accumulation, legitimation and the state. In D. Held, J. Anderson, B. Gibson, P. Hall, L. Harris, A. Lewis, R. Parker and T. Turk (eds), *States and Societies*. Oxford: Martin Robertson, pp. 487–99.

Held, D., J. Anderson, B. Gibson, P. Hall, L. Harris, A. Lewis, R. Parker and T. Turk (eds) (1983). *States and Societies*. Oxford: Martin Robertson.

Hoggart, K. and Kofman, E. (eds) (1986). *Politics, Geography and Social Stratification*. London: Croom Helm.

Holland, S. (1983). *Out of Crisis*. London: Spokesman.

Hudson, R. (1986). Producing an industrial wasteland: Capital, labour and the

state in North East England. In R. Martin and B. Rowthorn (eds), *The Geography of Deindustrialization*. London: Macmillan, pp. 169–213.
Hughes, W. M. (1970). Economic development in the 18th and 19th centuries. In J. C. Dewdney (ed.), *Durham County with Teesside*. Durham: BAAS, pp. 227–34.
Jessop, B. (1982). *The Capitalist State*. Oxford: Martin Robertson.
Keane, J. (1984). *Public Life and Late Capitalism*. Cambridge: Cambridge University Press.
Kilbrandon, Lord (1974). *Report of the Royal Commission on the Constitution*. Cmnd 5460. London: HMSO.
King, R. (ed.) (1983). *Capital and Politics*. London: Routledge and Kegan Paul.
Kinghorn, A. W. (1983). *Before the Box Boats*. Emsworth, Hampshire: Kenneth Mason.
Lane, T. (1988). *Liverpool – Gateway to Empire*. London: Lawrence and Wishart.
Lash, S. and Urry, J. (1987). *The End of Organized Capitalism*. Oxford: Blackwell.
Leadbeater, M. and Lloyd, J. (1987). *In Search of Work*. Harmondsworth: Penguin.
Lees, R. and Smith, G. (1974). *Action Research in Community Development*. London: Routledge and Kegan Paul.
Lefbvre, H. (1976). *The Survival of Capitalism*. London: Allison and Busby.
Little, K. (1947). *Negroes in Britain*. London: Kegan Paul.
London Edinburgh Weekend Return Group (1980). *In and Against the State*. London: Pluto.
Loney, M. (1983). *Community Against Government*. London: Heinemann.
Luxemburg, R. (1972). *Reform or Revolution*. Colombo: Young Socialist.
Mann, K. (1987). A new residuum or an old social problem. Paper presented at the Annual Conference of the Social Policy Association, Edinburgh.
Marris, P. and Rein, M. (1967). *Dilemmas of Social Reform*. London: Routledge and Kegan Paul.
Martin, R. and Rowthorn, B. (eds) (1986). *The Geography of Deindustrialization*. London: Macmillan.
Massey, D. (1984). *Spatial Divisions of Labour*. London: Macmillan.
Massey, D. and Catalano, A. (1978). *Capital and Land*. London: Arnold.
McCord, N. (1979). *North East England: An Economic and Social History*. London: Batsford.
Melling, J. (ed.) (1980). *Housing, Social Policy and the State*. London: Croom Helm.
Mess, H. A. (1928). *Industrial Tyneside*. London: Ernest Benn.
Metcalf, D. (1988). Quoted in *The Guardian*, 27 July, 15.
Miliband, R. (1969). *The State in Capitalist Society*. London: Weidenfield and Nicholson.
Miller, C. (1981). Area management: Newcastle's priority area programme. In C. Smith and D. Jones (eds), *Deprivation, Participation and Community Action*. London: Routledge and Kegan Paul, pp. 131–64.
Mingione, E. (1981). *Social Conflict and the City*. Oxford: Blackwell.
Mishra, R. (1984). *The Welfare State in Crisis*. Brighton: Wheatsheaf.
Mortimore, P. (1987). *The Last of the Hunters*. North Shields: North Tyneside Libraries and Arts Department.
Munday, N. and Mallinson, H. (1983). Urban development grant in action. *Public Finance and Accounting*, December.
Negri, A. (1979). Capitalist domination and working class sabotage. In *Red Notes*. London: Conference of Socialist Economists, pp. 93–117.
Nichols, T. (1979). Social class: Official, sociological and Marxist. In J. Irvine, I. Miles and J. Evans (eds), *Demystifying Social Statistics*. London: Pluto, pp. 152–71.

North Tyneside CDP (1976). *Some Housing and Town Planning Issues in North Tyneside*. North Shields: North Tyneside CDP.
North Tyneside CDP (1977). *North Shields: Working Class Politics and Housing*. North Shields: North Tyneside CDP.
North Tyneside CDP (1978a). *North Shields: Living with Industrial Change*. North Shields: North Tyneside CDP.
North Tyneside CDP (1978b). *North Shields: Working for Change in a Working Class Area*. North Shields: North Tyneside CDP.
North Tyneside CDP (1978c). *North Shields: Women's Work*. North Shields: North Tyneside CDP.
North Tyneside MBC (1984). *Proposed Initiatives to Positively Counter Vandalism in the Inner Riverside Area of North Tyneside*. North Shields: North Tyneside MBC.
North Tyneside MBC (1985). *Streetwise – Meadowell Detached Project*. North Shields: North Tyneside MBC.
North Tyneside MBC (1987). *The Plan for Jobs*. North Shields: North Tyneside MBC.
Northern Regional Strategy Team (1976). *First Interim Report*. Newcastle: NRST.
Northern Regional Strategy Team (1977). *Second Interim Report*. Newcastle: NRST.
Northern Regional Strategy Team (1979). *Strategic Plan for the Northern Region*. Newcastle: NRST.
Northern Trade Union Labour Left (1984). *Regionalism or Socialism*. Newcastle: NTULL.
Northumberland County Council (1959). *Seaton Valley Town Map – Written Statement*. Newcastle: NCC.
Northumberland County Council (1962). *County Development Plan – Written Statement*. Newcastle: NCC.
O'Connor, J. (1974). *The Fiscal Crisis of the State*. New York: St Martin's Press.
O'Connor, J. (1982). The meaning of crisis. *International Journal of Urban and Regional Research*. **5**, 301–328.
O' Connor, J. (1984). *Accumulation Crisis*. Oxford: Blackwell.
Offe, C. (1984). *Contradictions of the Welfare State*. London: Hutchinson.
Openshaw, S. (1983). *Cluster Analysis Programs*. Newcastle: Centre for Urban and Regional Development Studies, University of Newcastle.
Outhwaite, W. (1987). *New Philosophies of Social Science*. London: Macmillan.
Pahl, R. (1984). *Divisions of Labour*. Oxford: Blackwell.
Pahl, R. (1985). The restructuring of capital, the local political economy and household work strategies. In D. Gregory and J. Urry (eds), *Social Relations and Spatial Structures*. London: Macmillan, pp. 242–64.
Panitch, C. (1980). Recent theorization of corporatism. *British Journal of Sociology*, **30**, 159–87.
Parkin, F. (1979). *Marxism and Class Theory*. London: Tavistock.
Piven, R. and Cloward, F. F. (1979). *Poor People's Movements – How They Succeed and Why They Fail*. New York: Vintage.
Robinson, F., Wren, C. and Goddard, J. (1987). *Economic Development Policies*. Oxford: Clarendon Press.
Roderick, R. (1986). *Habermas and the Foundations of Critical Theory*. London: Macmillan.
Rowthorn, B. (1986). Deindustrialization in Britain. In R. Martin and B. Rowthorn (eds), *The Geography of Deindustrialization*. London: Macmillan.
Saunders, P. (1982). *Beyond Housing Classes: The Sociological Significance of Private Property Rights in Means of Consumption*. Working Papers in Urban and Regional Studies, 35. Brighton: University of Sussex.

BIBLIOGRAPHY 175

Saunders, P. (1983). The Regional State. A review of the literature and agenda for research. *Urban and Regional Studies Working Paper No. 35*. Brighton: University of Sussex.
Saunders, P. (1984). *Social Theory and the Urban Question*. London: Macmillan.
Saunders, P. (1985). Space, the city and urban sociology. In D. Gregory and J. Urry (eds), *Social Relations and Spatial Structures*. London: Macmillan, pp. 67–89.
Saunders, P. (1986). Comment on Dunleavy and Pretceille. *Society and Space*, **4**, 155–63.
Sayer, A. (1984). *Method in Social Science: A Realist Approach*. London: Hutchinson.
Seabrook, J. (1978). *What Went Wrong*. London: Gollancz.
Serge, V. (1977). *Birth of our Power*. London: Writers and Readers.
Serge, V. (1978). *Conquered City*. London: Writers and Readers.
Smith, C. and Jones, D. (eds) (1981). *Deprivation, Participation and Community Action*. London: Routledge and Kegan Paul.
Soja, E. W. (1985). The spatiality of social life: Towards a transformative retheorization. In D. Gregory and J. Urry (eds), *Social Relations and Spatial Structures*. London: Macmillan, pp. 90–127.
Stacey, M. (1971). The myth of community studies. *British Journal of Sociology*, **20**, 134–45.
Therborn, G. (1986). *Why Some People are More Unemployed than Others*. London: Verso.
Thomas, D. (1983). *The Making of Community Work*. London: Allen and Unwin.
Thompson, E. P. (1978). *The Poverty of Theory*. London: Merlin.
Tyne and Wear County Association of Trades Councils (1988). *Nissan and Single Trade Union Agreements*. Newcastle: Tyne and Wear CATC.
Tyne and Wear County Council (1979a). *Structure Plan – Report of Survey*. Newcastle: Tyne and Wear CC.
Tyne and Wear County Council (1979b). *Structure Plan – Written Statement*. Newcastle: Tyne and Wear CC.
Tyne and Wear County Council (1980). *Structure Plan – Report of Panel*. Newcastle: Tyne and Wear CC.
Tyne and Wear County Council (1981a). *Structure Plan – Response to Government Changes*. Newcastle: Tyne and Wear CC.
Tyne and Wear County Council (1981b). *Structure Plan – Annual Report*. Newcastle: Tyne and Wear CC.
Tyne and Wear County Council (1981c). *Structure Plan – Secretary of State's Proposed Modifications*. Newcastle: Tyne and Wear CC.
Tyne and Wear 2000 (1987). *A Regional Government for the North of England*. Newcastle: Tyne and Wear 2000.
Tynemouth CBC Surveyor (1961). *The Development of North Shields Town Centre*. North Shields: Tynemouth CBC.
Urry, J. (1981). *The Anatomy of Capitalist Societies*. London: Methuen.
Urry, J. (1982). Some theories in the analysis of contemporary capitalist societies. *Acta Sociologica*, **25**, 28–48.
Urry, J. (1983). Deindustrialization, class and politics. In R. King, (ed.), *Capital and Politics*, London: Routledge and Kegan Paul.
Urry, J. (1985). Social relations, space and time. In D. Gregory and J. Urry (eds), *Social Relations and Spatial Structures*. London: Macmillan, pp. 28–48.
Urry, J. (1986). Class, and disorganized capitalism. In K. Hoggart and E. Kofman (eds), *Politics, Geography and Social Stratification*. London: Croom Helm, pp. 16–32.

Urry, J. and Murgatroyd, C. (1985). *Localities, Class and Gender*. London: Pion.
Valentine, C. (1969). *Culture and Poverty*. Chicago: University of Chicago Press.
Walker, A. (1984). *Social Planning*. Oxford: Blackwell.
Williams, R. (1980). *Problems in Materialism and Culture*. London: Verso.
Williams, R. (1983). *Towards 2000*. London: Chatto and Windus.
Wood, E. M. (1986). *The Retreat from Class*. London: Verso.
Wright, E. O. (1985). *Classes*. London: Verso.

Index

Addison, P., 33
Ambrose, P., 9, 83, 96, 132
Anderson, J., 5, 33, 90
Anderson, P., 157
Ardagh, J., 7, 30, 133, 160
Avineri, S., 17

Ball, M., 24, 82–3
Banim, M., 48, 160
Bauman, Z., 24–5, 110, 136. 143
Bells (builders), 58
Benwell CDP, 78
Beveridge, W., 153
Beynon, H., 6
Blackman, T., 34, 58
Blyth Valley District Council, 57, 95–6, 126, 130
Braverman, H., 26
British Shipbuilders, 68–9
Byrne, D., 9, 21, 25, 47–50, 115, 141

Cameron, S., 93–4
Castells, M., 23
Catalano, A., 83–5
Centre for Environmental Studies, 8
Chaplin, Sid, 4, 7

Chapman, R., 40
Chirton Industrial Estate, 52, 74–5
civil society, 27–9, 39, 76, 133–5, 142
Cleaver, H., 6, 9, 17, 33, 79, 117
Cloward, R., 135, 166
cluster analyses, 10, 100–9
Cochrane, A., 34, 127
Cockburn, C., 20, 34
Colenutt, B., 9
Commission on Urban Priority Areas, 7, 113
Common, Jack, 7, 81
Community Development Projects (CDPs)
   national, 4, 7, 29, 61
   North Shields studies, 9, 14, 30, 65, 100
consumption cleavages, 23–4, 114, 141–3
Cooke, P., 6, 27–8, 39–40, 77, 80, 142
corporatism, 11, 31, 34–5, 122, 133
Coser, L., 137
Cowen, Joseph, 84
critical theory, 33

Dahrendorf, R., 9, 24, 110

Dawes, A., 17
De Toqueville, A., 7
Deacon, B., 152
Dickens, P., 8, 9, 26-8, 34, 38
disorganized capitalism, 3-4, 19-22, 140
Dockwray Square, 54, 94, 97, 102
Duncan, S., 23, 27, 122, 126-7, 131
Dunleavy, P., 47
Durham Regional Research Unit, 124-5

Elphick, P., 59
Employment Training Scheme (ETS), 164-5, 168
Engels, F., 7, 99
enterprize zones, 96, 136
European Economic Community (EEC), 149
Everitt, B., 101

Fabianism, 16
Ferge, Z., 12, 151
fishing, 72-4
Formica De La Rue, 53, 75
Forrest, R., 9
Foster, J., 23
Frankel, B., 28, 30, 133
Frankfurt school, 22
Friedland, R., 33
Friedman, A., 118

Garrahan, P., 116
gentrification, 11, 93-4
Giddens, A., 28
Greater London Council (GLC), 14, 155
Goodwin, M., 28, 34, 122, 126-7, 131
Gorz, A., 5, 12, 24, 33
Gough, I., 17
Gould, Brian M. P., 69, 137
Gramsci, A., 25, 36, 145
Greenwood Act (Housing), 51
Gregory, D., 17
Gregson, N., 27-8

Habermas, J., 32
Hailsham, Lord, 4, 123
Harvey, D., 82
Held, D., 31-2
HELP (Housing in Exchange for Land), 92
Holland, S., 149

Housing (Additional Powers) Act 1919, 5
Housing Act 1961, 56
Hudson, R., 6
Hughes, W. M., 42

indigenous workers, 165

Jessop, B., 4, 31

Labour against Militant, 92, 129
Labour groups, 12, 92, 127-9, 165
land development, 9, 49-51, 53, 56-9, 83-97
Lash, S., 19-22
Leadbeater, C., 137
Leech, William Ltd., 55-8
Lees, R., 100
Lefbvre, H., 9, 20
Little, A., 9
Lloyd, J., 137
locality, 26-7, 34
London Edinburgh Weekend Return Group, 162
Loney, M., 4
Luxemburg, R., 149

Mann, K., 109
maritime culture, 8, 72
Marris, P., 100
Massey, D., 8, 20, 26, 78-80, 83-5
McCord, N., 43
Meadowell Estate
  general, 7-8, 51-2, 135
  South, 102, 110-13, 141, 162
merchant shipping, 71-2
Metcalf, R., 143
Miller, C., 163
Miller, K., 9
Milliband, R., 126
Milne, Eddie, 10, 130
Mingione, E., 23
Mishra, R., 35

National Unemployed Workers Movement, 14, 52, 162, 164
National Union of Seaman (Seafarers), 52
Negri, A., 21
Nichols, T., 117
North Tyneside CDP
  analyses, 4, 48-50, 77-8, 84-7
  work of, 3, 43, 68, 71, 111, 166

INDEX

North Tyneside Metropolitan District Council, 112, 130, 152
Northern Economic Planning Council (NEPC), 123
Northern Regional Strategy Team (NRST), 14, 123–6, 140, 150, 153
Northern Trade Union Labour Left, 78
Northumberland County Council, 55–6, 130
Northumberland Structure Plan, 95–6

O'Connor, J., 21–2, 32, 138, 157
Offe, C., 21, 30–3, 150
offshore engineering, 67, 69–70
Openshaw, S., 9
Outhwaite, W., 36

Pahl, R., 24, 30, 114
Panitch, L., 34, 133
Parkin, F., 142
Parkside, 113, 141
Parson, D., 9, 21, 47, 115
partnership (housing), 92
People's Centre, 135, 163
Piven, F. F., 135, 166
Plan for Jobs, 152–3
Port of Tyne Authority, 84–5, 132–3
post-industrialism, 20, 115
post-modernism, 18
Poulson, J. G. L., 86

race, 11
RAWP (Resource Allocation Working Party), 131
realism, 6, 17–18, 35–6
regional government, 14, 156–7
Rein, M., 100
reserve army of labour, 10, 25, 110, 115–17
residualization, 9, 10, 115–18
Robens, Lord, 4, 43, 125
Robinson, F., 44, 61
Robson, Alex (Spike), 14
Roderick, R., 32–3
Rowthorn, B., 20

Saunders, P., 9, 17, 23–5, 114, 122–3, 137

Sayer, A., 6, 18, 35
Seamen's Minority Movement, 161
Serge, V., 7
Smith, C., 100
Smith's Dock Ship Repair, 49–50, 68, 70
social proletariat, 21, 143–4
Soja, E. W., 35
Spring, H., 7
Stacey, M., 26
Stockdale, Paul, 69
structural social planning, 13, 144
structure-action debate, 17, 33
Swan Hunters Ltd., 68, 70, 138

Therborn, G., 116–17, 139, 143, 152–3, 157
Thomas, D., 162–3
Town and Country Planning Act 1947, 56
Town Development Act 1952, 56
Trotter, Neville MP, 133
Tyne and Wear County Association of Trades Councils, 116, 140
Tyne Improvement Commission, 41, 50, 84
Tyne Ship Repair, 68
Tyne Tunnel Industrial Estate, 75–6
Tyne Wear Structure Plan, 87–90, 155
Tyne Wear 2000, 156

underclass, 10, 21, 25, 143–4
Urban Development Corporation
  and land development, 91, 93, 96–7, 136, 139, 141
  and the state, 9, 11, 35, 122, 127, 132–3
Urban Development Grant, 53, 89, 93, 141, 155, 168
Urry, J., 19, 20, 22, 26, 28, 167

Valentine, C., 29

Walker, A., 12–13, 144, 151, 154
Wilkinson Sword Ltd., 57, 80
William Press Ltd., 69–70, 80
Williams, R., 5, 8, 13, 19
Wright, E. O., 24